RIDDLES OF THE
SPHINX

By the same author

Egypt the Black Land
The Face of the Past

RIDDLES OF THE
SPHINX

PAUL JORDAN

WITH PHOTOGRAPHS BY
JOHN ROSS

SUTTON PUBLISHING

First published in 1998 by
Sutton Publishing Limited · Phoenix Mill
Thrupp · Stroud · Gloucestershire · GL5 2BU

British Library Cataloguing in Publication Data
A catalogue record for this book is available from the British Library.

ISBN 0-7509-1553-6

Endpapers: Sandstorm at the Sphinx

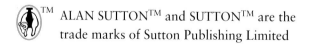 ALAN SUTTON™ and SUTTON™ are the
trade marks of Sutton Publishing Limited

Typeset in 10/14 Sabon.
Typesetting and origination by
Sutton Publishing Limited.
Printed in Hong Kong by
Midas Printing Limited.

CONTENTS

ILLUSTRATIONS

FOREWORD

The Great Sphinx has always had about it an aura of mystery as well as veneration. Its origins for long seemed lost in the mists of time, a puzzle and a matter of dispute even among the ancient Egyptians of the New Kingdom period, well before the time of the early Greek historians whose writings have come down to us. Yet even amid these and more recent controversies it seems crystal clear that the Sphinx is unquestionably the oldest truly monumental sculpture in the world. Many questions however remain. The precise date of this great work is still open to discussion. Its purpose is uncertain. There do indeed remain several 'riddles of the Sphinx'.

Paul Jordan is admirably qualified to investigate and to clarify for us the questions of date, and to adjudicate upon the various theories – some scientific, some fanciful, some just outlandish – which surround the Sphinx. He started his archaeological career as a pupil of Glyn Daniel, one of the first historians of archaeology as well as one of the great popularizers of the subject. He then moved to television and over the years has directed a distinguished series of well-researched programmes in the field of archaeology, with particular emphasis on Egypt and Egyptology.

With *Riddles of the Sphinx* he gives us much more than an account of this extraordinary and enigmatic monument. He guides us with a sure touch through the complications of chronology, showing how our knowledge of Egyptian history is built up. He deals effectively with the various theories about the Sphinx, including the recent arguments that the Sphinx might date from a period much earlier than the now widely accepted date of about 2500 BC. And he takes us through the early history of the archaeological exploration of Egypt, showing that even in ancient Egyptian times the Sphinx became an object of antiquarian curiosity. Paul Jordan skilfully uses the Sphinx as a fascinating and well-focused introduction to the whole field of Egyptology. Yet the veneration, and perhaps some of the mystery, still remain to intrigue the reader and to delight and awe the visitor.

COLIN RENFREW
Disney Professor of Archaeology in the University of Cambridge

ACKNOWLEDGEMENTS

I should like to thank Dr Rosalie David, Keeper of Egyptology at the Manchester Museum and Reader in Egyptology in the University of Manchester, for very kindly reading my manuscript and advising me on points of Egyptology. I should also like to thank Professor Lord Renfrew of Cambridge University for contributing his generous foreword to this book. My debt to Professor Selim Hassan's work will be evident to all who know their Egyptology.

Not only his fine photographs but also the bright idea that we do this book, and much else along the way, I owe to my old friend John Ross, whom I here salute. Except where stated in the captions, all the photographs were taken by him or come from his collection of historical photographs of Egypt. Text figures were drawn by Mike Komarnyckyj.

I should like also to thank Anne Bennett, my editor at Sutton Publishing, for all her calm capability and flair in putting this book together.

NOTE ON DATES
AND NAMES

Names written in the scripts of other languages are always difficult to transcribe into the Latin alphabet that we use (and vice versa, of course). Arabic place names present one set of problems, with many variants in use at different times and in different European languages – we can only settle for a consistent transliteration, in this case the one used by the *Times Atlas*. Similarly, we can only aim at consistency with personal names.

Ancient Egyptian names are much more difficult. The Greeks popularized their own versions of the names they heard on the lips of the (latter-day) Egyptians they ruled. These names are still with us: the builders of the pyramids at Giza are often called Cheops, Chephren and Mycerinus, though we spell these names in the Latin fashion and pronounce them like a sort of English! The same three kings are perhaps equally well known in versions of their original Egyptian names: Khufu, Khafre, Menkaure. But there are real uncertainties for us as to vowel values and syllable order with the ancient Egyptian scripts. You will see Khafre as Rakhaef, for example. Some people prefer the Greek versions in the light of these uncertainties, but the names of many Egyptian kings and places have no Greek equivalents. In this book, versions of the original Egyptian names of the kings of the Old and Middle Kingdoms are employed, but New Kingdom pharaohs are usually referred to by their more familiar and easy to pronounce Greek names. Where they exist, Greek place names are used (unless their Arabic equivalents are much better known), with the ancient Egyptian originals sometimes given for added interest.

In the matter of dates, I want to make a case for the use of the era system already adopted at some archaeological sites and museums of the ancient world. I think it is time to abandon the cultural imperialism of dating the whole world of different cultural traditions under the name of the Christian chronology, itself based on an arbitrary and erroneous estimate. It is better to regard this chronology as simply a common convention. Accordingly dates are given in this book as BCE, meaning Before the Common Era, or CE, meaning of the Common Era, in place of BC and AD. It seems to me appropriate to do this when we are dealing in the same book with dates in ancient Egyptian, Muslim and Christian chronologies. Occasionally, the even more objective designation BP is employed, a geological and archaeological usage with dates of immense antiquity, meaning Before the Present.

CHRONOLOGY

PREDYNASTIC EGYPT
c. 5000 to *c.* 3000 BCE

THE ARCHAIC PERIOD (DYNS. I AND II)
c. 3000 to *c.* 2700 BCE

THE OLD KINGDOM
c. 2700 to *c.* 2200 BCE
(Dyn. IV *c.* 2600 to *c.* 2450)

FIRST INTERMEDIATE PERIOD
c. 2200 to *c.* 2100 BCE

MIDDLE KINGDOM
c. 2100 to *c.* 1650 BCE

SECOND INTERMEDIATE PERIOD
c. 1650 to *c.* 1550 BCE

NEW KINGDOM
c. 1550 to *c.* 1070 BCE

THIRD INTERMEDIATE PERIOD
c. 1070 to 712 BCE

LATE PERIOD
712 to 332 BCE
(Second Saite Dynasty 664 to 525 BCE)

GRAECO-ROMAN PERIOD
332 BCE to 395 CE

The face of the Great
Sphinx above the Dream
Stela of Tuthmosis IV.

INTRODUCTION: THE RIDDLES

Two notions, not closely connected, come commonly to mind when we think of 'The Sphinx'. One is of a huge, decayed head sticking up out of the sand; the other, perhaps with vague recollections of the Greek myth or at least of a dubious rhyme, concerns a riddle somehow related to the beast. This book is all about the head in the sands, rather than the fearful creature of the classical myth, but it is right to associate the Egyptian monument with the posing of riddles, for there are many mysteries about that astonishing carving on the edge of the Libyan Desert by Cairo.

The latter-day ancient Egyptians of the last few centuries BCE were already in the dark about the origins of the Sphinx. After two thousand years of their own long history, they still remembered the names of the ancient kings who built the pyramids at Giza, but they had forgotten the identity of the ruler who ordered the carving of the Great Sphinx guarding the pyramid field. They had come to regard it as a deity in its own right, older than the pyramids and perhaps put there by the gods in the fabulous times before Egyptian history began.

The idea that the Sphinx is older than the pyramids has never gone away. The traditionalists of the Saite Dynasty (around 600 BCE) forged an anachronistic inscription – the so-called Inventory Stela, about which more later – that has Khufu, the builder of the Great Pyramid, claiming to have repaired the Sphinx in his own day. In the late nineteenth century, many Egyptologists were at first inclined to accept this record as at least an accurate copy of an original of Khufu's time. Further study of the language used in the inscription together with many anachronistic details that it contains makes that view untenable, and there has been no reason for a long time to regard the Sphinx as any older than the pyramids of Giza, indeed any older than the second pyramid, that of Khafre, to whom there are good reasons to assign the carving of the monument. That is not to say that the Sphinx could not possibly be older than Khafre's time (which Egyptologists generally put at about 2500 BCE) – it is simply that there has been no good reason to think it older and several good reasons for ascribing it to Khafre. The history of the ancient world is not easy to reconstruct and it has taken an immense amount of patient reasoning on the basis of rigorously sifted evidence, together with the necessary exercise of ingenuity of mind on the part of many scholars, to put together a coherent picture of the likely course of events in remote times and different parts of the world.

Inevitably, an orthodox scholarly view has emerged and Egyptology has its orthodoxy. That orthodoxy contends that the Sphinx was carved, most likely at Khafre's command, in about 2500 BCE, shortly after the building of the Great Pyramid of Khufu and perhaps at the same time as the construction of Khafre's pyramid. Working within that very reasonable orthodoxy, we are still faced with a satisfyingly wide range of riddles. We have to wonder where the idea of the man-faced lion came from and what this image meant to the Egyptian kings, priests, artists and common people of Old Kingdom times. We wonder, too, at the inspiration to make such a colossal sculpture at such an early date, with such a sureness of vision and execution. How was the work done and how came the Sphinx to its present highly eroded and battered condition? Could there be more to the Sphinx than we think: something inside it or underneath it? Who had the idea to turn a knoll of rock into this carving on a scale with no precedents and few rivals in subsequent Egyptian history, or anybody else's? Was the Great Sphinx of Giza the very first of the sphinxes of Egypt? Are there any traces of its ancestry in the archaeological record? And how was the sphinx idea taken on by the ancient Egyptians and developed into new forms? How did other peoples adopt the image later on and what did it mean to them?

But our main concern is with the Great Sphinx of Giza, and now there is a further riddle to be addressed. The idea that the Sphinx may be older than the pyramids, though hitherto unoccasioned, has persisted to this day. At last, a serious reason has been advanced to consider the possibility anew. A geologist has judged that the weathering of the Sphinx must be attributed to the agency of rainwater and not wind-blown sand as many people have thought: rainwater means wetter times, he thinks, than the days of Khafre; indeed, he concludes that we must look to times before 3000 BCE for the erosion of the Sphinx that we see, and he believes that the state of the rock around the monument indicates some time between 7000 and 10,000 BCE for the carving of the lion's body; the human head, though damaged, is less eroded than the body and is undoubtedly the work of an Old Kingdom ruler of roughly Khafre's time, if not, as remains most likely, of Khafre himself. Now here is a riddle indeed – the body much older than the face, and moreover much older than Egyptologists can possibly envisage, given their detailed knowledge of the prehistoric peoples living along the Nile Valley before the beginnings of Egyptian history in, as they carefully reckon, about 3000 BCE. And between 7000 and 10,000 BCE, there are no very obvious candidates anywhere in the world to drop by and carve the lion's body, even if such a visitation were a plausible possibility – which it is not, however much we may recognize that it is not an impossibility either.

To attempt to solve the riddles of the Great Sphinx, in particular this new version of the old riddle about its age, makes for an instructive exercise in investigating the nature of scholarly and scientific thinking. In this book, we want to show how scholars of ancient history – like scholars in any field and all who want to think logically and scientifically about things – have gone about constructing their schemes of human events in the remote past, in this particular case the remote past of Old Kingdom times in ancient Egypt, and how they must meet the challenge of new discoveries and new interpretations.

When Oedipus solved the riddle of the sphinx-hag of Thebes, she threw herself into the sea to her own destruction. Whether or not the Great Sphinx of Giza was ever tried by water, his condition is not good. In the first quarter of the twentieth century, his head on his badly eroded neck was judged to be in danger of being blown off in a severe storm and had to be supported with a cement restoration of the wig extensions that once reached down to the shoulders on each side. The wig and neck, incidentally, have certainly been badly eroded by wind-blown sand and not running water over the past four thousand years, whatever may be the cause of the major erosion of the body. The Sphinx will not last forever, but any solution of his riddles will not contribute to his downfall in the way that Oedipus put paid to the Theban sphinx.

The Giza Necropolis.

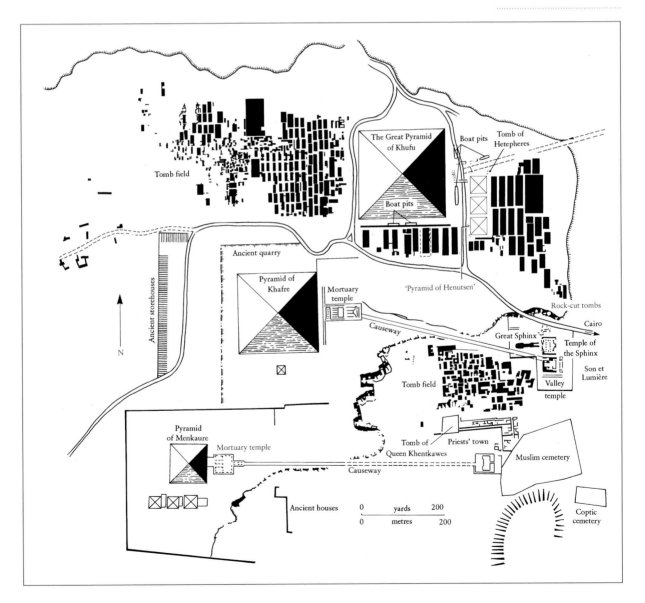

By what long road the Sphinx of the Old Kingdom Egyptians became the throttler of Thebes is a story that we shall look into later. But the Greek myth is worth recounting at this point, before we begin the investigation of the Great Sphinx of Giza that is the object of this book, for it retains, surprisingly enough, some ancient Egyptian elements that help to characterize the genuine Egyptian sphinx idea. For a start, the Greeks mistakenly thought that their word sphinx was derived from their native verb sphingein, meaning to strangle, constrict, bind tight, throttle (and contributing our English sphincter), whereas their sphinx was very probably derived in fact from an ancient Egyptian formula that transliterates as shesepankh with conjectured vowels, meaning 'living image' (of a king or a god: in the Old Kingdom kings like Khafre were gods). The Egyptians called sphinx sculptures in general by this name from Middle Kingdom times onwards, but the notion that they were all 'living images' of kings and gods almost certainly goes back beyond 2000 BCE to Old Kingdom times too. The Greek sphinx tightly bound her victims in death on the road to Thebes when they failed (as they all did until Oedipus) to answer her riddle about:

> A thing with one voice
> but four, then two, then three feet;
> nothing more changeable than this thing
> to be found in earth or sky or sea.
> When this thing goes on most feet,
> then its strength is at its weakest and
> its pace most slow.

In other words, the riddle of the sphinx might have come from a Christmas cracker: 'What has four legs in the beginning, two in its heyday, and three at the end?' Oedipus guessed that the right answer was, of course, a human being – who crawls on four limbs in the dawn of life, walks on two legs in his noon-tide and totters with a stick in the sunset of his days. And so the sphinx, hitherto the baleful guardian of the road to Thebes, was vanquished. Here, too, there is a hint of ancient Egypt, for the sphinxes in pairs in front of doors and gates or in double rows leading to temple entrances were above all guardians of the ways into significant places, taking their cue from the Great Sphinx of Giza who guarded the approach to the places of the illustrious dead buried in the rock-cut tombs and pyramids of the necropolis.

But there is more to the Theban sphinx's riddle of child, man and old crock. The inscription on a stela between the Great Sphinx's paws calls the sphinx, together with other names, by the triple denomination 'Kheperi-Re-Atum' and these were the three names given by the ancient Egyptians to the infant sun of the morning, the full-grown sun of midday and the fading sun of the afternoon. Something really important of the ancient Egyptians' imagery of the sun-god, whose living image was the Sphinx, had got through to the Greeks even when their story had an altogether different milieu and meaning.

The stela between the paws of the Sphinx was erected by a New Kingdom pharaoh at least a thousand years after Khafre's time. In the time of this Tuthmosis IV, the memory of some association of the Sphinx with Khafre of old still seems to have lingered on. The stela is damaged at the point where what seems to be Khafre's name is introduced and we can make nothing of the meaning of the apparent reference to him, but that his name might be there at all is really quite a powerful reinforcement of the modern Egyptologists' conviction that the monument was made by Khafre and bears his features. Evidently the New Kingdom Egyptians remembered Khafre in connection with the Sphinx, even if their successors eventually forgot.

A panorama of the Giza
monuments from the
Description de l'Egypte,
with the Great Sphinx
under inspection by
Napoleon's savants.

The Giza Plateau with, from left to right, the pyramids of Menkaure, Khafre and Khufu; Khafre's causeway leads down from his mortuary temple to his valley temple, with the Sphinx temple beside it immediately in front of the Sphinx; before the valley temple can be seen the seating area of the son et lumière.

The Sphinx from the north:
further to the south (at the
left of the picture) is
another knoll of rock like
the one from which the
Sphinx was carved.

ONE

THE GREAT SPHINX IN SITU

The Great Pyramid of Khufu at Giza has a rival for size and grandeur very close at hand: standing next to it is the pyramid of Khufu's successor Khafre, which from many angles looks bigger than the Khufu pyramid, being built on slightly higher ground. Indeed, the ancient Egyptians called Khafre's 'The Great Pyramid' and that of Khufu 'The Pyramid which is the Place of Sunrise and Sunset'. There were originally only a couple of metres in height between these pyramids, but our Great Pyramid of Khufu is the taller, has a shallower angle of incline than Khafre's and encloses a greater volume.

Just down the escarpment from the pyramids of Giza, the Sphinx stands alone, with no rivals either on site or elsewhere among all the sphinxes of Egypt. Truly, this is the Great Sphinx, as well as being very likely the first of the breed.

It might possibly have had a companion if its sculptors had cared to repeat the exercise of carving it. For the Great Sphinx started life as a knoll of rock (quarried in the course of pyramid building) on the slope down from the Giza Plateau towards the river valley of the Nile; and there is another knoll not far to the south, clearly visible to every visitor to Giza, which might have been fashioned into another giant monument. The later sphinxes of Egypt were often installed as pairs to guard entrances to significant places, but the Great Sphinx of Giza is a one-off, and perhaps the other knoll was just a little too far from the necropolis to be convenient. And perhaps the original meaning of the Great Sphinx was too particular to be shared with another of its kind. An eminent Egyptologist once spent some time looking for another Great Sphinx on the other side of the river, but eventually gave up the idea.

The Sphinx is in essence a carving out of the living rock, though parts of it have been repaired (and possibly were originally constructed) with cut blocks of stone. It is immediately apparent that the rock strata out of which the Sphinx has been made vary from a hard grey to a soft yellowish limestone. The head is formed of good, hard limestone of the same sort as was quarried all around for the core blocks of the pyramids. The bulk of the body, on the other hand, is made of poorly consolidated and therefore readily eroded limestone. The rock improves again at the base of the monument, with a return to harder (but brittle)

The heavily eroded Sphinx.

reef-formed limestone that has allowed some carved details of the beast to remain visible after at least four-and-a-half thousand years of natural and human attrition. In keeping with the whole Giza Plateau, these strata within the Sphinx run upwards from east to west, in other words from the breast to the hindquarters, and down from north to south. The Sphinx faces due east, with the same great precision of orientation as is seen in the disposition of the Giza pyramids. It seems inevitable that the monument was made from the start to point directly to the equinoctial sunrise. Interestingly, the face (but not including the ears) is a little awry in relation to the head as a whole: the left eye is slightly higher than the right and the mouth off-centre, and the entire face is tilted back a little.

Despite the generally better quality of the stone of the head, the face – as is immediately apparent – is badly damaged, and not just by natural erosion. The nose is missing altogether and the eyes and the areas around them are seriously altered from their original state as carved, as is the upper lip. Napoleon's artillerymen have been blamed for using the face of the Sphinx for target practice, but in fact the damage was done centuries before by a sheikh who regarded the Sphinx as a blasphemous infidel idol. Even so, traces of red paint have survived on the cheeks. The alteration of the face has brought an insinuation of mood to the features, changing with different lights (sometimes

The damaged face of the
Sphinx, smiling his
inscrutable smile.

Fragments of the Sphinx's beard: casts in the Cairo Museum.

into a knowing smile), that needs to be borne in mind when any attempt is made to compare the face of the Sphinx with the portrayals in sculpture of various Dyn. IV kings.

For the head and face of the Sphinx certainly belong with the Old Kingdom of the ancient Egyptians, and with their Dyn. IV in particular. The style of the head-dress (known as the 'nemes' head-cloth), with its fold over the top of the head and its triangular planes behind the ears, the presence of the royal 'uraeus' cobra on the brow, the treatment of the eyes and lips all speak of that historical period. The sculptures of kings Djedefre, Khafre and Menkaure all show the same configuration that we see on the Sphinx. The Sphinx was originally bearded with the sort of formally plaited beard to be seen on many Egyptian statues. Pieces of the Sphinx's massive beard found by excavation adorn the British Museum in London and the Cairo Museum: it was supported by a stone plate to the breast, parts of which have also been found. There is a hole in the top of the head, now filled in, that formerly located some further head decoration: depictions of the Sphinx from the latter days of ancient Egypt show a crown or plumes on the top of the head, but these were not necessarily part of the original design. The top of the head is flatter, however, than is the case with later Egyptian sphinxes.

Below the head begins the serious natural erosion of the body of the Sphinx, the leonine body of the man-lion hybrid. The neck is badly weathered, evidently by wind-blown sand during those long periods when only the head was sticking up out of the desert and the wind could catapult the sand along the surface and scour the neck and the extensions of the head-dress that are missing altogether now. The stone here is not quite of such good quality as that of the head above. In the 1920s it was deemed necessary to support the head with cement approximations of the absent parts of the head-dress, and it is these extensions that chiefly account for the altered appearance of the Sphinx's head in recent times, when compared with old photographs and drawings.

Erosion below the neck does not look like scouring by wind-blown sand. In fact, so poor is the rock of the bulk of the body that it must have been deteriorating since the day it was carved out. We know that it needed repairs on more than one occasion in antiquity. It continues to erode before our very eyes, with spalls of limestone falling off the body of the Sphinx in the heat of every day. The rock was of poor quality here from the start, already fissured along joint lines that went back to the formation of the limestone millions of years ago. There is a particularly large fissure across the haunches, nowadays filled with cement, that also shows up in the walls of the enclosure in which the Sphinx sits.

So severe is the erosion of the body of the Sphinx that, for example, what may have been in the first place an entire statue or attached column standing proud from the breast of the beast, has been reduced to a formless line of protuberances on the front of the monument between the forelegs. It is plain that extensive repairs have been made to the front paws of the Sphinx and in many other places over the body. Some of these repairs go back to the New Kingdom of around 1400 BCE (the time when King Tuthmosis IV set up his stela between the paws), and there is reason to believe that parts of the Sphinx must from the first have

The face of Khafre on statue fragments in museums in Copenhagen (left) and Leipzig.

been built on to the basically carved body, out of necessity arising from the poor state of the rock from the beginning. It is even possible that the body of the Sphinx was entirely plastered over at some stage.

Below the neck, the Sphinx has the body of a lion, with paws, claws and tail (curled round the right haunch), sitting on the bedrock of the rocky enclosure out of which the monument has been carved. The enclosure has taller walls to the west and south of the monument, in keeping with the present lie of the land: it is generally thought that quarrying around the original knoll (for pyramid blocks or blocks with which to build temples associated with the necropolis complex) revealed the too-poor quality of the rock for construction purposes at this point; whereupon some visionary individual conceived the plan of turning what was left of the knoll into the Sphinx; but, of course, the Sphinx may equally well have been planned from the start for this location, good rock or bad. The walls of the Sphinx enclosure are of the same characteristics as the strata of the Sphinx body and exhibit similar states of erosion.

There are three passages into or under the Sphinx, two of them of obscure origin. The one of known cause is a short dead-end shaft behind the head drilled in the nineteenth century. No other tunnels or chambers in or under the Sphinx are known to exist. A number of small holes in the Sphinx body may relate to scaffolding at the time of carving. The Great Sphinx is huge. The length of the

The Sphinx in a photochrome
print from around the turn of
the century, showing the
fissure across the haunches
that was filled with cement in
the 1930s.

The Sphinx temple in front of the Sphinx.

body is more than 74 m; its height from the floor of the enclosure to the top of the head some 20 m. The extreme width of the face reaches over 4 m, the mouth being 2 m wide; the nose would have been more than 1.5 m long, while the ears are well over 1 m high. The later Egyptians were accustomed to build big (but never again so big as the Giza pyramids) and to carve large statues, but even the giant New Kingdom statues of Ramesses II at Abu Simbel, sculpted thirteen hundred years later than the Sphinx, do not exceed the Old Kingdom monument, at 20 m high with faces about 3 m wide, and they have no long body behind them. The wrecked statue of Ramesses II that inspired Shelley's poem about Ozymandias was evidently about 18 m high. Similarly, the huge seated statues of Amenophis III called the 'Colossi of Memnon' are no taller than the Sphinx and, again, not so bulky – though they were entirely made out of single blocks and transported to their location. The statue of Zeus at Olympia, made by Phidias in the mid-fifth century BCE, was neither quite so tall nor made out of one piece of material; the Colossus of Rhodes was reputedly half as tall again as the Sphinx, but put together out of bronze castings. Mount Rushmore makes the closest comparison with the Sphinx carving in modern times, with its faces at 18 m in height, which took six-and-a-half years to create even with the aid of dynamite and pneumatic drills. The Statue of Liberty tops everything at 92 m, but is made out of copper sheets hammered together, over a framework of steel.

When viewed close-up, the head and body of the Sphinx look relatively well proportioned, but seen from further away and side-on the head looks small in relation to the long body (itself proportionally much longer than is seen in later sphinxes). In its undamaged state, the body is likely to have appeared still larger all round in relation to the head, which has not been so reduced by erosion. There could be a number of explanations for this discrepancy in our eyes.

This was, as far as we can tell, the first of the Egyptian sphinxes: the rules of proportion commonly employed on later and smaller examples may not yet have been formulated at the time of the carving of the Great Sphinx of Giza. In any case, the sphinx pattern was always a flexible formula, to an unusual degree in the context of Egyptian artistic conservatism. Then again, the Sphinx may have been sculpted to look its best when seen from fairly close by and more or less from the front. It is possible that there was simply insufficient good rock to make

The hind paws and tail of the Sphinx.

the head, where fine detail was required, any bigger; after that the fissure at the rear may have dictated a longer body, rather than one much too short. There remains the possibility that the head has been remodelled at some time and thereby reduced in size, but on sure stylistic grounds alone this is not likely to have been done after Old Kingdom times in ancient Egypt.

The Sphinx sits in an enclosure formed by the removal of limestone from around its body. This enclosure is deepest immediately around the body, with a shelf at the rear of the monument where it was left unfinished and a shallower extension to the north where important archaeological finds have been made. Without the excavation around it, the Sphinx would at best have no carved body below the level of the uppermost part of its back: it would look as it did when the sands buried it almost up to its neck in the nineteenth century, except that it would be the rock surface of the Giza Plateau out of which it would grow. The good, hard limestone that lay around the Sphinx's head was probably all quarried for blocks to build the pyramids; it was perhaps the removal of this limestone, leaving at some stage a suggestive lump of remaining rock (together with the discovery of poor rock beneath), that put it into someone's mind to create the Sphinx. The limestone removed to shape the body of the beast was evidently employed to build the two temples to the east of the Sphinx, on a terrace lower than the floor of the Sphinx enclosure – one almost directly in front of the paws, the other to the south of the first one. The core blocks of these two temples are of the same generally poorer quality and more easily eroded limestone as the body of the Sphinx. Thus these temples can be regarded as contemporary with the carving of the monument.

Of these two temples the southerly one was excavated by Egyptologists before the one in front of the Sphinx and so was regarded for a time as the temple of the Sphinx – the discovery of the other one, long buried under the ever-drifting sands, established that the Sphinx's own temple was this one straight in front of the eastward-facing monument. The two temples are similar in size and both face east in a north–south alignment; each has a pair of north and south entrances in their eastern façades. They are both built with core blocks quarried on site, around the body of the Sphinx: some of these core blocks of the Sphinx temple are three times larger than the core blocks of the Great Pyramid. Both temples were faced, inside and out, with finely dressed granite from Aswan in the far south of Egypt, and floored with alabaster.

The Sphinx temple is very ruined now, with little of its granite facing left and little of its alabaster floor. Any inscriptions it may once have carried, which might have told us much about its purpose, are long gone. Only the eroded limestone core of the structure remains, in part: enough to show that this temple once boasted a central court, about 46 m by 23 m, open to the sky and affording a good view of the Sphinx, and there was an interior colonnade of rectangular pillars. Large recesses in the inside eastern and western walls suggest the original presence of cult statues, very possibly to do with the rising and setting sun, but of decorative detail there is no trace. There was no immediate access to the Sphinx from inside the temple, whose west wall up to the height of 2.5 m was cut into the living rock,

The Sphinx lying in its
enclosure, mobbed by the
tourists of today.

thereafter topped with limestone blocks. It was necessary to go by passages to the north and south of the temple to reach the Sphinx. There is evidence that this temple of the Sphinx was never finished; perhaps it was never even used.

The interior of the other temple, to the south of the Sphinx temple, is quite different in layout, though the same granite casing of the limestone core blocks, the same rectangular style of pillar, the same presence of statue niches, the same overall size and method of construction mark both buildings as contemporary Old Kingdom temples. In the southerly temple, the remains of nine more or less complete statues of a king named on them as Khafre were found. Further fragments show that twenty-three statues of Khafre once stood in this temple, which Egyptologists identify as the valley temple of Khafre's pyramid complex: the temple on the edge of the Giza escarpment to which his body was brought by a canal from the river at the start of the process that would end with his being sealed within his pyramid up on the plateau above. Even in this century, the river in flood has occasionally come very close to the terrace of the temples by the Sphinx – and the water-table is not far below ground.

The valley temple of Khafre lies at the end of a limestone causeway that leads

Opposite: Khafre: the renowned statue from his valley temple, now in the Cairo Museum.

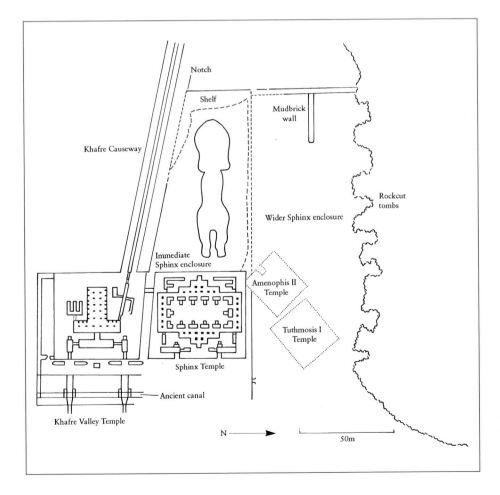

The site of the Sphinx, without the modern road which runs NNW over the temple of Tuthmosis I.

up the slope to a further temple at the foot of his pyramid. The Greek writer Herodotus, who never mentions the Sphinx as a feature of his visit to the pyramids (perhaps it was all but obscured by sand in the fifth century BCE), thought the causeway of the Great Pyramid was as wonderful in its way as the pyramids themselves. To judge by the causeways of slightly later pyramids, these long ramps were covered over, with slits in the roof to let in light, and possibly their walls even in the time of Khufu and Khafre carried sculpted and painted scenes on them, in contrast to the lack of decoration in the Giza pyramids themselves. The Khafre causeway was equipped with drainage channels which are interesting to us now because they indicate that rainwater run-off was an essential provision of the pyramid complex. We are accustomed to think of Egypt as a very dry place but even today, in times that are drier still than were the days of the Old Kingdom, rains can sometimes come and cause considerable damage in a context where they are not routinely expected. Evidently the monuments of the Giza necropolis needed precautions against rain. On the north side of the Khafre causeway, there is a ditch (2 m wide and 1.5 m deep) that forms a demarcation line between the pyramid complexes of Khufu and Khafre. This rock-cut ditch was large enough to channel a great deal of rainwater when heavy rains occurred. It is cut into by the corner of the Sphinx enclosure, and – were it not blocked at

The ruins of Memphis, with a statue of the god Ptah.

this point with pieces of granite – would allow water to pour in quantity into the basin out of which the Sphinx body was carved. These circumstances strongly suggest that the Sphinx enclosure and the Sphinx itself were created after the demarcation of the complexes of Khufu and Khafre and after the construction of Khafre's causeway. There are some tombs cut into the south-facing edge of the wider Sphinx enclosure to the north that belong to the same Dyn. IV as Khufu and Khafre, showing that the enclosure was not made after their time. Between them, the blocked ditch and the tombs indicate a narrow band of time in which the Sphinx enclosure, and by strong implication the Sphinx itself, could have been carved. It means that the Sphinx most likely dates to a time no later than a couple of reigns after Khafre and no earlier than his reign.

At the top of the Khafre causeway, 400 m in length, there was another temple, larger than the one at the valley end and immediately in front of Khafre's pyramid. This was the feature of a pyramid complex that Egyptologists call a mortuary temple. It is now a badly eroded ruin, but once measured over 110 m by nearly 50 m. It was again part-faced with granite from Aswan, but also with fine limestone from across the Nile at Tura. It featured an entrance hall, an open court, statue niches, storage magazines and a sanctuary close to the base of the pyramid, with an altar for offerings. The pyramid itself was surrounded by a high wall, and the area between the wall and the pyramid was paved. Khafre's pyramid was accompanied by one smaller pyramid to the south, but the slightly earlier pyramid of Khufu has three to the east, while the smaller Giza pyramid of their successor Menkaure has three to the south. All three main pyramids were equipped with mortuary and valley temples and causeways between these temples, though most of the causeway and the valley temple of Khufu is now invisible. The pyramids of Khufu and Khafre (and probably Menkaure too) were additionally accompanied by several boat pits in which wooden boats of some religious significance were buried. Around the Great Pyramid of Khufu there are numerous contemporary tombs of relatives, courtiers and officials, laid out in ordered lines. Subsequently, there was infilling with tombs of later reigns, and more tombs were built to the south-east of Khafre's pyramid.

To the south of Khafre's tomb field there is a priests' town, where the priests who maintained the religious duties of the necropolis were housed, and nearby there is another large tomb, of an Old Kingdom queen. Rock-cut tombs occur along the various natural and quarried edges of the escarpment including, as we have seen, the northern side of the Sphinx enclosure. To the west of Khafre's pyramid there is a line of ancient storehouses.

The whole Giza site was, you might say, a living necropolis for three millennia: living because, with varying degrees of dedication from time to time, the cults of the royal dead and their followers were kept up by the priestly administration of the place. There were periods of neglect, extreme at times, but also periods of renewal. We have described the complex of monuments that belonged together in Old Kingdom times, but Giza went on being an important place till practically the end of ancient Egyptian history. New Kingdom pharaohs, ruling a thousand years after Khufu and Khafre, built new temples close to the Sphinx, who had become in their time (whatever his original significance may have been) a god in his own right. In the latter days of ancient Egypt, two thousand years after Khufu and Khafre, an atavistic passion for an idealized and (not surprisingly) misremembered past led to more rebuilding on the Giza site and fresh interpretations of the origin and meaning of the Sphinx.

The Giza complex lies at an elevation of about 100 m above sea-level on a

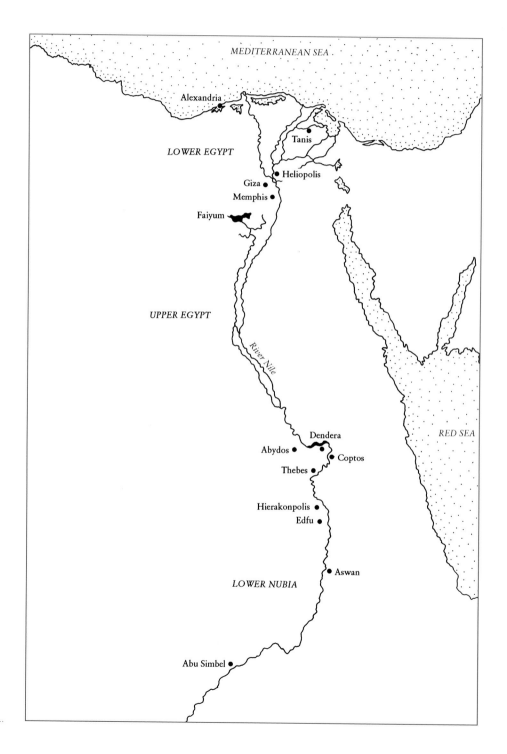

Ancient Egypt, with places mentioned in this book.

latitude 30° north of the equator, towards the northern end of a vast cemetery of the ancient Egyptians associated with their Old Kingdom capital city of Memphis. Both city and cemetery lay on the west bank of the Nile. About 10 km north of Giza is the northernmost station of the cemetery, where the very ruined pyramid of Khufu's successor Djedefre (sometimes rendered Radjedef) lies at Abu Rawash. About 7 km south of Giza, another pyramid was left unfinished at Zawyet el-Aryan: to what king it belonged is now unknown. There is also evidence of an unfinished Dyn. III structure. About the same distance south again is Saqqara, with more than a dozen royal monuments ranging from Dyn. III to Dyn. XIII, though none of them from Dyn. IV like the Giza pyramids. There are more Dyn. IV pyramids at Dahshur, about 10 km south of Saqqara, where the father of Khufu (his name was Snofru) built two pyramids, one with a noticeably gentler slope than those of any of his successors and the other with a change of angle like a mansard roof that has earned it the modern name of the Bent Pyramid.

Old Kingdom pyramids.

Down in the river valley east of Saqqara lies all that remains of the great city of ancient Egypt that the Greeks called Memphis. Picturesquely forlorn and shrunken today, Memphis was really the capital city of Egypt in Old Kingdom times, reputedly founded by the first king and unifier of the ancient state, Menes as he is named by the Greek writers. In a long history, until rivalled by the southern city of Thebes in New Kingdom times (and totally superseded by the Arab foundation of Cairo, on the east bank of the Nile) Memphis probably stretched at various times up and down the west bank of the river for many kilometres. Its no doubt abundant archaeological remains are buried now under successive inundations of silt and modern settlement. It got its Greek name under curious circumstances, after the whole town had come to be known by the name of one of the pyramids at Saqqara (that of Pepi I) called Mennufer. In Old Kingdom times, the town was commonly called The White Wall, probably because the king's residence was fortified with such a wall. Much later there was a temple there of the god Ptah, who was always closely associated with Memphis, called Hikuptah, and from this word it seems the Greeks derived their name for the entire land of Egypt, Aiguptos. (Why the Greeks called the southern city Thebes, after their own city of the same name, is a mystery.)

At all events, Memphis was the greatest and most important city of Old Kingdom Egypt, the seat of Menes and his successors. It is because of Memphis that the pyramids of Giza (et al.) are where they are – they and their associated tomb fields are the cemeteries of the top people of the Old Kingdom.

City and cemeteries were on the west bank of the Nile. On the east bank at the time, south of modern Cairo, were the quarries at Tura from which the hard high-quality limestone used to case the pyramids at Giza was extracted, to be rafted across the river on the annual flood to the foot of the plateau on which the pyramids were built, with cores of softer stone quarried on site.

About 20 km north of Memphis the river fans out in the branches that form the Delta of the Nile as it runs to the Mediterranean Sea, which the Egyptians called 'The Great Green'. Formerly there were more streams than there are today and the whole

In a photograph taken earlier this century, the Nile flood reaches to the foot of the Giza Plateau. The Sphinx is below and between the two large pyramids of Khafre and Khufu. Photo: Lehnert and Landrock.

area of the Delta constituted quite a different world, with its manifold creeks and brooks running among swamps and patches of dry ground, from the situation south of Memphis where the single stream in its fertile flood plain was soon bounded on both sides by desert and rock. These two different worlds, Lower Egypt in the north and Upper Egypt in the south, were throughout Egyptian history culturally rather distinct, and more so in prehistoric times before the unification of the state. The eastern part of the Delta was probably the readiest way by which influences from the other civilizations of the ancient world might come into Egypt from the peoples at the eastern end of the Mediterranean and beyond. Egypt was unusual among the early civilizations in the degree of its isolation from the outside world, as a result of geography. The route to Palestine up the eastern Mediterranean coast was not the only avenue to the wider world but it was probably always the likeliest.

It was also possible to go east from Memphis across the desert to the top of the Gulf of Suez and on to Sinai, in search of turquoise and copper for example; to go south down that arm of the Red Sea into the Sea itself and so reach the coasts of modern-day Sudan, Ethiopia and Somalia; and to cross the Red Sea to the Arabian Peninsula. The Eastern Desert along the whole length of the Nile in Egypt was never as barren as the desert to the west. Probably nomad pastoralists tending their flocks were often to be found there, and there was the attraction of minerals and precious metals to draw the ancient Egyptians on expeditions away from their river valley home. Granite and greywacke, tin, copper and gold were to be found there, and more routes to the Red Sea. In the Western Desert, stretching away from Memphis to the Libyan Plateau, there was less to lure the ancient Egyptians away, even in the wetter days of old before the far Sahara became completely desiccated, though there were substantial oases of considerable importance to the Egyptians in later times.

South of Memphis, into Upper Egypt, the valley of the Nile reached for about a thousand kilometres towards the African interior but still within the land of Egypt itself before, above Aswan, the border of the state was crossed into Nubia and tropical Africa. The first cataract of the Nile marked the frontier in Old Kingdom times, the place where the river first becomes seriously difficult to navigate as the waters tumble over rocks. The Old Kingdom Egyptians of Dyn. IV exercised some kind of influence over the region between the first and second cataracts – and this was, of course, the place where imports from the African interior made their way into Egypt: ivory, spices, ostrich feathers among them. There were probably many middlemen along the route these goods travelled into Egypt and few if any Egyptians are likely to have travelled far into the African interior. (In those days, of course, some of the African megafauna could be encountered well within the bounds of Egypt itself – lions and crocodiles included.)

But the sources of the great river which made the civilization of ancient Egypt possible were deep inside the continent. Above the fifth cataract first the Atbara, and then above the sixth the Blue Nile flow down from the Ethiopian Highlands into the waters of the White Nile, which rises in central Africa. It is the seasonal flooding of the Nile in Egypt as a result of the mingling of the rivers in the Sudan that supplies Egypt with the means to sustain life. Without this happy state of affairs, there would have been no settlement of the Nile Valley, no unification of the state, no great kings – and no Great Sphinx.

The Sphinx in an engraving
from the *Description de
l'Egypte*.

TWO

THE SPHINX BEFORE EGYPTOLOGY

The scholarly discipline called Egyptology came into being at the end of the eighteenth century as a result of Napoleon's military expedition to Egypt, which was accompanied by a team of savants who first described the monuments of Egypt in a thoroughly accurate way. The expedition moreover turned up the Rosetta Stone, which was the key to deciphering the hieroglyphs and translating the ancient Egyptians' own records so as to get directly at their history. The combined study of Egyptian writings and the physical remains of Egyptian civilization constitutes Egyptology, which has been tremendously successful in reconstructing the course of ancient Egyptian history from its beginnings in about 3000 BCE to its end with foreign conquests by Persians, Greeks, Romans and Arabs. The prehistory that underpins the historical civilization has similarly been elucidated. Before Egyptology, everything about ancient Egypt – not just the Sphinx – was something of a riddle. There was little or nothing from ancient Egypt itself to go on. The language was not understood at all and the hieroglyphs were usually thought of as some complicated sort of picture writing with mystical meanings rather than as an everyday script representing the sounds of everyday words. The Bible made fairly frequent mention of Egypt and Pharaoh, but almost always (and especially in its earlier sections) without much in the way of specific detail as to time and place or named Egyptian personalities. Before the nineteenth century, nearly everyone who was interested in ancient history relied on the Bible as certain fact and tried to fit everything else in with its account. So the fabled adventures of, for example, Joseph and Moses in Egypt were fixed points about which all other conjectures had to circle. The Bible contributed to the prevalent notion that the ancient Egyptians were great sorcerers and workers of magic, with scenes like the one where Moses and Aaron struggle with Pharaoh's magicians; the supposed magical powers of the Egyptians have never been popularly forgotten. And the Bible is silent about the Sphinx.

Second only to the Bible and frequently regarded as equally unassailable were the classical authors in Greek and Latin: among these, Herodotus of the fifth century BCE was the principal source. Solon, the law-giver of Athens, had visited Egypt before him, but Herodotus was the first Greek writer to present a detailed account of what he had seen and heard there. The cautionary thing to note in his case is that, despite his having been dubbed the 'Father of History', he sometimes behaved like a modern tourist out at Giza who believes everything his fifty piastre guide tells him. Not all of Herodotus' Egyptian advisers can have known what they were talking about, or been in earnest if they did.

Herodotus travelled the whole country as far as Aswan at the Nubian border, and wrote vivid accounts of life along the Nile. He coined the apt characterization of Egypt as 'The gift of the Nile': he had even taken hold of the idea that the fertilizing Nile rises and falls each year because of rains in the distant mountains of the African interior. He is a witness to the fact that the Great Pyramid still boasted its finely finished casing stones in his day, before they were taken away over fifteen hundred years later to build the Arab city of Cairo. On the other hand, he credulously tells us that there is an artificial lake under the pyramids – and he does not mention the Sphinx at all.

The Greek ruling class of latter-day ancient Egypt after Alexander's conquest of 332 BCE, and the Romans after 30 BCE, resembled the colonial rulers of the various nineteenth-century empires of western Europe. Their writers' accounts of the country and its ways are much less adequate in truth than a British civil servant's reminiscences of India. They never developed the study of anthropology that arose among the scholars of the European imperial powers. Worse still, they never bothered much with the language of the Egyptians or the various ways of writing it. So it is unfortunate that the history of Egypt written in Greek in the third century BCE by a native Egyptian priest named Manetho did not survive the end of the classical world into the European renaissance. All we have is excerpts quoted by later writers. It was itself a late work and evidently, from the remains of it that we can read, not entirely reliable especially for the early history of Egypt, but even today after so much Egyptological progress it would be a valuable work if we had it in full. The bits of Manetho available to us do not mention the Sphinx. Nor was it mentioned by the Greek writers Diodorus and Strabo when they dealt with Egypt – perhaps it was all but submerged in sand in the last century BCE.

The Roman author Pliny the Elder, writing in the next century, does have some interesting things to say about the Sphinx. 'In front of the pyramids,' he says, 'is the Sphinx, perhaps an even more wonderful work; it is regarded as a divinity by the local people. They believe that it is the tomb of King Harmais, and they further maintain that it was brought there from a distance. But the truth is that it was carved there from the natural rock. For religious reasons the face is painted red.' Pliny, we know now, reported correctly that in his time the Sphinx was regarded as a divinity in its own right: 'King Harmais' reflects the Egyptian concept of the Sphinx as the image of the sky-god Horus in his manifestation as Horemakhet (to render the ancient Egyptian name), Horus on the Horizon. Pliny is right, too, to have no truck with the idea of the Sphinx's having been transported in from elsewhere, and there are still traces of red paint on the face in this century.

Pliny gets the measurements of the Sphinx mostly wrong but his remarks on the pyramids and Egypt in general in his *Natural History* are perfectly rational by comparison with the ideas of some of the late classical authors. The so-called *Hermetic Corpus*, for instance, and Horapollon's *Hieroglyphica* promote notions of the hieroglyphs as mystic signs of ineffable truths and Egypt as the fount of all wisdom, mixing some garbled late Egyptian concepts with elements of Hellenistic philosophizing. These works were rediscovered in the early years of the Renaissance and exercised a profoundly misleading influence on the early development of European interest in ancient Egypt.

The last of the ancient Egyptians, in the latter days of the Roman Empire, were not concerned to pass on any heritage of the great days behind them. The Empire had exploited Egypt very comprehensively, bleeding it into a ruinous state for its agriculture and mineral wealth. A taste for otherworldliness, generated by the growing unpleasantness of everyday life, made Egypt vulnerable to Christianity years before Theodosius imposed it by degree at the end of the fourth century. The most otherworldly form of Christianity – monasticism – was pioneered in Egypt. The old religion was abandoned, along with the impossibility of continuing to live in the old ways. Christian monks closed the last of the old temples and destroyed what they could of the pagan Egyptian heritage. The first monks were among the last Egyptians who could read hieroglyphs and related scripts. Among such writings, there was nothing they wanted to read or pass on to later generations. They might speak their Coptic tongue (a direct evolution out of the ancient Egyptian language, about as close to it as modern English is to Anglo-Saxon) but they wrote it now in a modified Greek alphabet. Nothing about the Sphinx was likely to be transmitted by these people.

The Arab conquest, in 640–1 of our Common Era, found a Christian Egypt that had already rejected and suppressed its own past. In the last days of Roman Egypt, tourists could still go inside parts of the Great Pyramid, whereas five hundred years later in the ninth century CE al-Mamun, son of Harun al-Rashid, had to force his way in, for the entrance was by then blocked with rubble. It is unlikely in the extreme, by the way, that anything of Khufu's burial was left inside when al-Mamun's men got in there: that must have been robbed away in the days of the pharaohs. The Arabs were generally interested in the treasure potential of the ancient Egyptian tombs. The story of Aladdin and the great treasure behind the magically opened door goes back to tomb-robbing reports: the treasure is the funerary equipment of some dead Egyptian and the magically opened door is what Egyptologists call the 'false door' of the tomb inscribed with hieroglyphs. 'False doors' were imitations of real entrances set up as the scene of ritual offerings to the dead in ancient Egyptian tombs.

The Arabs went on to rob the Great Pyramid of all its fine casing stones and the neighbouring Khafre pyramid of nearly all of them, though at the top the remaining courses still shine a little in the sun. The stones were taken away for the building of the new city of Cairo in the thirteenth century. To about this time date a few references to the Sphinx in the writings of Arab travellers in Egypt. A doctor from Baghdad named Abd al-Latif reported that 'Near to one of the pyramids is a colossal head emerging from the ground. It is said that its body is buried in the ground, and to go by the dimensions of the head, the body would have been seventy cubits in length. The figure is painted red.' Abd al-Latif was impressed by the Sphinx as by nothing else in Egypt, remarking on 'the wonder that in a face of such huge size, the sculptor should have been able to maintain the exact proportion of every part, when nature presented him with no model of a similar colossus or anything at all comparable'.

Abd al-Latif saw the pyramids and Sphinx before much damage had been done to them, but a hundred years or so later, in 1402, al-Makrizi found a now damaged face on the Sphinx. A Sufi zealot had organized an assault on it. 'This man wanted to remedy some religious errors, and he went to the Pyramids and disfigured the face of Abul Hol [The Sphinx], which has remained in a damaged state from that time until now. From the time of this disfigurement, the desert sand has invaded the cultivated land of Giza, and the people attribute this to the disfigurement of Abul Hol.' The Arabic name Abul Hol for the Sphinx has an interesting history, going back to ancient Egypt, as we shall see. Of the Sphinx al-Kodai reports that 'it is a large idol situated between the two pyramids, and only the head is visible. The mob calls it Abul Hol and Balheeb, and believe that it is a charm to keep the sand of the desert from invading Giza.' Al-Kodai mentions a book called 'The Wonders of Building' that says that the local people believed that the Sphinx body was buried under the sand: perhaps folk memory went back to a time when the benefits of one of the many historical clearances around the Sphinx had not yet been buried in the drifting sands.

Apart from the learned Arab visitors who saw the pyramids and Sphinx, few outsiders ventured to Giza in the Middle Ages. There were stray European travellers, pilgrims looking for the Egyptian locations of the Gospel stories and associated relics. What they took in of ancient Egypt, they tried to interpret in the light of the Bible: the pyramids, for example, they called 'granaries of Joseph'. The study of Egyptian antiquities began in the sixteenth century in Rome, where numerous Egyptian monuments looted by the Roman Empire were to be found, notably the many obelisks covered with hieroglyphic inscriptions. There were some sphinxes too. Unfortunately the fatal course set by the writings of Horapollon et al. only encouraged general belief in the magical essence of ancient Egyptian civilization, and new study of the classical authors such as Herodotus, with his manifold errors and gullibilities, could do little to dispel this attitude.

More people were passing through Egypt in the sixteenth century, and now as curious-minded travellers rather than pious pilgrims. One, the chaplain of Catherine de Médicis remarked on the 'head of a colossus, caused to be made by Isis, so beloved of Jupiter' – a notable multicultural garbling, derived from late classical religious speculation. Another, Johannes Helferich, published an account in 1579 which picked up this interpretation and took it on, complete with an illustration. 'The head is the height of three men. It is a portrait of the goddess originally called Isidis, who was a daughter of King Inachus of Greece, whom the Egyptian god Osiris took as his wife, who changed her name to Isis, and after her death she was held to be a goddess, and in her honour this figure was fashioned.'

Helferich adds a teasing detail that echoes down to our own day when he tells that 'from afar, under the ground, through a narrow hidden passage, one can pass unseen. By this passage the heathen priests get inside the head and speak to the people out of it as if the statue itself had spoken.' Helferich's woodcut illustration of the Sphinx makes one doubt whether he can ever actually have been there and seen it, showing as he does a female face and full-breasted torso. And yet his circumstantial accounts of entering the pyramids ring true.

In the seventeenth century, travellers were bringing back to Europe both small and portable antiquities and Coptic manuscripts, the study of which was an important part of the background to eventual decipherment of the hieroglyphs and understanding of the ancient language of the Egyptians. The first traveller to come back with halfway reliable drawings of the pyramids and Sphinx was George Sandys in 1610: a woodcut in his book shows him riding with his companions towards the Giza complex, with pyramids that are too tall for their bases but a quite surprisingly well-rendered Sphinx head, its damage and erosion accurately detailed. Sandys reported seeing only the head, 'though Pliny gave it a belly'. John Greaves, Professor of Astronomy at the University of Oxford, visited Egypt in 1638–9 and made a thorough examination of the pyramids. When he published his discussion of the Giza complex in 1646, he drew on the writings of the classical authors and the Arab historians to make sense of what he had seen, coming to the rational conclusion that the pyramids were royal tombs whose grandeur had been motivated by religious belief in the preservation of the body.

In the eighteenth century, real progress was made in the accuracy with which the monuments were described and illustrated. The prejudices of the European artistic tradition were gradually shed in reproducing the true character of this alien art. The Sphinx as drawn by Pococke in 1743 still wears a classical sort of expression, but the Sphinx by Norden in 1755 looks much more like the real thing. Thomas Shaw, who examined the Sphinx in the 1720s, found the hole in the top of its head and speculated about tunnels to the pyramids. The century ended with the military expedition to Egypt which Napoleon had persuaded his government to undertake as a first step towards wresting India from British rule. In the Enlightenment spirit, he took with him a team of scholars in all fields to investigate every aspect of the Egyptian scene. During their three years in Egypt, before the British and the Turks finally defeated the French force, the members of the commission of savants travelled all over the country measuring, describing and illustrating the monuments of ancient Egypt, along with the rest of their scientific tasks. The results were published in nineteen volumes between 1809 and 1828 as the *Description de l'Egypte*. They had done some clearing around the Sphinx's breast, but the monument remained essentially just a battered and eroded head and neck sticking up out of the sand, with only the top of the back visible behind it. This head they measured accurately and depicted in wonderful engravings that record the appearance of the Sphinx and the rest of the Giza monuments on the eve of the breakthrough in understanding about them, and about ancient Egypt in general, that came with the decipherment of the hieroglyphs in the 1820s.

Champollion was not the first to make some progress with the phonetic system of the hieroglyphs but he was the first to work out an extensive list of sound values and to use his knowledge of the Coptic language, that late descendant of the old Egyptian tongue, to understand the words whose sounds were represented by the signs. You might think that once the ancient Egyptian language was understood, progress in knowledge of ancient Egypt would be rapid. Much progress was soon made, but Egyptology long remained a very academic study and the vast amount of archaeological material that started to come to light during the nineteenth century posed many perplexing questions; not least among these were the problems of ancient Egyptian chronology. On the one hand there was the system of thirty dynasties set out by Manetho. But this history of Manetho's, though it named king after king and gave the lengths of their reigns, was known only in excerpts quoted by later writers and its reliability was suspect on several counts: Manetho wrote late in Egyptian history, thousands of years after the early history of his country; and the people who quoted him might well have misrepresented him, wilfully or carelessly. On the other hand, first looting and then archaeological excavation were turning up material frequently inscribed with the names of kings absolutely unrecognizable as entries of Manetho's and difficult if not impossible to place in his scheme. Scientifically conducted excavation had a long way to go in the whole world of archaeology in the mid-nineteenth century, and nowhere more so than in Egypt, where the sheer wealth of easily recoverable material put no premium on careful procedure and accurate recording.

It is hard now to re-imagine the general landscape of Egyptological understanding in which Champollion and his nineteenth-century successors were operating. Manetho and Herodotus and the Biblical references to Egypt were inevitably to the fore. There were the pyramids, assigned to rulers that Manetho indicated came early in Egyptian history. There were the extensive ruins of the ancient city that was clearly to be identified with the Egyptian Thebes of Manetho's Dyn. XVIII and later ones. There were the beguiling temples of Greek times, lavishly decked with carvings and hieroglyphic inscriptions whose late and aberrant character was not always appreciated. Nothing was known until the end of the century of the prehistory of Egyptian civilization. Much remained to be determined about the complexities of the ancient language as it evolved over the thousands of years of Egyptian culture.

Where the Sphinx was concerned, the ancient writers, as we have seen, could contribute little beyond the implication that there was more of the monument to be found below the drifted sands and that it represented for the ancient Egyptians a divinity called something like Harmais or Harmachis, and therefore having to do with their god Horus, known from the philosophical writings of late classical times. Plainly the Sphinx had its place in the Giza complex, but its relationship with the pyramids as to its meaning and date of construction was not obvious.

Stories persisted among the local people at Giza that Napoleon's engineers, digging down in the sand in front of the Sphinx, had just uncovered a door that led into the monument (and, better still, up to Khafre's very pyramid) when the work had to be broken off, never to be resumed by them. It is quite likely that in attempting to clear sand beneath the head, the soldiers and savants had gone down far enough to begin to reveal some details between the paws (which were to be rediscovered a little later) that were for the moment mistaken by local onlookers for just the sort of door to treasure that folklore predicted.

Those details were to come to light again in 1816 when an Italian sea captain named Giovanni Battista Caviglia was employed by the British Consul-General in Egypt to investigate the Giza site, which he did with considerable archaeological skill for the time. At the Sphinx, he began with a trench towards the left shoulder of the monument. Digging in sand, he recognized the great danger of collapse (that had probably deterred Napoleon's engineers from carrying on with their clearance) and used planks to shore up his excavation. He was able in this way to reach right down to the base of the monument in this area and to measure the height to the top of the head. He found that there were in places two layers of casing stones added to the rock-hewn body of the beast and to its extending paws. He also reported traces of red colouring. When his trench perforce was narrowed from a width of 6 down to 1 metre he gave up for the moment, returning later with some sixty to a hundred men to continue the work on a larger scale. He thus discovered a fragment of the Sphinx's broken-off beard, then the head of the cobra that was part of the head-dress, and then something that would turn out to be of immense interest and importance once the writing it bore could be understood. This was probably what Napoleon's diggers had got down to previously, what had given the locals the idea of a door into the monument. Covered in hieroglyphs as it was, it could not for the moment be interpreted. It was what archaeologists call a stela, an upright stone slab, commonly found on ancient Egyptian religious sites.

Caviglia found two more of them subsequently in the remains of a little temple or chapel between the Sphinx's paws. This chapel was guarded by a small stone lion, and there were in addition fragments of other such lion sculptures, and the head of a small sphinx figure, all painted red. Also in the space between the paws, Caviglia found a granite altar with traces of combustion on it, which caused him to speculate about burnt offerings at the Sphinx. At this time, before the decipherment of the hieroglyphs, it was not possible to determine when or by whom these things had been placed between the paws. It turns out that they were the products of a much later age than the one in which the Sphinx was first carved.

Caviglia then excavated about 30 m east along the paws, noting Greek inscriptions on them as he went. Next he discovered thirty mud-brick steps leading up to a landing on the higher ground to the north of the Sphinx, and thirteen more after the landing, on which there was a small rostrum with a Greek poem inscribed on it in honour of the Sphinx. Evidently all this belonged to a very late period, in Greek or more likely Roman times. There were also traces of a 40 m approach ramp up to the Sphinx with a mud-brick wall on its south side. Caviglia could not know it, but this ramp ran entirely over the ruins of the ancient temple that we now know to stand in front of the Sphinx, all trace of which had been long lost before the ramp was constructed.

Champollion achieved the decipherment of the hieroglyphs and the translation of the ancient Egyptian language in the early 1820s. The stela that Caviglia had found in front of the Sphinx was soon translated and found to record a much earlier excavation around the Sphinx that had been undertaken as a pious exercise by a pharaoh of New Kingdom times, known from Manetho and called (in Greek) Tuthmosis: Tuthmosis IV, in fact. The ancient Egyptian form of this name was something like Dhutmose. The stela is nowadays known as the 'Dream Stela', for it was a dream that it says caused Tuthmosis IV to refurbish the Sphinx. By New Kingdom times the place of the Sphinx was called Setepet, meaning the select place, and the Sphinx himself was identified as Horemakhet, Horus on the Horizon (which name was later Graecized to Harmachis, or Harmais, as we saw with Pliny). The Sphinx was also known at this time by the triplet name of Kheperi-Re-Atum: the sun of dawn, of midday and of sunset. Tuthmosis caused the circumstances of his dream to be recorded on the stela, a dream that came to him before he was pharaoh while taking a nap on a regular hunting trip out at Giza.

> Now when the hour came for giving rest to his followers, it was always at the Setepet. . . . The very great statue of Kheperi rests in this place, great of powers, upon which the shadow of Re lingers. . . . One day it came to pass that the king's son Tuthmosis came hunting at the time of midday, and rested in the shadow of this great god. Sleep seized him when the sun was at the zenith, and he found the majesty of this revered god speaking with his own mouth, as a father speaks with his son, saying, 'Behold thou me, my son Tuthmosis. I am thy father Horemakhet Kheperi-Re-Atum. I will give to thee my kingdom on earth. . . . My face is directed to you, my heart is to you, you shall be to me the protector of my affairs, because I am ailing in all my limbs. The sands of Setepet upon which I am have reached me; listen to me in order to do what I desire . . .'. The king's son awoke hearing this. . . . He understood the words of the god, and he put them in his heart.

After this point, the inscription on the stela became harder to read, on account both of damage in antiquity and subsequent erosion. Sad to report, it is in an even worse state now than when it was discovered, thanks to the ongoing process of erosion. But the text went something like this:

> They shall protect the offerings to this god, which we bring for him, oxen, fruit . . . and all vegetables, and we shall give praise to the ancestors . . . august . . . Khaf . . . the statue made for Atum-Horemakhet.

Clearly Tuthmosis IV has asserted that, before ever he became pharaoh, he was singled out by the god to rule Egypt, in return for restoring the 'ailing limbs' of the Sphinx and restituting the religious offerings that ought to be made to him.

Evidently Tuthmosis kept his side of the bargain, cleared the sand out of the Sphinx enclosure and carried out some repairs on the monument. It is the apparent reference to the Old Kingdom ruler named Khafre that intrigues. Tuthmosis would have known that the huge pyramid to the west of the Sphinx had been constructed for Khafre of old – did he also know that the Sphinx itself was somehow associated with this same remote king? Egyptologists calculate the date of Khafre's reign to about 2500 BCE and that of Tuthmosis IV to just before 1400 BCE; they are separated by about eleven hundred years. It is the same order of time as that which separates us from Alfred the Great. It is quite possible, then, that Khafre's name was represented by the fragmentary writing of Khaf on the stela – that suggestion was made by Thomas Young, one of the pioneers of hieroglyph decipherment. But it is only in the context of what we know about the history of ancient Egypt that the suggestion has any force. For the developing discipline of Egyptology in the nineteenth and twentieth centuries, it was essential to construct a chronological scheme into which the names and events and products of the ancient Egyptian civilization could be put. Until that chronology was in place, the dates of the ancient kings like Khafre – and their mighty works like the pyramids and the Sphinx – could only be conjectured: even their true order in time, let alone their absolute dates, could only be guessed.

Seti I with his son Ramesses
at the head of the Abydos
king list, from a nineteenth-
century photograph.

THREE

DATING ANCIENT EGYPT

Before the infant discipline of Egyptology could tackle questions like the origin and dating of the Great Sphinx of Giza, many strands in the study of ancient Egypt needed to be brought together. Above all, the chronology of this ancient civilization needed to be established in as much detail as possible, somehow combining the discoveries of archaeology in the field (and not in Egypt alone) with the surviving ancient chronicles and whatever other stray sources were available from classical times and from other cultures contemporary with ancient Egypt.

Until the discovery of the Rosetta Stone paved the way for the decipherment of the ancient Egyptians' own writings, the best estimates of Egyptian chronology were based on what had survived of that history of Egypt written in Greek by Manetho in the early third century BCE. The Bible made references to Egypt and to 'pharaoh' but always without any hard chronological context and rarely naming the pharaoh in question. Greek writers like Herodotus related largely anecdotal material about ancient Egypt. Until the middle of the nineteenth century, scholars really only had Manetho to go on.

Manetho was an Egyptian priest, a native Egyptian-speaker with access to the annals of his people, who was commissioned by the Greek ruler Ptolemy II Philadelphus to write a history of Egypt for the benefit of the new ruling class who came in with Alexander's conquest. The Egyptians had been maintaining their annals, written on papyrus, for two-and-a-half thousand years by the time Manetho came to make use of them. None of those annals survives now, except for the small selections from them that were edited and transferred to stone, and these latter only survive in very fragmentary form. If we had them complete they would be invaluable to us in helping to solve remaining problems of Egyptian chronology. If we had Manetho's complete history, we should perhaps be well on the way to solving those problems, though it is doubtful that Manetho, writing late in Egyptian history and for a foreign readership, made as accurate a use of his material as we would have liked. For instance, his Greek versions of Egyptian rulers' names are not always easy to relate back to their originals and sometimes impossible.

In any event, Manetho's history (called *Egyptian Memoirs*) has not come down to us – only garbled abstracts in other writers giving some kings' names and the

The full king list of Abydos.

lengths of their reigns. The writers who used him in this way were the Jewish
historian Josephus of the first century of the Common Era and the Christian
chroniclers Sextus Julius Africanus of the third century, Eusebius of Caesarea of
the fourth century and George the Syncellus of the late eighth century. Partly by
accident and partly by design, they failed to reproduce Manetho with unanimity
or complete accuracy: in particular there was a Christian tendency to equate
Manetho's first Egyptian king with Adam, inflating the reigns of the early rulers to
extend Egyptian history back in time to the supposed creation of the world.

Manetho as related by the later historians makes a rather poor guide to
Egyptian history. But for all that, his division of the native rulers of his land into
thirty houses, or dynasties as he calls them, has remained a basically useful
scheme, employed by Egyptologists despite the rich discoveries made since the
Rosetta Stone was found on the eve of the nineteenth century. Because of the
dynastic scheme of Egyptian history pioneered by Manetho and adopted by
Egyptologists, what would be called prehistoric in other branches of archaeology
is called predynastic in Egyptology.

Scarcely anything of predynastic Egypt was known even as recently as a
hundred years ago. Since Egyptologists could only guess at the dates of the
known kings of the Old Kingdom such as Khufu and Khafre who built their
pyramids at Giza, they were even more ignorant about the chronology of
prehistoric, predynastic Egypt when archaeological excavations started to turn
up evidence of Egypt before the pharaohs. Manetho's first two dynasties, before
the pyramid age, were shadowy enough: before them, he talked mysteriously of

an epoch of demigods ruling between the eras of the gods and the first human kings.

It is the consensus view among Egyptologists today that Egyptian history began, with Manetho's first dynasty and its first king whom he called Menes, in about 3000 BCE. This is not a precisely calculated benchmark but a best estimate based on extremely ingenious scholarship in the light of the fragmentary evidence available.

In common with most of the cultures of the ancient world, the Egyptians had no framework of universal chronology into which to set their history: indeed, they probably had no concept of history as a continuously unfolding, evolving process as we think of it in modern times. They thought of their world as essentially eternal and unchanging, though going through natural cycles of the days and years. Of course, they recognized that with the years different rulers ruled, the Nile flood rose to different heights, there were lean times and fat times, enemies came and went on their borders and so on. These were the sort of events that they saw fit to record in their annals, assigning them to such and such a year of such and such a king. But they did not say, for example, that the greatest flood on record occurred in the year 1953 of Egyptian history: there was no 1953. Their annals noted the principal events and numbers of years of a given king's reign, then reverted to year one for the next king. If the annals had been complete, an ancient Egyptian scholar such as Manetho could have added up the years of given dynasties and whole periods of his country's history – even its complete history, in theory. Of course, matters could never be that simple, since records are in practice damaged, lost, misunderstood, edited, censored, falsified.

A later ruler might not think much of a predecessor, disapprove of him enough to have him written out of history altogether, rather in the manner of the old Soviet Encyclopaedia. And after a thousand years, or two, what had once seemed important might mean little or nothing to a later writer. So it is clear that what has survived from Manetho and from various other ancient Egyptian written sources must be handled with caution, and tested against archaeology wherever possible. The inscriptions on the monuments and remains uncovered by Egyptologists, where they indicate a particular year of a named king's reign, can be measured against the figures given by Manetho and the other ancient listings. Some kings' names have only come to light through archaeology.

If we were to go by Manetho, as related by the Christian writers, we should put the first king of the first dynasty at about 5800 BCE – nearly three thousand years earlier than Egyptologists want to put him today. But there are other ancient Egyptian records that contribute towards a broader chronological account, despite their various shortcomings.

The shortcoming of the chief of these other records is that it is in tatters! This chronicle, written in the time of the New Kingdom pharaoh Ramesses II, was reputedly in good condition when it was found in Egypt at the beginning of the nineteenth century. By the time it came to be studied properly (by Champollion among others) in the Turin Museum, it was in many small fragments. Painstaking work on it since has coaxed out of the remains a record essentially similar to Manetho's, but differently divided and with some different names and reckonings. The Turin Canon agrees with Manetho in making Menes the first king of a united Egypt, preceded by demigods of fabulously long reigns, and it often lists similar numbers of reigns until the end of the Middle Kingdom.

Manetho and the Turin Canon are supplemented by other king lists carved in stone at Abydos, Saqqara and Karnak. Reconciling these sources is not easy, since different inclusions and omissions confuse the overall picture, and sometimes different names are used for the same kings – not surprisingly, since Egyptian kings had more than one name and, while the Abydos list for example uses religious names, Manetho prefers the kings' secular names. The discovery of inscriptions giving several of the names of particular kings has helped to clear up this confusion.

Manetho, the Turin Canon and the king lists mentioned above all drew on the annals kept on papyrus by the ancient Egyptians from early times: we know of their existence because New Kingdom texts refer to them, but none has come down to us. All that we have that resemble the annals are fragments of an inscribed stone (or of several identical inscriptions) evidently based on them. The chief piece of this inscription is called the Palermo Stone, as it is housed in the Sicilian capital; there are further small pieces in the Cairo Museum. The Palermo Stone was evidently a free-standing slab with inscriptions on both sides. They began at the top of the front face with the names of various predynastic rulers, without any record of lengths of reign. Below that, the lines list years as well as names, and heights of Nile flood year by year. If complete, and starting line two with the first king of the first dynasty (as it undoubtedly did – but this part is broken off) the Palermo Stone would tell us, subject to editing by its compilers, the names and lengths of reigns of the kings of Egypt from the unification of the country until well into Dyn. V, after the pyramids of Giza and the Sphinx were made. This information would overlap with the Turin Canon and other king lists and, taken with Manetho, get us well on to a chronology, in years, for ancient Egyptian history.

There would still be the problem that all the lists expire before the end of the New Kingdom, leaving a gap of unknown but calculable duration until the first certain dates for ancient Egypt that are tied into Greek history. Manetho's account of the New Kingdom succession, as reported by the other writers, is a very garbled affair, often completely at odds with the evidence of archaeology. On the other hand, Manetho does agree fairly well with the other sources for the Old and Middle Kingdoms. Unfortunately there were three major periods of social breakdown during the long course of Egyptian history, with short-lived and sometimes overlapping reigns in different parts of the country. These periods of unknown duration make it difficult, without additional chronological information, to establish the likely total span of Egyptian history, despite the good records that appear to exist for certain dynasties.

But Egyptian chronology has been rescued in the eyes of the majority of Egyptologists from most of its remaining uncertainty by a quirk of the ancient Egyptian calendar. The Egyptians reckoned their year at twelve months of thirty days each, plus five extra days to bring it up to 365 days. They had not hit upon the idea of the leap year, when an extra day is added every four years to accommodate the fact that the time taken by the Earth to move right round the Sun is very nearly 365¼ days. The formal Egyptian year consequently slipped out of synchronism with the real solar year by a quarter of a day per year, by a day every four years, by half a year every 730 years, only returning to full synchronism after 1,460 years.

The Egyptians took the day when the star Sirius, after a period of invisibility, rises just before the Sun itself (the so-called heliacal rising of the star) as the start of the new year. This date more or less coincided with the inundation of the Nile, when the river's waters overflowed its banks to fill up the irrigation channels and spread fertile mud over the fields. The phenomenon has now been severely modified by the building of dams on the Nile in Upper Egypt. In the days of ancient Egypt, this was a terrifically significant moment – a fit time to start the new year. Only once every 1,460 years could the formal new year's day coincide exactly with the real, observed new year's day, the day when Sirius rose with the Sun. The Egyptians apparently called this day 'the going up of Sothis', Sothis being the Greek form of their name Sopdet for the star we call Sirius.

There are three useful instances in which ancient Egyptian records mention, specifying the day of the month of a particular year in a king's reign, that Sirius did indeed rise heliacally: so we infer that these were three moments in the long history of Egypt when the real new year was recorded as beginning at a specified number of days away from the formal new year. Calculation makes it possible to determine the year in question in terms of our own calendar, with its reckoning forwards and backwards from year one of the Common Era. This calculation rests on the fact that the Roman historian Censorinus records that the formal and real new years' days actually coincided in 139 CE: hence we can calculate that they also coincided 1,460 years earlier in 1322 BCE (there was no year 0) and 1,460 years before that in 2782 BCE. Actually, the star Sirius, which is relatively close to Earth, has proper motion of its own (rather than seeming to move solely by virtue of the Earth's movement), so the figures need very slight adjustment.

The oldest of the ancient records with mention of the heliacal rising of Sirius is dated in ancient Egyptian terms to the sixteenth day of the eighth month of the seventh regnal year of a king identified as Senwosret III of the Middle Kingdom. Theory has it that all that is necessary in order to know the year in our own terms is to count back the number of days that had passed since the first day of year seven of Senwosret (226), multiply that figure by four and then count down by that many years from 2782 BCE. The date arrived at by these means is about 1875 BCE. (This date depends on the latitude of observation – in the far south of Egypt, it would come out as about 1830 BCE.)

And so, some date at around 1860 BCE is arrived at for year seven of a certain Dyn. XII ruler. Since the ancient records and archaeology all agree fairly well as to the number of kings and their regnal years for the Middle Kingdom (to which Dyn. XII belongs) then a fairly sound basis for ancient Egyptian chronology from around 2100 to 1650 BCE is achieved. This was the next period of social stability after the pyramid age, when Egyptologists believe the Sphinx was carved.

Dating this epoch by means of a reference to the rising of Sirius depends on certain assumptions. In particular, it is clear that the Sothic dating method only works if no ancient attempts to reconcile the formal and real new years' days were made before the recorded date of day sixteen of month eight of year seven of Senwosret III. But there is no reason to think such adjustments were made: certainly in late New Kingdom times the discrepancy between real and formal years had not been adjusted, for a papyrus records that 'winter comes in summer, the months are reversed, the hours in confusion'. The Greek rulers tried to reform the calendar, but it took the Roman emperor Augustus to force the Egyptians to use the Julian system of 365¼ days. The very fact that Sirius was to rise heliacally on the sixteenth day of the eighth month of the year shows that the formal and real years had not been adjusted back to synchronism: this should have been new year's day, day one of the first month of the first season of the year.

But even if we accept this Middle Kingdom date (and forget, for the purposes of our investigation into the Old Kingdom Sphinx, the problems of Egyptian chronology after the Middle Kingdom) we are still faced with uncertainties in trying to get back beyond 2100 BCE to the age of the pyramids. For a start, there was a period of social collapse (and consequently of extreme chronological uncertainty) after the end of the Old Kingdom, before the Middle Kingdom got under way. Then there is the difficulty of reconciling Manetho, the Palermo Stone and the other chronicles with the discoveries of archaeology to arrive at a plausible estimate of the length of the Old Kingdom (Dyns III to VI) and the early dynastic period (I and II). Only when we have arrived at such an informed estimate shall we have a chronological context in which to put the pyramids, the Sphinx and the developments that led up to them.

The period of collapse between the Old Kingdom and the Middle Kingdom amounted to 143 years according to one of Manetho's Christian reporters; another says 100 years; the Abydos king list names eighteen ephemeral rulers, some of whom are shown, by archaeological finds with their names on, to have really existed. We can only estimate a figure of about 100 years for this period, taking us back to 2200 BCE for the end of the Old Kingdom. The Turin Canon gives 955 years from the time of Menes, first king of Egypt, to the end of the Old Kingdom, whereas the version of Manetho passed on by Sextus Julius Africanus gives 1,497 (a figure probably inflated by Biblical considerations). Most scholars prefer the figure from the Turin Canon over Manetho as it accords better with plausible lengths of reign for the number of kings mentioned in the various lists and/or evidenced by archaeological finds. The Palermo Stone, broken though it is, seems to allow for only a shorter estimate too.

And so we arrive at about 3100 BCE for Menes, founder of the Egyptian state, first king of the first dynasty; before this date, we are in the realm of predynastic Egypt. The pyramids of Giza and, according to most Egyptologists, the Sphinx belong to Dyn. IV, at around 2500 BCE.

There are two other avenues by which dates for Old Kingdom times might be arrived at. One is cross-dating with other civilizations of the ancient world, notably those of Mesopotamia; but contacts between Egypt and Mesopotamia at this remote time, in the very first centuries of written history, are not sufficiently frequent and historically clear-cut to make this method of dating of much use. No Mesopotamian text of the third millennium BCE mentions Egypt. The other avenue is C14 dating, by radiocarbon analysis, which has transformed the study of European prehistory in a spectacular fashion since its invention in the 1950s. Its application to ancient Egypt has been much less impressive, partly because Egyptian dates have perhaps been too well established in Egyptologists' minds for them to feel the need of C14 dating, and more importantly because the inherent imprecision of C14 dates has rendered them less useful in settling fine-detailed questions of Egyptian history than they are when brought to bear on prehistory elsewhere. Nevertheless, as a general check on the overall reliability of the scholars' scheme of Egyptian chronology, C14 dating can make a valuable contribution.

C14 dating is restricted in application to objects of organic origin (or, by extension, to contexts associated with datable organic material); and its date determinations come with a built-in blur of probability rather than sharp focus of certainty that does not always help with narrowly defined historical problems. The quotation of any given C14 date with a plus-and-minus range always indicates only a likelihood that the true date of the sample falls somewhere between the highest and lowest limits, with no preference for the midway date. For example: suppose a C14 date is given as 130 BCE plus-and-minus fifty years. This does not mean that the true date of the organic remains in question is most likely 130 BCE but might just range from 180 to 80 BCE. Rather it means that there is an equal probability (a 68 per cent probability with the usual quotation of C14 datings) that any date between 180 and 80 BCE is the right one. To increase the probability to 95 per cent, the range would extend from 230 to 30 BCE.

As a matter of fact, the first C14 dates that were determined in order to check the potential of the method were derived from Egyptian material. Pieces of wood from Dyn. III and Dyn. IV pyramids were dated, and from a boat of that same Senwosret III. The results of these early tests were close enough to bolster confidence in the new method (or to encourage the Egyptologists in their own system) but thereafter divergences between C14 and received Egyptian chronology were revealed when more tests were made. There are always some considerations to be borne in mind with C14 dating, quite apart from the implications of the probability ranges of the dates. You have to be quite certain about the provenance of the sample, for example, and its association with the context you wish to date; you have to be sure that no contamination with organic material of a different age has taken place; and you have to remember that wood, for example, may have been already old (even by hundreds of years in a country like Egypt where building timber was hard to come by) when it was last used by the people you are hoping to fix in time.

The most reliable C14 dates for any given historical context are those where several different samples of material of known association with the period come out at very much the same dating when tested. Four well-spaced clusters of C14 dates do much to buttress the chronological scheme arrived at by the Egyptologists. Dates for late predynastic material at *c.* 3400 BCE, and for Dyn. I at *c.* 3100 do confirm the Egyptologists' estimate for the very beginnings of Egyptian history. Wood from the Step Pyramid of King Djoser of Dyn. III at *c.* 2700 BCE supplies a confirmatory date for the early part of the Old Kingdom. The New Kingdom pharaoh Akhenaten (Dyn. XVIII), the predecessor of Tutankhamun, is C14 dated to about 1330 BCE, with a plus-and-minus range of fifty years that squares well with his Egyptological dating of 1367–50 BCE. Ramesses II of Dyn. XIX comes out by C14 at 1230–96 BCE, while Egyptologists had arrived at 1290–24 for his reign.

For the Middle Kingdom, there are dates that agree with the Sothic dating of Senwosret III, but also C14 dates that are too early to agree. The use of wood that was already going on for a hundred years old may account for one discrepancy.

Where the Old Kingdom of Dyn. IV is concerned (the age of the pyramids and also the Sphinx according to Egyptologists), there is good agreement between C14 dates of Nubian material of this dynasty and the scholars' scheme. But several C14 determinations for pyramids at Saqqara, Giza and Abu Rawash are too old, by up to several hundreds of years, for the conventional chronology. The C14 samples were of mortar with organic content taken from between the stones. In the case of the Great Pyramid, fifteen samples are reported to have been dated, the youngest coming out at *c.* 2870 BCE, some three hundred years too early by the standards of the received chronology. Khufu's successors, Djedefre at Abu Rawash and Khafre at Giza, show results by C14 that are similarly too early, by up to three hundred years. Menkaure, the builder of the third and smallest pyramid at Giza, comes in his expected place after Khufu and Khafre, but like them too early, as does Wenis of Dyn. V. Sekhemkhet of Dyn. III is likewise dated some hundreds of years too early for conventional chronology, but relatively earlier than Khufu and Khafre as the conventional chronology would expect. In other words, we have a range of Old Kingdom dates that are as expected in terms of their relative chronology, but all too old in terms of their absolute chronology. It has been suggested that the habitual use of old wood for fuel in making the gypsum mortar may be responsible for the discrepancy with the conventional chronology. As we have seen, other predynastic, early dynastic and Old Kingdom C14 date clusters do significantly concur with the scheme so cleverly constructed by the Egyptologists on the basis of Manetho, the Turin Canon, the Palermo Stone, the king lists and the Sothic calendrical calculations. The Egyptian Old Kingdom may therefore be dated with some confidence to between about 2800 and 2200 BCE, and Dyn. IV in particular to a time between about 2650 and 2450 BCE.

The Sphinx certainly carries the head of an Old Kingdom ruler – of Dyn. IV, to go by the style of the head-dress. The face itself bears a strong resemblance to the known faces of Dyn. IV kings like Djedefre, Khafre and Menkaure. The Sphinx could only be older than Dyn. IV if the head was an alteration at that time of an older, and necessarily bigger head (or unfinished lump of rock), attached to an older body. The lion's body cannot be usefully dated on stylistic grounds, because it is badly eroded and was added to in later times. As we saw in Chapter 1, the Sphinx cannot be younger than the building of the pyramids at Giza and their associated rock-cut tombs. The next sphinxes in order of age that we know of after the Great Sphinx belong to late Old Kingdom and Middle Kingdom times and were evidently carved after the Giza model.

The rock out of which the Sphinx is carved cannot at present be directly dated: there have recently been geologically based claims that the weathering of the Sphinx's body points to an age greater (even greater by far) than Old Kingdom times. And it has recently been proposed that the Sphinx rock might be dated by a method based on chemical change (after exposure by carving for example) as a result of cosmic ray bombardment, but it remains to be seen how much credence could be put in this procedure at the Sphinx, in the light of the continual erosion of the surface of the monument.

There are powerful reasons, besides the Dyn. IV head of the monument, to associate the carving of the Sphinx with the building of the pyramids and the two temples close to it (one of which certainly belongs to the pyramid complex of Khafre); moreover, the Sphinx's situation in an enclosure evidently cut into the ditch alongside Khafre's causeway strongly indicates that enclosure and Sphinx constitute a late addition to that complex. In order to understand how the Sphinx might have come to be made as a part of the Dyn. IV necropolis at Giza, it is essential to know about the historical and cultural context of ancient Egypt, its technical capabilities, its religious traditions, its social organization. In order to judge the plausibility of new ideas about the Sphinx's age which want for various different reasons to push its date of carving back into very distant times, it is furthermore essential to know something of the entire course of human evolution and cultural progress on this planet. If at times our review of global prehistory, and even the early days of Egypt itself, seems to take us a long way from the Sphinx at Giza, it must be remembered that all this background is absolutely essential for the understanding of the Sphinx – and certainly for any judgement we can come to about those recent speculations that it might be much older than we thought.

FOUR

BEFORE EGYPT

Herodotus famously called Egypt 'the gift of the Nile'. He was right to emphasize the role of the river in making life not just so abundant but even possible at all in a place with such low rainfall and bounded by deserts. The Nile is the world's second longest river, overtaken only by the Amazon, and the extent of the Nile system from tropical Africa to the Delta is only exceeded by the Mississippi–Missouri system.

It was not always as long a river as it now is. Until about 25,000 BP (before the present), its headstream was probably not the White Nile of today, but the Atbara from the Ethiopian Highlands. Then changes in the drainage system associated with Lake Victoria filled up Lake Sudd in the Sudan until the course of the White Nile was forced through to the north to join up with the Blue Nile and the Atbara. Since the end of the last ice age about ten thousand years ago, when rainfall increased after the cold and dry preceding period, the situation has been that the waters of the White Nile flow north and are augmented by the Blue Nile and the Atbara, after which no more tributaries further feed the river until it runs out through the Delta into the Mediterranean Sea. The rains of early summer falling on the Ethiopian Highlands swell the Blue Nile and the Atbara to the point where their inflow is able to hold back the waters of the White Nile and at the same time send up the level of the true Nile below the fifth cataract throughout the length of Nubia and Egypt, carrying nutrient silt from the highlands with it. (The silts are spread during the season of Nile flood over the extent of the river valley and the Delta – the Delta is in fact an old gulf of the Mediterranean Sea filled with silt from the Ethiopian Highlands.) When the declining rains cease to supply the Blue Nile and Atbara from September on, the waters of the White Nile resume their flow until the following May, preventing too rapid a drop in the level of the Nile in Egypt, and maintaining the river over the winter months.

It was this annual summer phenomenon of inundation with fertilizing waters that made possible the benign pattern of ancient Egyptian agriculture, with a reliable growing season and harvest and an equally reliable season when there really was not much to do in the fields. And it was successful agriculture with

Opposite: A great stone tower of prehistoric Jericho. Photo: Paul Jordan

surplus wealth and time for civilized pursuits, not trade or foreign conquest, that was the main support of the ancient Egyptian state from first to last. It was Nile-based agriculture that made possible the emergence of Egyptian civilization and the social organization that could undertake irrigation schemes to increase production, build pyramids, carve the Great Sphinx. Agriculture was adopted (late by world standards) in Egypt after about 5000 BCE, and metalworking – also vital to large-scale constructional efforts – after 4000 BCE.

Food production, followed by metalworking, writing and ordered civilization were a chain of social inventions whose impetus goes back to the challenge posed to Stone Age hunter-gatherers by the vast alteration of the world at the end of the last ice age. Human beings of some sort, ancestral forms of modern man, had been on earth for more than two million years before any of them turned from hunting and gathering as the main means of subsistence to food production by way of agriculture and pastoralism, with possibilities of regular surplus and settled living in larger groupings. During the time-span of man on earth, previous ice ages and their aftermaths had issued their challenges to human ingenuity, but the breakthrough to food production was never made until the end of the last ice age. This state of affairs may have resulted from the interplay of many factors but it seems clear that it required the full establishment of the modern species of human being, Homo sapiens sapiens, with many millennia of experience in social organization, in language, and in technical progress to prepare the way for the decisive change from hunting to farming.

Humanity and the apes may have parted evolutionary company as recently as five or six million years ago, to go by the genetic correspondences of human beings and chimpanzees. One or two million years later, an animal that is an ape but more like a human being than any living chimpanzee or gorilla was thriving in east and southern Africa. It is called the Southern Ape, Australopithecus, and its remains have been recovered in some quantity (showing a range of species within the genus), with the occasional survival of rarer bits and pieces, such as limb bones and even digits, that are always less likely to be still around after millions of years than skulls and teeth. The bones of Australopithecus render it possible to produce reconstructions that make him out to be a very plausible ancestor to the human line: he was short of stature, with a small brain (bigger than any modern ape's), but capable of regularly walking on two legs like no ape. In particular, the more slender variety of australopithecines appears to have evolved around two million years ago into the first representatives of the genus Homo, to which we ourselves belong as Homo sapiens. With this evolution, there appeared a momentous development in the human story: the habit and tradition of toolmaking. Other animals (including birds) may be said to use tools, in the form of adventitious objects in the world around them, to facilitate their acquisition of food: chimpanzees, for instance, will sometimes use sticks to poke out what they want. But man and his direct ancestors are the only animals to have systematically gone about the manufacture of tools for regular use.

Toolmaking marks a great intellectual advance in the evolution of man: its invention not only denotes an increase of intelligence among our ancestors, but it has also played its own part in fostering that very increase in terms of intellectual and imaginative stimulation under the pressure of Natural Selection. A tool made to a regular pattern, however crude (and the first tools were crudely modified pebbles), was a new concept for evolving mankind – one might even say the first concept, for here was a wholly new sort of relationship with the natural world that must have made our ancestors think hard and gave them, perhaps for the first time, something to try to talk about. Needless to say, toolmaking conferred immense survival benefits on its practitioners by enhancing their scope for the manipulation of the world about them, in catching and cutting up food in shapes and sizes and quantities beyond the means of non-toolmaking creatures (in particular energy-efficient meat), and working aspects of the environment into more useful forms, like shelters against the weather which are archaeologically attested at this time. Toolmaking was the harbinger of all the revolutionary inventions of the human race, including the innovations of farming and metalworking after the end of the last ice age that made civilizations such as that of ancient Egypt possible, and all their works.

A succession of ice ages is the backdrop of the story of toolmaking man's further evolution and spread over the whole globe. Since about two-and-a-half million years ago, the Earth has been locked into a phase of continually fluctuating climate, with many periods colder than the present and a few that were much warmer. The last eight hundred thousand years, the time when the genus Homo has spread all over the world (save Antarctica till absolutely modern times), has been a period of often very severe glaciation, with great extension of the polar ice sheets and the pushing south over presently temperate zones of subarctic climates. With so much precipitation locked up in the glaciers, worldwide sea level has often been much lower than it is today. During the phases of glaciation, conditions well away from the ice in subtropical and tropical areas have been drier and cooler than they are now. We are living in an interglacial episode that may already be past its peak of warmth and precipitation (which occurred before about 3000 BCE) and on its way back to glaciation – give or take man-made climatic interference in the shape of global warming. The evidence indicates that ice ages come on slowly and hesitantly with frequent fluctuations, but end more rapidly, with relatively sudden rises of temperature, flooding and the return of temperate patterns of vegetation and animal life to areas that have been subarctic during the cold years.

Homo erectus was the human species that spread all over the Old World after about one million years before the present. The species' name reflects the old belief that this was the first upright walking form of 'man' – the australopithecines have turned out to take that laurel. But certainly it was with erectus that the skeleton below the neck achieved more or less its modern form. It is important to note that the generally modern look of the erectus skeletons that we can reconstruct may all the same cloak some important differences from fully modern man: the size of the hole through which the nerves run down the backbone is smaller than ours, for example, and may have implications for the degree of voluntary muscle control that these animals could muster. This would have been very important for the control of breathing that plays such a part in speech and the development of language. At the same time it has been conjectured that the voice-boxes of no form of man until the arrival of Homo sapiens sapiens were capable of uttering speech. Speech and language are crucial in human evolution – without them, the conscious formulation of thought is impossible. The ancient Egyptians appreciated the creative role of speech when they imagined their god Ptah bringing things into existence by uttering them with his tongue.

A gradual physical evolution marks the half million years or so of the erectus heyday, and a gradual evolution of the tools of these first human beings. Of course, it is the stone tools that have survived in abundance, though there is some evidence for the use of wood, too, in the form of spears, but clearly most of the non-stone products of these people have inevitably disappeared. The commonest implement was the so-called hand-axe, an all-purpose tool that lasted for hundreds of thousands of years as a favourite piece of technology. Hand-axes are to be found at the Kharga Oasis, about 200 km west of Thebes in Egypt, and along old shorelines of the river Nile, formed when a broader river flowed at higher levels than the present stream. In time, the preparation of the cores of flint (or other suitable stones) from which these tools were made was elaborated, and flakes from the cores were made into a widening range of additional tool types. By two hundred thousand years ago, flake technology was to the fore, and the first appearances of more modern forms of man occur in the human fossil record. The heavy faces, with huge jaws and massive brow-ridges, and small brain-cases of erectus are rivalled from now on by finds of individuals with reducing jaws and bigger brains. The first really modern forms of man have been discovered in South Africa at over one hundred thousand years before the present.

As the latest series of severely cold times came on in about 75,000 BP, a pronouncedly cold-adapted form of human being evolved in Europe whom all the world knows as Neanderthal Man, Homo sapiens neanderthalensis, wielding a developed flake technology and exhibiting, for the first time, such a truly human trait as careful burial of the dead, with provision of grave goods such as tools and pieces of meat that suggest the idea of continuity of existence after death. Whether Neanderthal Man could speak anything worthy of the name of language is debatable, though he was probably capable of it. But he produced no works of art as far as we have discovered in any of his dwelling places (mostly caves, though there is evidence of skin-covered huts), but with the furnishing of his graves we detect the first signs of a concern that human beings have since made much of, none more so than the ancient Egyptians.

More fully modern forms of man are attested in the Near East and south-east Europe by forty thousand years ago. With their full appearance in the fossil record as Homo sapiens sapiens there goes an explosion of technological inventiveness in the forms and types of flint tools and a great extension in the use of other materials, notably bone and antler. Needles bear witness to the making of elaborate clothing. These people possessed clear survival advantages over the

Neanderthals, which must have included language and all that that implies of abstract thought and sophisticated communication.

Most famously in the cave sites of France and Northern Spain, but also notably in Central and Eastern Europe, these people of the last ice age, which reached its peak about eighteen thousand years ago, exhibited a range of achievements not just in technology but also in art that makes them the equals of any hunter-gatherer societies that have existed since. Indeed, in their art they are at the forefront of all human achievement. The paintings of Lascaux, and other places like it, with their acutely observed depictions of the wild animals of the time, are sufficient reminder of this truth. It must have taken the coming together of many strands of physical, mental and social evolution to reach the point where all this was possible. The brain needed to be large enough and organized to be capable of language, voice-box and breathing control required to be ready for the task of speech. Speech itself needed to have evolved, perhaps over a long period, from simple concepts and mere chatter (a sort of sociable grooming, not to be despised as social cement) into sophisticated language and abstract thought, able to remember the past and imagine the future, to learn from shared experience and plan new strategies in concert.

Such were the accomplishments of the human race as the last ice age entered its final and hardest stage, between about 18,000 and 13,000 BP. By thirteen thousand years ago, around 11,000 BCE, worldwide sea levels were rising again as the glaciers started to melt and retreat. The modern species of man, albeit in small numbers, was now to be encountered in all the habitable places of the world, including Australia and the Americas. Everywhere men and women got their livelihood by hunting game and gathering plants. In Europe the hunters possessed an advanced Stone Age tool kit with finely finished little blades of flint, bone and antler harpoons, fowling forks and fish hooks, to exploit the rich game potential of the woods and creeks that replaced the tundra of the ice age. In Africa and the Far East stone technology with blades, scrapers, and bone-working tools is similarly in evidence; in Australia we find tools made from flakes of stone and in the Americas finely worked projectile points that tipped the spears of the hunters. The world of 10,000 BCE belonged everywhere to hunter-gatherers with an advanced Stone Age technology.

The climatic changes that followed rapidly upon the end of the ice age brought warmer conditions to the higher latitudes and wetter ones to more southerly zones. Flora and fauna that had been pushed out of the way by the cold and dry conditions before about 11,000 BCE now moved north again to recolonize old habitats previously lost to the harshness of the ice age. Wild cereals migrated back to the Near East as the steppe retreated north and east to Central Asia. The importance of such wild cereals to the hunter-gatherers in the region to the east of the Mediterranean is attested in the archaeological record by flint sickle blades and bone sickle handles used to gather in the wild grains, which constituted an easily storable supply of food. This was not yet the controlled growing of crops, but rather the extensive exploitation of a wild resource that preceded real agriculture. (It had happened before in recent human history, notably in Nubia and Egypt during the dry times before the end of the ice age: flint blades with the characteristic edge sheen produced by gathering grasses have been found there. But these instances did not lead to agriculture and settled living; there are no archaeological signs of larger communities with permanent dwellings and no traces of cultivated strains of cereal.)

In the postglacial world of the eastern Mediterranean hinterland, the immense innovation of crop growing in place of mere gathering was finally accomplished, for the first time in the archaeological record.

This oldest known development of agriculture occurred in an area called the Fertile Crescent, arching from the eastern Delta borders of Egypt through Palestine and southern Anatolia to Mesopotamia, with an eastern extension to the Zagros Mountains. The postglacial pattern of vegetation over this area included the large-seeded grasses that are the wild ancestors of wheat and barley. In the seeds of these grasses, able to withstand summer drought, an attractive source of food was stored for the gatherers of postglacial times, if they could gather enough of them. At the same time, across North Africa and on through Palestine and Syria to the Zagros, there was a tradition of hunting the herd animals that were the wild prototypes of sheep and goats, cattle and pigs. None of this gathering of seeds and hunting of herds was actual farming practice, but it prepared the way.

The same sort of seed-gathering that had already gone on in Nubia and Egypt had now been practised in Palestine, and developed further. Among the remains of some groups of hunter-gatherers of about 9000 BCE in this area, excavation has turned up sickle flints and mortars that testify to the collection and preparation of grass seeds. These people seem moreover to have deliberately sown seeds away from the places where the grasses were growing naturally, which represents an even bigger interference with nature than at first appears: for to be able to preserve seed-heads for transport to other sites, the less easily shattered heads must have been selected from among the wild grasses (whose heads tend to shatter all too easily), and thus was initiated the human selection of breeds of plant to evolve the domesticated forms of wheat and barley and so on that we know today. At Jericho, about 20 km from where wild grasses still grow today in the Judaean hills, the seeds were grown in ground watered by the spring, with rapid benefit to the community who occupied the site. By 8000 BCE, there was a large settlement here with houses built to last out of mud-brick, a stone wall around the village with a rock-cut ditch and a stone tower 9 m high with interior staircase. In the archaeological record of the world, nothing of the like has ever been found that pre-dates Jericho. Over the next millennium after 8000 BCE, there was a great spread of farming villages over the ancient Near East, and plants were cultivated not just for food. Flax was grown to provide fibres for weaving and soon quite complicated textiles were being made. For all the cultivation of wild grasses, the hunting of wild animals still supplied a great deal of the food of these people.

But what could be done by way of domestication with plants could also be done with animals. To the east of the Levant, in the Zagros range, archaeology turns up to begin with less evidence of plant exploitation but shows that a wider range of animals was hunted, among them wild sheep and goats, ripe for domestication. Sheep may have begun to be herded as early as 9000 BCE, though sheep breeding really got under way only after 7000. Both sheep and goats could be fed on a more varied and so more easily obtainable diet than other potential domesticates, and goats could be milked. Goats and pigs were added to the list of domesticated animals around 7000 BCE, cattle at about 6000. At Ganj Dareh in the Zagros the abundant imprints of hooves bear witness to the exploitation of sheep and goat already in the eighth millennium.

The earliest traces of agriculture and pastoralism known to archaeology have been found in the region of the Fertile Crescent, but farming was developed in other parts of the globe at a not much later date. This could have happened on occasion as the result of the diffusion of the idea around the ancient world, but more likely the farming way of life was sometimes invented quite independently in different places. After the evolution of Homo sapiens sapiens, people everywhere were clever enough to see the possibilities of the world around them, especially when environmental pressures – changing climates, for example, or population growth – put a premium on innovation. Farming spread to Europe by 6000 BCE, and was probably independently developed in Middle America at about the same time, in Africa in the middle of the sixth millennium, in the Far East possibly before 5000 BCE.

But farming did not get off to a particularly early start in Egypt, probably because the hunter-gatherer way of life followed along the Nile provided an easy living without it. Along the banks of a river flowing broader than it does nowadays, fed by more abundant rains in Ethiopia than today's, with swamps and wadis that had not yet run dry, there was ample game to be had in the Egypt of 6–7000 BCE, and the seeds of the wild grasses could go on being collected without recourse to domestication. Between the end of the ice age and about 3000 BCE, and to an extent for a few hundred years more, there was (with some fluctuation) more rainfall in Egypt and to its south and west than there is now. The full return of wetter conditions after the end of the dry period of the ice age has been moderated since about 3000 BCE. In Egypt, farming arrived a little late, after 5000 BCE in Upper Egypt and possibly slightly earlier in the Delta. By that time, further technological and social innovations had already been pioneered in the wider world.

As the first few millennia of the farming way of life went by, after about 8000 BCE, and more plants and animals were added to the repertoire of domestication, with an increase in yield and the provision of real surpluses to be stored and administered, so divisions of wealth and power became marked, along with big increases in population. Whereas the hunter-gatherers had worked hard together from time to time and the first farmers had worked very hard together most of the time, now there were poorer or landless peasants working drudge-hard all the time and richer landowners (in the form of chiefs and medicine men) directing them, administering their production and living off their labour. There was seafaring and trade, too, around the eastern end of the

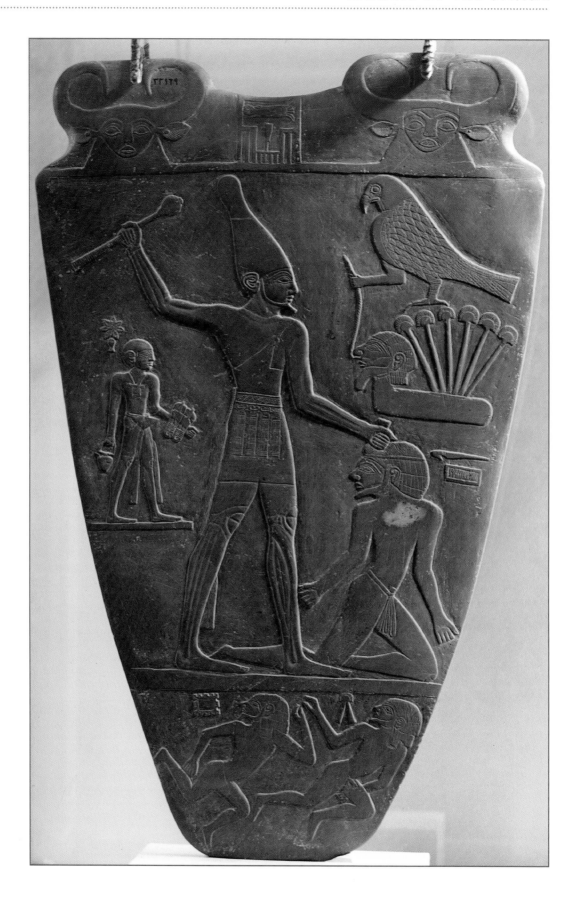

Mediterranean as farming spread wider. Pottery-making was added to the technical accomplishments of the farming societies. It too seems to have been independently invented in different parts of the globe: even as early as about 10,000 BCE in Japan, but only after 7000 BCE in any substantial way in the Near East; in Africa (but not in Egypt) it dates back to the eighth millennium BCE, in India to the sixth, in the Americas and in most of Western Europe to the fourth. Metals like copper and gold were fashioned by hammering and cutting from about 9000 BCE onwards, but copper smelting was first pioneered after 7000 BCE in the Near East and south-east Europe. Once again human cleverness appears to have hit upon smelting and casting quite independently in different places at different times. Metalworking reached the rest of Europe and North Africa after 4000 BCE. Irrigation as a means of increasing crop yield was extensively applied in Mesopotamia from about 5000 BCE onward.

This was the world context in which the civilization of the Nile Valley began to take shape after the introduction of farming there between 5000 and 4500 BCE, two thousand years or more before the building of the pyramids and the reign of King Khafre to whom Egyptologists attribute the carving of the Sphinx. Without farming to create surplus wealth and leisure and promote social inequality, the organization needed to build the pyramids would not have come into being and Egypt would not have been unified under a king able to command the resources for the job; without the availability of metal technology, the tools needed to shape the blocks out of which the pyramids were built would not have existed; without their basically agricultural religion, which measured its seasonal round by the Sun, Moon and stars, it may be doubted whether the ancient Egyptians would ever have wanted to build the pyramids or carve the Sphinx.

Opposite: The Narmer Palette, from the earliest days of Egyptian history, shows the king in identification with the hawk god Horus and wearing the White Crown to smite his enemies. Cairo Museum.

FIVE

FROM EGYPT'S FIRST FARMERS TO ITS FIRST DYNASTIES

Egyptological reasoning and C14 dating indicate that the Egyptian state and civilization came into being at about 3100 BCE. It was at this date that full and final unification of the communities along the Nile Valley and over the Delta took place (give or take later periods of social turbulence) under kings decked with royal attributes that were to persist throughout Egyptian history; at this time, too, a system of writing was adopted which would similarly continue until the end of the civilization, and which made possible the recording of historical events, among other things.

Egypt was not the world's first civilization, nor the place where writing was first employed: some of the impetus for these developments in Egypt may well have come from the slightly older civilizations to the east around the head of the Persian Gulf. But among the world's first civilizations, Egypt was by 3000 BCE the only unified state. Self-sufficiency in agriculture and the topographical isolation of the Nile Valley promoted the unity of the land. There was trade from predynastic times onwards with the east, and with the south via Nubia, but on the whole Egypt was a self-contained culture – even when it took in influences from abroad.

At the time (around 8000 BCE) when the people of Jericho in Palestine were living in mud-brick houses by their spring, sowing grass seeds, harvesting the crop, hunting gazelle, and defending themselves with their great stone towers, the archaeological record can show no comparably advanced settlement to have existed anywhere in the world, and certainly not in Egypt. Along the Nile, there were bands of hunters and fishers, reaping but not sowing, making an undemanding but perhaps equally unstimulating living off the land they roamed over. They were to go on like that for another three thousand years. The pictures they sometimes engraved on rocks in the wadis where they hunted show the animals they could easily bag for food – Barbary sheep, antelope, even elephant.

By the time that farming was adopted in Egypt (probably as a result of an acquaintance with the idea of farming rather than the invasion of new farming people) in about 5000 BCE, there had already been some spectacular progress in

Opposite: The other side of the Narmer Palette shows the king with the Red Crown, celebrating his success in battle. The intertwined necks of the serpent–feline hybrid animals probably symbolize the unification of Egypt.

Finds from predynastic Egypt. Photo: Paul Jordan.

social organization, technology and trade in other parts of the ancient world, as we have seen. In southern Mesopotamia towards the Persian Gulf, village communities that pre-date the appearance of the world's first civilization – that of the Sumerians – were established on the basis of irrigation fed by the twin rivers Tigris and Euphrates. Irrigation made agriculture possible where it had not been possible before and promoted higher crop yield: at the same time it called for a greater degree of co-operative labour and a more elaborate form of social organization, with leaders and led. The prototypes of kings and priests emerged from the ranks of village chiefs and medicine men: seals and seal impressions hint at authority and ownership.

While the people who lived along the Nile Valley and among the Delta streams were not among the first beneficiaries of the spread of the farming way of life, in fact their land was ideally suited to the practice of irrigation agriculture, far more reliably so than Mesopotamia. For the annual inundation of the land on the river's banks, when waters laden with fertilizing silt spread over the flood plain, made growing crops a profitable and not so very arduous proposition. With some effort put into planned irrigation, things might be better still. Agriculture had a bright future in Egypt from the moment of its inception, down to the time when latter-day Egypt would be the bread-basket of the Roman Empire.

Nonetheless it was in Mesopotamia, in the land of Sumer at the head of the Persian Gulf, that human civilization first arose on this earth. Here it was that villages became cities, village shrines became temples, chiefs became kings and medicine men became priests. Here writing was first devised, initially to keep records of wealth and property in about 3500 BCE. But Sumer remained, like ancient Greece later on, a land of city-states, and its kings never put on the divinity of the kings of Egypt.

The village chiefs of the first farming communities of Egypt back in about 5000 BCE cannot have dreamed of the grandeur of the rulers of the Old

A restored wall painting from Tomb 100 at Hierakonpolis, with human figure and lions at top left. Cairo Museum.

Kingdom some two thousand years after them, but there was probably always some ideological strain in the tradition of the predynastic Egyptian leaders that emphasized their quasi-divine role among their people. It is tempting to relate this status to the African traditions of chiefdom that have lasted into modern times. Dim memory of the long line of revered petty kings who preceded the named rulers of unified Egypt accounts for the Egyptians' belief in historical times that their land had been ruled, after the reigns of gods like Osiris and Horus, by demigods following in their footsteps.

The first evidence of agriculture turns up in both the Delta and in Upper Egypt, and also in the Faiyum region, at around the same date of 5000 BCE. The Faiyum today is the shrunken remains of a once extensive lake, to the south and west of Cairo, fed by a western branch of the Nile that leaves the main river still further south and flows roughly parallel to the Nile for more than 200 km before emptying into the Faiyum Depression. Prior to 6000 BCE, there were hunters around the Faiyum, who have left behind their late Stone Age flints at the edges of the larger and deeper lake of old. After 5000 BCE, hunting of mainly gazelle, but also hippopotamus and elephant (for the African megafauna, including lions and crocodiles, extended this far north in those wetter days), was supplemented by the cultivation of emmer wheat and barley. Animal domestication was very limited: these people could only just be called farmers. Their agricultural produce was stored in basket-lined pits, but their pottery was of poor quality. They milled their flour on stone querns and they grew flax to make linen. In the western Delta, archaeological evidence of a similar culture has been found, again with rather plain pots but perhaps more in the way of animal domestication. These people lived in wicker houses which were sometimes plastered with mud at the

The Battlefield Palette.
British Museum.

base. In general, the Faiyum and Delta farmers had more in common with farming communities of the eastern Mediterranean than with the farmers of Upper Egypt.

The farmers of southern Egypt are known by some of their settlement sites, but more particularly by their graves on the desert's edge. The graves were dug into the ground and lined with basketwork or skins. From the burials comes evidence of linen cloth, of bracelets and necklaces of shell, of ivory needles and combs, of blue-glazed beads. Their flint work was not as good as that of the Lower Egyptians of the time, but their pots are more impressive, red-brown in colour and with darker, burnished rims. Their art, seen in examples of little (usually female) figures from the graves, carved in ivory, gives off no hint of the distinctive character of Old Kingdom art, from which it is separated in time by fifteen hundred years. Stone palettes on which malachite was ground to make eye paint, some stained green with use, do suggest a continuity of personal grooming habits with the historical Egyptians.

In Upper Egypt, this first farming culture evolved over perhaps a thousand years without any indication of input from outside, spreading more widely along the Nile Valley but still showing little sign of social stratification in any marked differentiation of wealth in grave goods. The graves were now perhaps roofed with branches and heaped over with a little tumulus. Pottery improved, with highly polished red bowls and tall vases, occasionally decorated with white geometric patterns and sometimes depictions of animals like goats and hippos. The cosmetic palettes continued in geometric and animal shapes, some of them seeming to go beyond the simply practical and suggesting ceremonial intent: large ceremonial palettes are a feature of the very earliest semi-historical times, hundreds of years later than these early predynastic finds. There are bone combs, too, sometimes with animal carvings to the handles, and the figurines continue, again usually of women. And still the distinctive elements of the historical Egyptian style are only to be glimpsed now and then: the hairstyle of one carved figure suggests the wig fashion so favoured by the later Egyptians. Stone vases were hollowed out with some sort of brace and bit (the bit was of hard stone, not metal). Flint was mined for knives and scraping tools. Some of the graves have yielded hard stone mace-heads, clearly on the pattern of weapons, but again – like some of the cosmetic palettes – of no obvious use in terms of size or adequate provision for shafting. Probably these things were specials, made for the furnishing of the graves. The later Egyptian preoccupation with provision for the afterlife is well foreshadowed here.

After 3500 BCE, a change comes over the entire network of cultures along the Nile. It is worth recalling that at about this time the first real civilization was appearing in southern Mesopotamia, with formal state and religious organization and the invention of writing. At this time in Egypt a more uniform culture than before is in evidence over the entire country from the First Cataract to the apex of the Delta, with the development of distinct concentrations of population at certain places. For the first time, clear signs of contact with the outside world are to be seen in the archaeological record, with new items

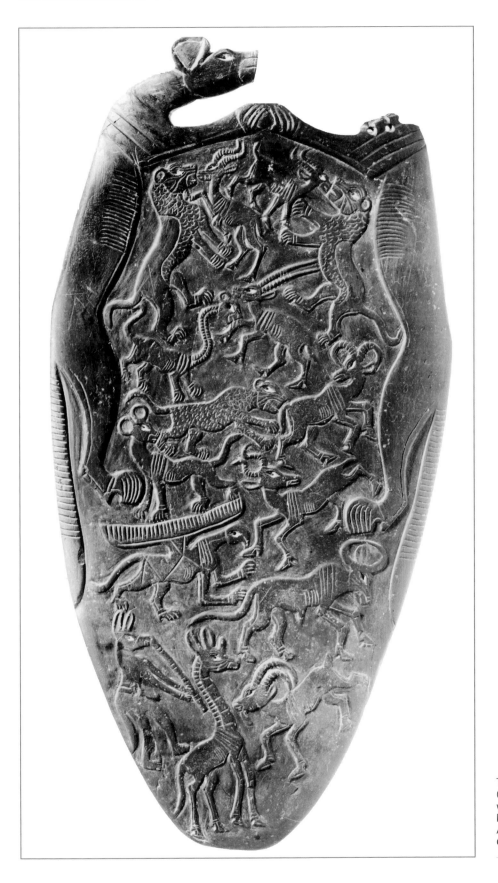

The Oxford Palette with (left below centre) a winged, falcon-headed and lion-bodied 'griffin'. Ashmolean Museum, Oxford.

appearing among the grave goods. This has suggested to some scholars the infiltration, perhaps even invasion, of outsiders in Egypt, but it might just as well indicate the effects of trade and the diffusion of ideas. The language of historical Egypt evinces mainly Semitic traits mixed with North African elements, but the origins of this situation may be very complex. Despite the new items among the grave goods, there is also clear continuity with the preceding earlier predynastic culture, whose origin was in Upper Egypt. The new elements could have entered Egypt via the eastern Delta area, or much further south across the desert from the Red Sea. The extensive use of copper only comes in at this period, suggesting trade with Sinai or expansion into the Eastern Desert, where copper ore was mined. Copper now became the commonplace material for weapons and tools, though flint was still used for fine carving implements and for sickle blade segments. There is as yet little evidence for the carving and shaping of large pieces of stone, but the adoption of copper tools paved the way for this development.

The graves of this later predynastic culture tend to be rectangular rather than oval in shape, and more often lined with mud-bricks. In this they probably follow the pattern of the new housing of this period, built out of brick and rectangular in form. The pots of these people are more highly decorated than ever before, with depictions of people, animals, plants and, most strikingly, of boats with cabins and oars and ceremonial standards. In one case, there is on a boat a dancing figure, apparently of a woman, with hands over head: similar figures carved in ivory have come from the graves.

Opposite: Early dynastic 'mastaba' tombs at Saqqara.

One tomb at Hierakonpolis in Upper Egypt (a very important late predynastic centre) features boat pictures and the image of a human figure with two lions.

The Hunters' Palette. British Museum.

A feraciously snarling lion from Coptos. Ashmolean Museum, Oxford.

This association of lions with human or divine power faintly prefigures the sphinx icon of historical times. But all the same, this tomb (which is floored and lined with bricks) shows very little of the unmistakable character of historical Egypt, even of early dynastic Egypt, though only a few hundred years separate it from the first flowering of the civilization. But a circle of sandstone blocks at Hierakonpolis, forming the base of some large predynastic shrine, does look forward to the building achievements of the historical Egyptians.

The mace-heads and palettes of early predynastic times continue in the late predynastic period, but there are some definitely exotic novelties. Mesopotamian cylinder seals are among them, actual imports from abroad, whose pattern was afterwards adopted by the Egyptians. Fantastic animal motifs of contemporary Mesopotamian inspiration appear for a while among Egyptian decorations: a pair of serpent–feline hybrids, with their long necks intertwined, decorates one side of a cosmetic palette, for example, while another shows, among many other animals, hunting lions and a 'griffin' with the body of a lion and the head and wings of a hawk. Many of the same artistic tendencies that were to produce the sphinx icon are in place here, on this late predynastic palette called 'The Oxford' because of its location in the Ashmolean Museum. There is the strong presence of the lion motif, the hybridization of beasts (though not yet of man with beast), the nearly sphinx-like conjunction of lion body with hawk head and the winging of the lion body that was to be seen again in much later historical times. Indeed, we may be looking at the remote beginnings of the sphinx idea: certainly the hawk's head calls to mind the falcon-god Horus of historical Egypt. But as yet, on the very eve of historical Egypt, there has nowhere occurred in the archaeological record a single depiction of the classic lion-bodied man-headed sphinx.

The king of beasts, which still roamed the Nile Valley in predynastic times (and indeed well on into Egyptian history), is frequently pictured on late predynastic objects, but nowhere is the lion depicted in a way that closely resembles the body of the Sphinx. On various palettes the lion is shown standing up and in action, goring his prey ('Battlefield Palette') or being hunted ('Hunters' Palette') and the mane is treated in a very distinctive style, all over the head and shoulders of the beast, in a way not seen again in historical times, not even on the maned Middle Kingdom sphinxes. Where carvings in the round are concerned, late predynastic or early dynastic lions are shown in ferocious mood, heads raised and mouths open in a snarl, and tails curled right over the top of their haunches – like the 30-cm-long little lion in speckled granite that is now in a Berlin museum, or the little lion from Coptos in the Ashmolean. A larger pair of lions (1.3 m long) found at Coptos, in the same fierce style, may have been placed as guardians of a late predynastic temple there: if so, they prefigure the guardian role of the sphinxes of historical times and hint at the early development of religious notions about guardian deities that underlie the evolution of the sphinx idea. The famous Gebel el-Arak knife handle, carved in ivory, shows much more clearly than the Hierakonpolis tomb the motif of the hero subduing two lions. Though both lions and man are here depicted in a heavily Mesopotamian style, it is possible that the Egyptians already interpreted this motif in their own terms, as we shall see later. What all these late predynastic lion depictions do is to demonstrate the potency of the lion image for the emergent civilization of ancient Egypt. The king is readily to be identified with the lion for obvious reasons of strength and prowess – likewise with the bull, which also features on the palettes, and with the falcon. From late predynastic Coptos, interestingly, there also comes the earliest evidence in Egypt of a taste for larger-than-life statuary, in the form of 4-m-tall figures that foreshadow the historical god Min. This tendency towards the gigantic would also play its part in the creation of the sphinx image.

The most important thing that seems to have been imported into Egypt from Mesopotamia was writing. It was the idea of writing that the late predynastic Egyptians adopted, not the specific signs used by the Mesopotamians. Writing

A pair of lions from Coptos in University College, London.

was developed among the Sumerians in about 3500 BCE, a few hundred years before it appears in Egypt on the very eve of dynastic times. It first occurs in Egypt on some of those slate palettes, in particular on the very important 'Narmer Palette' from Hierakonpolis that clearly dates to the time when Egypt was first unified under a single ruler of all of Upper and Lower Egypt. Here for the first time Egypt's king is shown in the garb and stance of the rulers of the historical kingdom, effortlessly subduing his enemies in a posture of smiting that was to be repeated on umpteen temple walls over the following three thousand years. Doing that, he wears what later ages called the 'White Crown' of Upper Egypt, while a falcon faces him: on the other side of the palette, he wears the 'Red Crown' of Lower Egypt to review his standards and survey the headless corpses of his enemies. Before him here is written his name in early hieroglyphs, Nr Mr, Nar-mer. The same name is prominently displayed at the top of both sides of the palette. Whether this Narmer (or Meri-nar) is the Menes of Manetho, the Meni of the Turin Canon, the first king of unified Egypt according to the later Egyptians, cannot now be exactly determined. A clay jar sealing with the name of Narmer also carries the hieroglyphs for the sounds of m and n, but then so does a docket with the name of another early king called Aha. The full word represented by the letters mn probably meant 'He who endures' and may have been a royal title – one that was later remembered as a personal name. At all events, the Narmer Palette clearly belongs to the time when Egypt came into being as a unified state in about 3100 BCE. This political unification was probably preceded by a period of cultural unification, during which the culture of Upper Egypt spread to the north. Political power may have long been concentrated into a unit in the south: it is not so certain that a single political entity existed in the north before 'Menes'; it may have been more a matter of many chiefdoms in the Delta, with more cultural affinity to the east than to the south until the culture of Upper Egypt spread north in the centuries before full unification. The united kingship of Egypt put the organization of irrigation and agriculture and of mining and trade under a single rule from Nubia to the Delta, with obvious benefits to the growing economy of the time, and at whatever cost to the previous political arrangements in different parts of the country. But the ancient Egyptians of historical times liked to think dualistically about their world: life and death, field and desert, day and night, east and west, north and south; and so Upper and Lower Egypt were considered to be always two poles of an eternal duality.

The five hundred years that began in about 3200 BCE and ended with the close of what Egyptologists call the Archaic Period, after Dyn. II, were times of rapid growth and astonishing change. In truth, little of the sophisticated civilization of Old Kingdom times (Dyns III–VI) was in evidence at the beginning of those five hundred years, yet at the end of the Archaic dynasties everything was in place. Social and political organization, better managed agriculture, writing and bureaucracy paved the way for the achievements of the next five hundred years.

Though the rulers of united Egypt were of Upper Egyptian origin, at the time

A small ivory docket showing King Den of Dyn. I in smiting pose. British Museum.

of unification they established their capital city at Memphis, a place ideally suited at the apex of the Delta to exercise their power both south into Upper Egypt and north over Lower Egypt. A strong religious tradition associated with their southern origins led these first kings to continue to have themselves buried near Abydos, but some of their high officials were buried in large mud-brick tombs close to Memphis at Saqqara, thus initiating a funerary tradition that lasted throughout the Old Kingdom. Saqqara was the principal burial ground of Memphis during the early dynasties, but tombs were also built at Giza just to the north. The oldest tomb at Giza lies about 1.5 km south-east of the Great Pyramid: it is a large flat-topped mud-brick tomb of Dyn. I; nearby there is a tomb of Dyn. II. Both of these tombs pre-date the building of the Giza pyramids by several hundreds of years.

Coming as it does at the very beginning of Egyptian history, when written material is exiguous and harder to con, when moreover the records of later times that deal with it are at their most obscure, the Archaic Period of Dyns I and II presents many problems of archaeological interpretation. Nonetheless, the sequence of rulers can be established in some detail and the names of the kings (and a queen regent) unearthed by archaeology can be partially married to the names given by the later ancient Egyptian king lists and by Manetho.

Even the royal tombs of the Archaic Period were modest affairs by comparison with the Old Kingdom pyramids and the New Kingdom tombs in the Valley of the Kings. They were built mostly of mud-brick and all of them were, of course, comprehensively ransacked in antiquity, long before the Egyptologists unearthed them. But the finds that have sometimes been made in them despite the robbing of the past do demonstrate that they were originally furnished with vast quantities of grave goods, like finely worked stone vessels and objects made of copper. Even in historical Egypt it was still copper rather than bronze (which required tin to alloy with copper) out of which tools, weapons and vessels were usually fashioned. Hammered copper could produce very sharp tools which, when used with a quartz sand abrasive, were capable of cutting up stone blocks, like those of the pyramids. Iron was rare in the extreme until after 1000 BCE, and what little there was of it was probably derived from meteorites. The tombs of the early dynasties have also yielded stray finds, missed by the robbers of old, of gold, turquoise and amethyst, and fragments of furniture have been found.

The superstructures of the tombs of the Archaic Period sometimes mimicked the exterior appearance of the sort of houses that kings and high courtiers inhabited in life. Some wood (probably imported from Lebanon) and much mud-brick were used to construct them, with decorative recessed buttressing on the outside. But there was occasional use of stone, for door jambs for example, and the last king of the Archaic Period, whose own tomb chamber was hewn into stone, is recorded as having built a temple, called 'The Goddess Endures', out of stone. Much was to come of this precedent: copper tools and the cutting of stone prefigure the architectural achievements of the pyramid age. And so does the presence, buried within some of the Archaic tombs, of a tumulus mound – looking back to the little tumuli that covered some predynastic graves and forward to those great mounds of stone that the Greeks called 'the pyramids', jesting about their resemblance in shape to cakes.

The common toilers of ancient Egypt in the Archaic Period, and indeed until New Kingdom times or later, could look forward to no such elaborate tombs and funerary provisions as did their kings and high officials. They were probably popped into shallow desert graves like their predynastic ancestors. But the idea of trying to preserve the body after death, as a religious prerequisite of the afterlife, was probably derived from the observation that burial in the hot dry sands did indeed prevent decay and promote tissue preservation. In fact, burial in tombs made a much worse job of preservation than the desert sands, unless some technique of mummification was applied to the corpse. The first prototype mummies are known from tombs of the Archaic Period: here was another tradition that would last throughout subsequent Egyptian history. The entire preoccupation with provision for the afterlife that distinguished the ancient Egyptian civilization is clear from the very beginning.

There is one aspect of the funerary practices of the Archaic Period Egyptians that mercifully did not persist into later times. Associated with some of the main tombs, in a way that clearly points to their having been dug and occupied at the same time, are the graves of some numbers of women and practitioners of various professions connected with the court, perhaps even a few high officials. Evidently in these early days a barbarous tradition of simultaneously burying

King Khasekhemwy.
Cairo Museum.

alongside the dead king the servants of his earthly life was still in force. This resembles the larger-scale mass funeral sacrifices uncovered at Ur in Mesopotamia, dating to four or five centuries later than the Egyptian cases. There is no evidence to suggest that in Egypt the practice survived into the pyramid age.

Narmer was depicted on the palette called after him in an early version of the smiting pose that never lost its popularity in Egyptian temple reliefs: King Den, later on in Dyn. I, is shown on a small ivory plaque in a more developed version of the pose, and the hieroglyphs that go with it – though crudely engraved in a disorderly way – clearly state that this was 'the first time of smiting the Easterners'. The written language was progressing: the hieroglyphs were becoming more standardized and capable of greater expression. Papyrus came into use for the writing of portable documents and a more cursive version of the hieroglyphs, suitable for rapid writing in ink, was devised.

The close association of kingship with the cult of the falcon-god Horus is shown by the frequent recording of kings' names (their 'Horus names') within boxes (modelled on the panelled façades of the royal palaces of the time) surmounted by falcons. Meanwhile, lion imagery continues into Dyn. I from its predynastic beginnings with a frieze of recumbent lions on a limestone lintel from a royal tomb at Saqqara and the depiction of a lion on a stela from the tomb of a queen.

In two small statues of the last Dyn. II king, Khasekhemwy, from Hierakonpolis we encounter the earliest known royal sculpture, clearly in line with the style of later statuary. The king is seated on a throne, with one arm resting across his lower chest and the other extended along his thigh: this was a posture commonly seen in statuary of Dyns III and IV. Khasekhemwy wears the White Crown of Upper Egypt in this case, while the later Old Kingdom royal statues usually wear wigs and head-dresses. But all in all, this figure of a late Dyn. II king of about 2750 BCE looks thoroughly 'Egyptian' in character, as we apprehend the style of ancient Egypt from Dyn. III onwards. The civilization of ancient Egypt was poised to make its first clear-cut statement in the world.

In the wider world of the early third millennium BCE, the peoples of Mesopotamia remained Egypt's only rivals in the progress of full civilization with writing. In the city-states of Sumer there were lavish temples and ziggurat mounds dedicated to the local gods. The cuneiform script was fully developed. Full bronze metallurgy was practised after about 2600 BCE, with sophisticated casting techniques. In the region of the eastern Mediterranean and its hinterlands, there was maritime trade which included the Aegean, and the growth of towns and small city-states. In the western Mediterranean, people living in farming villages were burying their dead in communal graves, and on Malta starting to build stone temples which, though crudely fashioned and small by comparison, pre-date the first extensively stone-built monuments of Egypt's Dyn. III. The megalith tombs of western Europe, though assembled out of boulders and stones (split and broken where possible) rather than constructed out of regularly cut blocks, similarly pre-date Egypt's first real stone buildings, by many centuries in some cases. But writing was quite unknown in all these places.

Across the Middle East to India, the inspiration of Mesopotamian civilization was spreading east in the first few centuries of the third millennium, but it was not until about 2600 BCE that the Indus civilization, with a script we still cannot read, got under way. In the Far East, the farming way of life continued to spread against a background of hunter-gatherer subsistence. In the Americas, a similar situation obtained, with the familiar pattern of basketry, pot-making and weaving being added to the farmers' repertoire in some places, though metalworking was unknown. In subtropical and tropical Africa, the hunter-gatherer way of life inevitably persisted long after the spread of farming elsewhere: cattle herding spread over the Saharan area (wetter before 3000 BCE than it is now) but the crops of the Fertile Crescent simply could not be grown outside Egypt and Ethiopia. Other plants were domesticated in time, but in the first few centuries of the third millennium BCE when Egypt was coming into its own, the African interior beyond the Nubian border zone was a land of mystery from which exotic items like ostrich feathers, spices, ivory, ebony and baboons could be imported.

Old Kingdom Egypt traded south into Africa and eastwards with the Levant and Mesopotamia, but after the brief period of clear foreign influence from Sumer at the very beginning of its history, Egypt went its own way – to the glories of the pyramid age.

SIX

THE PYRAMID AGE

After the end of Dyn. II, the siting of the royal cemetery was moved from Abydos to be close to the capital at Memphis, to Saqqara to begin with and then a little further to the north at Dahshur and later still to Giza. At Saqqara (even at Giza) there were already some impressive tombs belonging to officials of the kings of the Archaic Period. The first ruler of Dyn. III is a shadowy figure, soon succeeded by a king whose grandiose monument at Saqqara makes him the first great name of Egyptian history. His name was Djoser, and the name of his architect was as well known as his own throughout Egyptian history. For the enduring fame of Imhotep grew in the latter days of ancient Egypt into a cult in which this chancellor, architect, doctor of Old Kingdom times was regarded as a god of healing, to be equated with the Greeks' Asclepius. Manetho, as retailed by Africanus, says that 'Imuthes was reckoned by the Egyptians as Asclepius, on account of his medical skill, and he invented building with hewn stone; he also devoted attention to writing.' Imhotep was evidently a polymath who excelled in several different fields: the record of his invention of 'building with hewn stone' is an accurate one, for the Step Pyramid complex of Djoser was the world's first large-scale construction out of cut stone.

Opposite: Djoser's head seen through one of the eye-holes in his serdab's north wall.

The Mesopotamians had already built some of their ziggurat temple mounds with mud-bricks, Europe had seen megalithic tomb-making with boulders and rock-cutting and the Egyptians themselves had pioneered some small-scale use of stones, but no-one in all the world had attempted anything like the vast tomb complex of Djoser in 'hewn stone'. It had required the convergence of religious belief, political will, social organization and technological accomplishment to make the project feasible. Copper tools, a workforce used to communal enterprise as the result of long experience with irrigation and a wealthy unified state under a king invested with divine authority – these were the background to the achievement. But it took also the individual genius of Imhotep to imagine the daring scope and detail of the work. All this in about 2650 BCE.

The world of Egypt's Old Kingdom has come down to us mostly in the form of royal and upper-class funerary equipment. The whole world of the common people, and most of the everyday world of the rich and powerful, has not left

A head of Imhotep, now in Copenhagen, from the latter days of ancient Egypt, when he was regarded as a god.

behind imperishable relics. Houses for the living were built of mud-brick, wood, reed bundles, palm thatch, wattle and daub. Kings' tombs, and after a while nobles' and officials' tombs, were built of stone and have more often survived. The contents of the tombs have not quite entirely vanished despite four-and-a-half thousand years of plunder. What remains, together with the wall pictures that appear in some of the tombs, can give us a good impression of life in the Egypt of the Old Kingdom, even of ordinary people's lives where they are illustrated. But it is as well to remember that nearly everything we have comes from a mortuary context. Because the ancient Egyptians evidently loved their life along the Nile and wanted more of it to come in the hereafter (though kings could look forward to something rather more transcendental), this mortuary context does not promote a morbid impression of their culture, but it does mean that what we see now of them makes a selective picture of their world.

At Saqqara, the creation of the Step Pyramid and its extensive complex involved Imhotep and his associates and workmen in a task for which nothing in their previous experience could have prepared them. Working in wood when it could be got (for useful timber was imported from Byblos on the Levantine coast of the Mediterranean) and mud-brick, in wattle and daub and lashed papyrus stalks, in wicker fencing and rush matting, the architects and craftsmen before Djoser's time had built up a body of expertise and ways of doing things that suited their old materials very well but were not tailored to the qualities of the new material, stone. Small wonder that the details of Djoser's complex often display the characteristics of the older materials rendered in stone. Ceilings of wooden beams are reproduced in stone, wall hangings of coloured reed matting are imitated with blue-glazed tiles, even a half-open section of stake fencing is carved out of solid stone blocks. Columns imitating lashed and mud-plastered reed bundles but made in stone, that could have stood up all by themselves, are engaged into a stone wall, as though the innovators were feeling their way with the possibilities of the new material. But there was another motive behind these devices: to make stone replicas of things that for everyday use were made of perishable materials was to render immortal the idea of those everyday things. On behalf of Djoser, Imhotep was making an eternal version of his palace and domain where his body, preserved by mummification, could reside for ever. It was all right for the everyday dwellings, even of kings, to pass away, but in death Djoser was to have an eternal home.

The centrepiece of the Djoser complex is the Step Pyramid, rising in six terraces of stone blocks to a present height of 60 m. This was Egypt's first pyramid and its interior construction demonstrates the evolution of the pyramid idea out of previous patterns of royal tomb. It started life as the sort of flat-topped bench-like tomb (called mastaba after the Arabic for bench) of earlier dynasties, but built of cut stones instead of mud-bricks. The first change of plan was evidently to build up the mastaba with three more steps on top, of diminishing size, thus creating a stepped tumulus not unlike the smaller tumuli sometimes incorporated into the superstructure of older tombs, ultimate descendants one supposes of the tumuli heaped over predynastic graves. Creative confidence must have run high, for the plan was changed yet again, and the whole project greatly enlarged, when the decision was made to build a six-stepped structure over the four-stepped halfway house.

The burial of Djoser was sited in a deep shaft under the mastaba tomb that formed the basis of the pyramid, and a very complicated pattern of galleries and corridors runs under the whole structure. It is possible that some of these were adapted from Dyn. II tomb excavations.

The pyramid, the base of which is not a square as were the later ones, is orientated with its four sides very nearly in line with the cardinal points of the compass. On the north side are the remains of a mortuary temple of complex interior design and an interesting small chamber, paralleled in non-royal tombs of the Old Kingdom but not seen in later pyramids. This serdab, as Egyptologists call such chambers, contained a life-sized seated statue of King Djoser gazing north from the base of his pyramid. The front wall of the chamber is pierced with two small holes, like eye-holes, through which today's visitor can see the head of Djoser in replica – the original enthroned statue is conserved in the Cairo Museum. Whether the holes were symbolically intended to permit Djoser's image, in eternal stone, to see out of his tomb or whether they were meant to allow the scents of offerings to reach him cannot be known. It is tempting to think that he was meant to be able to gaze eternally towards the imperishable, never-setting north stars to which some part of his own immortal being had migrated after death. Beliefs recorded in the Pyramid Texts of later times associated dead kings with the polar sky.

The whole Step Pyramid complex was surrounded by a 10-m high sanctuary wall with only one real entrance among its fourteen apparent portals. (Djoser's palace in his lifetime was probably similarly walled, with fourteen gates.) Within the wall, as well as the pyramid there were dummy chapels, mostly without interior features, and at the southern end of the enclosed rectangle another apparent tomb, duplicating many of the features of the pyramid hypogeum but without the pyramid itself. Whether this was perhaps the tomb of a close relative, a child of Djoser's for example, or more likely of his separately mummified internal organs or even his preserved placenta (regarded as a sort of predeceased twin), or whether it was a cenotaph with some symbolic dualistic significance for the burial of the king of the two lands of Upper and Lower Egypt is not to be determined now.

It is interesting to note that a throne-base or table of Djoser's is decorated with fourteen lions' heads whose teeth-baring ferocity harks back to the late predynastic style of lion depiction. Were these the guardians of the fourteen gates of his pyramid complex?

Tens of thousands of fine vessels made of alabaster, rock crystal, serpentine and other fancy stones were left behind in the chambers and galleries of Djoser's monument by ancient tomb robbers whom we can rely on to have removed everything that was really valuable. The robbers gouged out the eyes of the seated statue of Djoser in his serdab, probably because they were made of rock crystal, but the figure remains a most powerful expression of the unchallenged authority of

Djoser's Step Pyramid with a reconstructed length of wall and entrance.

Djoser running in his jubilee, in a relief from an underground corridor of his pyramid complex.

the rulers of Egypt's Old Kingdom. The pose is in line with Khasekhemwy's statue of the end of Dyn. II, one arm across the chest, the other along the thigh. But Djoser wears an early version of the folded head-dress seen on later Old Kingdom royal statues (and on the Sphinx), but here with pointed lapels, over a bulky wig which hangs down over his shoulders. Some other pieces of Djoser statuary have been found lying about the enclosure, but these are, interestingly, unfinished: it seems that the Step Pyramid complex was never brought to full completion after Djoser's death, as though his successor wanted to get on with his own funerary arrangements rather than using the workforce to complete his predecessor's. This pattern seems to have been often repeated in later Egyptian history.

There are other depictions of Djoser in bas-relief in the underground galleries of the complex, evidently performing (forever, in stone) an important rite of royal renewal that the kings of Egypt observed at intervals during their reigns. It involved the running of a ceremonial race, to demonstrate the king's powers. Divine kings upon whom the entire future of their kingdom depended needed to keep vigorous and prosper: in prehistoric times, one can plausibly speculate that kings were ritually put to death when they ceased to be the young lions and strong bulls they once were, to give way to fresh players; by the time of Djoser, symbolic rejuvenation by jubilee seems to have been the style and his tomb enshrined that cycle of rejuvenation for ever in the form of the pictures in the bas-reliefs. In them, the hawk of Horus flies over the running Djoser. The hieroglyphs that accompany these reliefs are more assured in form and layout than previously but still without column marks, as are the hieroglyphs on the remarkable wooden panels from a private Dyn. III tomb belonging to a physician (like Imhotep, who also 'devoted attention to writing') named Hezyre. Among them are the lion ideogram with very naturalistic depiction in profile of the lion's head and forequarters with outstretched paws, and the recumbent lion phonogram (with the sound of rw, roo) which resembles the general layout of the Sphinx (without the human head, of course) except that the tail is raised high into the air. No image of a sphinx occurs in any of these Dyn. III reliefs. A painting from Hezyre's tomb shows a gaming board with pieces in the form of little lions and dogs. And the importance of the lion as an image of power is underlined by pieces of lion statuary from contemporary contexts: there is an unusual red pottery lion, about half a metre high, from Hierakonpolis, seated on its hindquarters like a domestic cat, with the tail curled round the right back paw, but otherwise nothing like the Giza Sphinx. This and fragments of a similar piece from Coptos probably date to early Old Kingdom times.

Djoser's pyramid enclosure on the desert's edge at Saqqara, overlooking the fertile flood plain of the river where Egypt's people lived and toiled, must have

A red terracotta lion ascribed to Djoser's dynasty. Ashmolean Museum, Oxford.

The interior court of the Step Pyramid with dummy buildings; newly cut restoration blocks (at the right) start white and then turn warmly yellow.

A wooden panel from the
tomb of Hezyre: note the
lion hieroglyph at the top.
Cairo Museum.

appeared more wonderful than anything else in the world when it was (more or less) completed, without precedent or parallel. The archaeological record shows that his successors followed his lead and embarked on similar monuments for themselves, but these were never brought to anything like completion. One of them, belonging to a king called Sekhemkhet, would have included a step pyramid higher than Djoser's, to judge by the first two steps, and built of bigger individual blocks. Remains of ramps found here hint at the construction method for these early pyramids – huge ramps, that nearly cover the whole of what remains of the stepped structure. In the burial chamber an alabaster sarcophagus was discovered by archaeologist Zakariah Goneim in the 1950s, with an unusual sliding panel at one end rather than a lid on top. What seemed to be the remains of wreaths on top of the sarcophagus led to high hopes that an intact Dyn. III mummy might still be found inside, but when the sliding panel was raised, the sarcophagus proved empty. This has caused some to wonder whether the sarcophagi and burial chambers of the pyramids ever necessarily contained the bodies of the kings whose tombs they appear to be: perhaps the actual burials were made elsewhere, for reasons of religion or security. But the Sekhemkhet pyramid was far from finished when construction work was abandoned and, then again, perhaps what looks like remnants of a wreath is actually a greatly decayed wooden lever employed by robbers to open the sarcophagus. A very unfinished monument essentially similar to the Sekhemkhet pyramid was discovered at Zawyet el-Aryan, between Saqqara and Giza. There was no sarcophagus and, unlike the cases of Djoser and Sekhemkhet, no item with any inscription on it to name the owner of the pyramid, but it seems likely that we have here, only a few kilometres from Giza, another step pyramid of Dyn. III.

The evolution of the pyramid can be followed through the end of Dyn. III into Dyn. IV, when the immediate predecessors of Khufu rapidly achieved (over only some fifty years) the pyramid proper in place of the stepped pyramid. The last king of Dyn. III, Huny, may have begun work on a pyramid at Maidum, 50 km or so south of Saqqara, at around 2600 BCE, which the first king of Dyn. IV, Khufu's father Snofru, attempted to finish off. What is left of the Maidum pyramid today constitutes an extraordinary tower-like monument, standing up out of a mound of rubble, that does not resemble a pyramid at all. Its modern appearance is the result of a collapse following an attempt to clothe a step pyramid in a smooth and stepless coat of facing stones. The tower shape attests to the original step-built construction of the core, from which not only the smooth casing but also the lower outer steps have fallen away. There is evidence that the Maidum pyramid was never finished in the first place – perhaps design difficulties had already become apparent and some of the casing had already fallen off. But the major collapse must have occurred much later on, since the rubble was revealed by archaeology to have covered up a New Kingdom graffito. Interestingly, some blocks were found in the course of archaeological excavation at Maidum upon which the ancient quarrymen scratched drawings showing pyramids of two, three and four steps. Perhaps these drawings chart the early stages of changing plans for this construction.

The serdab building at the foot of Djoser's pyramid, with a statue of the king inside (seen through a modern glass panel), gazing north to the never-setting pole-stars.

Not only was the Maidum pyramid the first to have been cased with a smooth, sloping and stepless outer layer: it was also the first to feature the same general sort of arrangements of entrance shaft, in the north face, and burial chamber, to be seen in the later pyramids of Dahshur and Giza. The mortuary temple was now on the east side of the pyramid, rather than the north as in Djoser's case; again this was the pattern subsequently followed, and it probably indicates the growth of a solar element in beliefs about the afterlife alongside the older stellar component. Dead kings might now journey with the sun-god across the day- and night-time skies, as well as going to dwell with the never-setting polar stars.

The Maidum pyramid had not only a mortuary temple but also, for the first time, a causeway and valley temple like the later pyramids. Inside the mortuary temple up against the pyramid was an altar for offerings and two stelae of the sort that the Egyptians used to carry royal and religious inscriptions – like the one that Tuthmosis IV of Dyn. XVIII set up in front of the Sphinx after his dream. In the mortuary temple of the Maidum pyramid, the stelae are blank and uninscribed, which supports the view that this complex, too, was never finished. But there are graffiti on the walls that show that in New Kingdom times this temple was considered to belong to Snofru of Dyn. IV: with what justification we cannot tell. The entire pyramid complex at Maidum might be tentatively ascribed to Snofru on the basis of these graffiti in the mortuary temple, but for the fact that Snofru can lay claim to two more pyramids much closer to Saqqara, at Dahshur about 8 km to its south. The seemingly unsatisfactory conversion of the Maidum pyramid from stepped to smooth-cased profile, with collapse and without completion, suggests that Snofru simply tried here to finish off his predecessor's job before turning his attention north to Dahshur. There the

The Maidum Pyramid.
Photo: Paul Jordan.

southern one of the pair of pyramids was certainly built by Snofru, and it looks as though he built the northern one too. Inscriptions of Old Kingdom date mention Snofru's having two pyramids, and his very name was written in red ochre, presumably during building operations, in two places on the southern pyramid of Dahshur. Moreover the same named king is shown on a stela before the chapel of a smaller pyramid to the south but within the enclosure of the southern pyramid – a situation that reminds us of the other tomb within Djoser's complex.

This southern pyramid of Snofru at Dahshur is another unexpected sort of pyramid, for its angle changes about halfway up, giving it the mansard look: it is commonly called the Bent Pyramid. It has been suggested that it was finished in a hurry, or that adverse experience with the Maidum pyramid caused the builders to lose confidence in their ability to finish it as intended. It carries more of its outer casing of fine limestone (from the Tura quarries on the other side of the Nile) than the later pyramids of Khufu and Khafre at Giza. Its internal arrangements are complicated with two separate but connected chambers and, uniquely, two entrance shafts – one in the north face, like other pyramids after Maidum, and another high up on the west face. With this pyramid of Snofru's at Dahshur, something of the unfathomable complexity of the interior arrangements of the Great Pyramid at Giza is foreshadowed, though details differ. It simply is not possible after four-and-a-half thousand years to puzzle out all the changes of plan and other vicissitudes that went into building these monuments. In the Bent Pyramid we also arrive at a greater sophistication of anti-theft measures than had been seen in earlier pyramids, with two interior portcullis blocks that could be let into position by knocking away props.

The Bent Pyramid is not very exactly aligned on the cardinal points of the compass by the standards of Khufu and Khafre, and its mortuary temple seems to have been completed as something of an afterthought, but its valley temple at the other end of the temple causeway was altogether more impressive: monumental in size, faced with Tura limestone, with entrance hall, open court and pillared portico, all carrying scenes carved in bold relief to do with royal rituals like the jubilee renewals depicted in Djoser's pyramid. Fragments reveal that there were also several statues of Snofru in this temple.

Since Old Kingdom inscriptions relate that Snofru had two pyramids, it is likely that the northern pyramid at Dahshur is the other one of the pair. His name is written on a casing block at one corner and the tombs close by belong to courtiers of Snofru's reign. If both these pyramids at Dahshur do belong to Snofru and he also had a hand in finishing the Maidum pyramid, then the suggestion arises that pyramid building may have been as much a rolling exercise in public works as a religious provision for individual kings: pyramid building may have been a permanent occupation of the Old Kingdom; when you finished one, you started another, whether the king of the moment lived or died. And when a king died, his successor buried him and wound up work on his pyramid as quickly as possible, to get on with the next. In the case of Snofru, it looks as though two or three pyramids were being worked on simultaneously from time to time. It has been speculated that the extensive and highly organized workforce that had come into being to maintain irrigation and plant and sow in season needed something to keep it occupied – or, at least, was available for work – out of season, and that pyramid building fitted the bill. In much later times, tradition had it that Snofru had been a good ruler, but his successors Khufu and Khafre had not. If there is anything in them, these stories may hint that it was in Snofru's twenty-four-year reign that the balance between communal labour in a good cause and royal aggrandizement was last maintained.

Snofru's northern pyramid at Dahshur is the first real pyramid, without steps and bends and with all its stones in horizontal layers rather than inclined upwards to the outside, although its slope is noticeably gentle by comparison with later pyramids (and about the same as the top part of the Bent Pyramid). A northern entrance passage leads to three chambers within the built body of the pyramid, whereas only one of the Bent Pyramid's two chambers was above bedrock and the earlier pyramid's burial chambers were in the ground under their structure. In size and volume, in constructional detail and in interior arrangements, Snofru's pyramids at Dahshur, and in particular his northern one, begin to approach the grandeur of his son's Great Pyramid at Giza.

Khufu's pyramid is not a great deal larger than that of his later successor Khafre next door, but it has features which are unique to it among all the pyramids of Egypt. In particular, its complicated arrangement of internal shafts, corridors, chambers, gallery and robber-deterrents is unparalleled elsewhere. Much ink has been spilt about the possible significance of these details, ranging from rational discussion as to how robbers may have contrived to get into it all the way down to crazy interpretations of its mystical meaning for all the ages. In a complex monument built four-and-a-half thousand years ago, almost certainly robbed over four thousand years ago (if not immediately upon completion), visited by tourists in Greek and Roman times, roughly penetrated anew by Arab explorers over a thousand years ago and open in virtually its present state for more than a hundred and fifty years, there are bound to be insoluble puzzles. Quite when and by whom some particular bit of damage or alteration was done is often now impossible to decide.

It is important, to begin with, to note that the ancient Egyptians of the latter days of their history, in the times of Herodotus and Manetho, certainly believed that this pyramid had been built by King Khufu. We know from archaeology that Khufu's father Snofru built at least one and almost certainly both of the pyramids at Dahshur. Those pyramids clearly have their place on an evolutionary scale between the earlier pyramids of Dyn. III kings like Djoser and the pyramids of Giza, in terms of constructional details, shape and size. Khufu's name has been found inside the Great Pyramid, utterly hidden away among the original quarry markings left on undressed surfaces of blocks used to construct the pressure-relieving compartments above the burial chamber. That Khufu's name is casually written, in graffiti that are not very literate as we might expect from quarry gangs, on blocks high in the Great Pyramid's interior, is a very strong indication that this pyramid was under construction during his reign. The king lists, Herodotus and archaeology tell us that Snofru's son Khufu was succeeded (after the brief reign of another) by Khafre – and Khafre's named statues were found in the valley temple of his pyramid alongside the Great Pyramid. The third and smaller pyramid of Giza is similarly proved by archaeology to have belonged to the king named Menkaure and known from the king lists, Herodotus and Manetho. The obvious conclusion is that Khufu built the Great Pyramid, in about 2550 BCE.

The internal disposition of the pyramid of Khufu indicates that at least three changes of plan occurred during its building. When Khufu determined to build his pyramid at Giza, he found a fairly flattish site on the edge of the desert plateau, with knolls of limestone rising here and there out of it and probably some visible natural fissures in the rock. There were also one or two mastaba tombs from the earlier dynasties and he may have decided to incorporate an existing tomb, as evidently Djoser did before him at Saqqara, or a natural fissure into the underground part of his pyramid. The so-called 'grotto' where the well-shaft inside the pyramid passes into the bedrock may be the remains of such a pre-existing feature. The large underground excavation that seems to have been intended as the burial place of Khufu in the first stage of the monument was abandoned well short of completion and a new chamber (often mistakenly called the Queen's Chamber) created higher up, within the built structure, as the pyramid rose layer by layer.

The most extraordinary feature of Khufu's pyramid, not seen in any other (but constructionally foreshadowed in the Dahshur pyramids), is the Grand Gallery which continues up inside the monument beyond the level of the second stage burial chamber. The likeliest explanation of the Grand Gallery is that it represents the most ambitious scheme ever tried by the pyramid builders to block the entrance after the king's burial with the utmost security against robbery. It may have developed out of earlier methods of closing pyramids with blocks chuted into the entrance shafts from external ramps. Here the idea was to build the ramp into the pyramid and trigger the slide of the blocks after burial, perhaps by remote control or perhaps (less securely) from inside by personnel with a secret means of escape – the well-shaft being cut out for this use.

Such a method of closing up the pyramid would have served to protect the second stage burial chamber, lying above and beyond the blocked ascending corridor that had given access to it. But in fact, as the pyramid rose higher, its designers chose to embark on a third stage burial plan, with a new chamber high up inside the pyramid, at the top of the Grand Gallery, which we now correctly call the King's Chamber. Additional security was provided for this final resting place with a further great block and multiple portcullis arrangement at its threshold.

Any blocks that may ever have been introduced into the entrance shafts of earlier pyramids have long ago been removed by robbers, but three blocks are still in place at the bottom of the Khufu pyramid's ascending corridor. The Arabs under al-Mamun who broke into the upper parts of the pyramid in the ninth century CE simply tunnelled round these blocks. The reports of their adventures are unclear as to whether they found anything at all in the two upper chambers: some say they found nothing, some add that al-Mamun offset the potentially dangerous disappointment of his men by smuggling in a bogus treasure sufficient to pay their wages, some tell of a statue in the sarcophagus with a gold breastplate set with gems and covered in mysterious writing. This latter tale sounds like a description of an Egyptian mummy and probably relates to garbled

The pyramids of Dahshur, seen from Saqqara – the Bent Pyramid to the left, and the Northern Pyramid of Dahshur to the right.

Hemon in a relief from his tomb at Giza. Museum of Fine Arts, Boston.

folk memories of finding real mummies in other Egyptian tombs. It is highly unlikely that anything of value was left in the pyramid after the ancient robbers, of various periods in Egyptian history, had done their worst with it. The well-shaft, that might have served to let out any workmen left in the tomb after the dramatic closure following the burial, may equally well have served to let in robbers, perhaps robbers in the know about the interior details of the pyramid.

This is not to say that further small discoveries may not yet be made inside Khufu's monument at Giza. The narrow shafts that lead out of the King's Chamber towards the exterior casing of the pyramid have recently been explored in part by a robot camera, which has discovered a blockage a long way up in one of them: it is possible that, for example, a small statuette of the king or a god (it could only be a few centimetres tall) might be found beyond this point, having been put there when the pyramid had reached the level of the exit of the shafts. Speculation suggests that these shafts (and those leading out from the Queen's Chamber) may have been orientated for religious reasons on various stars, including the Pole Star of the day.

Just as we have the name of the architect of Djoser's Step Pyramid at Saqqara, the famous Imhotep, so we probably know the name of the man responsible for the building of Khufu's pyramid at Giza. He was a relative of the king named Hemon, with titles we may translate as Vizier and Master of Works. His tomb lies close to the Great Pyramid and, thanks to images in the tomb, we can still look upon the features of the man who most likely masterminded this wonder of the world.

Khufu was succeeded for a few years by a king named Djedefre who started to build his pyramid away from Giza to the north at Abu Rawash. It was evidently to have been a large and steep pyramid but probably it was never quite completed and has since been robbed away (in a process that continued into the last century) into virtual non-existence. But some important pieces of Dyn. IV sculpture were found at Abu Rawash, apparently deliberately smashed and thrown into a ritual boat-pit by the pyramid. One of them, a broken-off head of Djedefre in life size, so closely matches the head of the Great Sphinx in treatment of the face and details of the head-dress that it quite clearly establishes the general date of the Sphinx head, if not body, at Giza, and gives us a better idea of what the Sphinx looked like before its face was so damaged. Another statue from Abu Rawash shows Djedefre with his queen kneeling at her husband's leg. Yet another, tantalizingly, is of a female sphinx, painted yellow to render the untanned colouring that Egyptian women aspired to.

If this small sphinx (74 cm long) belonged with the Old Kingdom statuary of Abu Rawash, it would constitute the oldest real sphinx image that we know, just pre-dating the reign of Khafre to whom the Giza Sphinx is attributed. Sad to say, we cannot be sure that this sphinx does belong with the Djedefre material at Abu Rawash, though the site does not seem to have been extensively developed after Djedefre's time there until Graeco-Egyptian days. Its general form is certainly in line with the Giza Sphinx, though the head is bigger in relation to the body, as

The female sphinx from Abu Rawash, which might just predate the Great Sphinx; its age is not certain, but it looks stylistically like an Old Kingdom piece (after Jéquier).

with most sphinxes after the Great Sphinx, and it carries leonine ears like some sphinxes of the Middle Kingdom. Emplacements for sphinxes that evidently stood guard before his valley temple were discovered during excavation of Khafre's complex, together with some broken sphinx fragments, so sphinxes besides the Great Sphinx do seem to appear in the archaeological record at about the time of Djedefre and his successor Khafre. If the Sphinx is, as Egyptologists believe, an image associated with the sun-god, then the Re component of these kings' names, appearing for the first time with them, is of great significance in the development of the sphinx idea at this time.

Khafre's pyramid closely parallels Khufu's in shape and size, but not in interior arrangements. His burial chamber is at bedrock level, with little of the complexity of galleries and shafts seen in the Khufu pyramid, though there are two entrance passages and a sort of vestibule off the lower one. Here again there are signs of a change of plan with regard to the location of the actual burial chamber, and very likely of the whole pyramid over it; and, interestingly, it seems that it was planned to cut narrow shafts out from the burial chamber to the exterior of the pyramid, like the ones in Khufu's monument, but here the plan was first changed by repositioning the shafts and then abandoned altogether after only about a third of a metre.

The whole pyramid may have been relocated slightly to the south after building began in order to exploit the discovery of rock suitable to make the pyramid's causeway down to the valley temple site to the east. At the same time, the builders of Khafre's pyramid needed to keep the northern sighting line of their entrance passage clear of Khufu's pyramid, so that the north polar stars could be kept in view. This served the practical purpose of facilitating orientation of the pyramid and its shafts, and religious purposes too. When Menkaure came to build his pyramid at Giza, the same provisions had to be observed. It is the lie of the land, the usefulness of the rock, and the clear north sighting requirements that explain the staggered disposition of the three pyramids at Giza.

Khafre's proprietorship of the second pyramid at Giza is indicated by later tradition and by the occurrence of his name at entrance openings in both the mortuary temple and the valley temple of his pyramid, and upon statues of this king in the valley temple. Menkaure's authorship of the third pyramid at Giza is attested in a similar way with the discovery of named statues of this king in his mortuary and valley temples; moreover, his name was written in red ochre on the roof of the burial chamber of one of his subsidiary pyramids. On some of Menkaure's constructions, original levelling marks and measurements have been noted. Menkaure's mortuary temple, incidentally, is another building at Giza besides the Sphinx temple and Khafre's two temples that is constructed of an inner core of huge limestone blocks, faced with granite: core plus casing was the standard building style for mastabas, pyramids and temples in the Old Kingdom. There is evidence that Menkaure's complex was hurriedly finished off by his son Shepseskaf, who opted to have himself buried not in a pyramid but in a huge rendition of a sarcophagus at Saqqara. Khentkawes, who may have been his queen, was buried in a similar tomb at Giza between the causeways of Khafre and Menkaure: from her valley temple

The broken-off head of Djedefre from Abu Rawash that closely resembles the head of the Sphinx, especially in pictures taken before the addition of the Sphinx's cement head support. Louvre Museum.

comes the figure of a standing lion with missing front legs and head which might have been a sphinx, albeit of a different pattern from the Great Sphinx.

Dynastic and perhaps religious strife may lie behind the altered funerary arrangements of Shepseskaf's time. In about 2465 BCE, a new dynasty arose with King Userkaf: a huge head of this king is a pioneering example of sculpture much larger than life. After him, the rest of the kings of Dyn. V had names that featured the sun-god Re. This custom had been prefigured in the names of Djedefre and Khafre, but now the identification of the king with Re was total and the solar religion of Re dominated belief and practice. The royal and divine pretensions of the kings of Egypt reached their apogee: but the tombs of their courtiers and officials show that they too were feeling their feet in these prosperous times. The mastabas of Dyn. V are more spacious and elaborate than those of Dyn. IV and more highly decorated with scenes of their owners' lives in painted relief. Evidently the owners of these tombs were rising in importance in relation to the kings and were no longer such self-effacing servants as they had been. This situation may be reflected in the increasingly jerry-built nature of the royal pyramids erected in Dyn. V. Userkaf's pyramid at Saqqara already displays recourse to rubble-filled interiors, faced with fine stone, in place of solid construction through and through. This decline in building standards is seen at Abusir, between Giza and Saqqara, too: a bold design, which must have looked splendid at the time, is nowadays reduced to mere tip-like heaps of rubble because roughly piled interiors were only faced with a cosmetic outer layer of finely finished stone, and once that facing was disturbed the pyramid could only slide into what a casual visitor might not recognize at first sight as a pyramid at all.

For all that, Dyn. V was a wealthy time, with an increase in foreign trade and involvements. Sahure, who has a pyramid at Abusir, is known to have fought against the Libyans to the north-west and Asiatics to the north-east. A damaged relief from his Abusir complex features a trampling sphinx with the body of a lion and the plumage and wings of a hawk – a slightly later version of this imagery confirms the suspicion that this figure would originally have had a hawk's head too. The lion–falcon sphinx idea is thus continued here in a tradition that goes back to the late predynastic 'Oxford' palette with an essentially similar image on it.

Wenis was the last king of this dynasty, and it is in his ruined pyramid at Saqqara that the best executed of the so-called 'pyramid texts' are found. These are the first lengthy writings of the ancient Egyptians that we know. They are religious texts and, like comparable material from other religious traditions, they reflect in frequently obscure language beliefs that relate back to earlier and more primitive times. Some of these beliefs are to do with the stars. We shall see later on what they can tell us about the religion of the people who built the pyramids and carved the Sphinx, but it is interesting to note at this point that the pyramids that contain these texts do not have shafts leading out from their chambers to point to any stars.

Dyn. VI was marked by increasing limitations set upon the royal power by the rise of the nobles. Parallel with the rising power of high officials at court ran the recovery of those provincial powers that had waned under the kings' centralized

The pyramids of Giza: Menkaure's to the fore, Khafre's in the middle, and Khufu's at the back.

Opposite: Pyramid texts in
the burial chamber of King
Wenis.

A large restored statue of
Menkaure, with a relatively
small head, recalling the
disproportion of the
Sphinx's head and body.
Museum of Fine Arts,
Boston.

domination since Dyn. III times. Provincial families were on their way to becoming little independent principalities. At Saqqara, the badly built and much decayed pyramids of Teti and Pepi I and II seem to bear eloquent witness to this circumstance. Continuity of the sphinx motif is evidenced by the discovery of the base of a sphinx statue belonging to Pepi I and of a relief of Pepi II showing the same trampling sphinx with hawk's wings (and this time hawk's head too) that was found on Sahure's pyramid temple. The very first appearances of sphinx styles we usually associate with later periods have been detected at the end of the Old Kingdom. To a king who ruled for less than a decade between Pepi I and Pepi II have been ascribed a sphinx statue in Moscow that prefigures the Middle Kingdom variants with lions' manes and ears and a tiny sphinx in Edinburgh that holds out offering pots in a manner commonly seen in the New Kingdom.

Pepi II's long reign (longer than Queen Victoria's) seems to have witnessed an accelerating decline of central authority in favour of the rise of the provincial power groups and, after his death in about 2200 BCE, serious internal trouble broke out. It was evidently not a question of outside interference in Egypt's affairs: what probably happened was that the burden imposed upon the country during a long and complacent reign by the royal and priestly centres had become too great to be borne. There is also evidence of a period of low Niles, with serious implications for the agricultural and economic prospects of the time.

It was perhaps during the First Intermediate Period, before order was restored in the Middle Kingdom times after about 2100 BCE, that the monuments of Giza (Khafre's valley temple, for example) were first vandalized and the pyramids systematically robbed of their contents – if they had not been plundered, occasionally at least, by well-informed robbers soon after closure. More pyramids were built in Middle Kingdom times, but there would never again be anything on the scale of the Giza pyramids in terms of size and quality of construction. The kings of the Old Kingdom were great kings indeed and their pyramids, particularly those of Dyn. IV, were suitably great works. On these grounds alone, it is to Dyn. IV and the time of the pyramids of Khufu and Khafre that we should first look, to find a context for the creation of the Great Sphinx.

Opposite: The broken base of a sphinx statue belonging to King Pepi I. Cairo Museum.

SEVEN

ARCHAEOLOGY AND THE SPHINX

In the early days of Egyptology, there was a tendency to assign the Sphinx to Middle Kingdom times. Herodotus had not mentioned it in connection with Khufu and Khafre, and the other sphinxes of Egypt were seen to be of Middle Kingdom or New Kingdom date, so it seemed reasonable to attribute the Great Sphinx to no earlier than Middle Kingdom times (unless one concluded that it might even pre-date the Old Kingdom pyramids).

It was the inscription on the stela of Tuthmosis IV, discovered between the Sphinx's forelegs by Caviglia, that inclined scholars to seriously consider an Old Kingdom date for the monument. The apparent but fragmentary reference to Khafre was soon noted, but even on the assumption that the reference really was to the Khafre of the Turin Canon (Chephren of Herodotus), the damaged text left no clue as to Khafre's role in relation to the Sphinx. But an apparent historical reference of some sort to the builder of the second pyramid of Giza found between the paws of the Sphinx was bound to suggest an association between the two monuments.

Archaeological excavation reinforced this association. After Caviglia's first work at the Sphinx in the second decade of the nineteenth century, he was employed for a time by Howard Vyse in the course of his operations at the pyramids in the 1830s and '40s. Howard Vyse is known today for his rather violent methods of investigation, which could include the use of gunpowder on stubborn rock, so it is not surprising to learn that he and his associate Perring drilled a hole in the top of the Sphinx's back to look for hidden chambers inside the monument, finding none. Howard Vyse was able to send back to England two stelae of the New Kingdom pharaoh Ramesses II that were found in the little chapel between the Sphinx's paws by Caviglia. These are now in the Louvre in Paris. The chapel was again cleared and drawn by the German Egyptologist Lepsius in 1843.

It was a pioneering French Egyptologist, Auguste Mariette, who next worked at the Sphinx, from 1853. He was unable to make a thorough clearance of the sand around the monument, which had inevitably swept in again after the bold work of Caviglia, and he went so far as to think that the Sphinx had always been

Opposite: Scaffolding at the Sphinx, as archaeology and conservation go on today.

The valley temple of
Khafre's pyramid complex,
to the south of the Sphinx
and its temple.

The Dream Stela of
Tuthmosis IV. On it the
Sphinx is shown as the
restorers of Dyn. XVIII
ideally pictured it.

intended to be viewed from a distance and half buried in the sand. He thought
sand had been brought in for the purpose. He was the first to note that masonry
blocks had been applied to the flanks as well as the paws of the Sphinx. With
some excuse in its sand-swamped condition, Mariette believed that the Sphinx
was largely a natural rock formation and that repairs with blocks of stone added
on had distorted the original proportions of the body. It was Mariette who first
cleared some of the sand out of the large fissure across the Sphinx's hindquarters,
and discovered those box-like attachments at the base of the monument that are
probably the remains of shrines added to the Sphinx in New Kingdom times. He
also found fragments of a large statue of Osiris that could have come from one
of these shrines.

   The temple in front of the Sphinx was quite unknown in Mariette's day, being
buried deep in the sand, but he was the first to excavate in the other temple
immediately to the south of it, discovering among other things the wonderful
statues of Khafre that had once stood in it (all save one deliberately smashed in
the past and all tumbled into pits in the temple). These statues carry Khafre's
name and their presence in the temple by the Sphinx persuaded many scholars
that the Sphinx had indeed been carved by Khafre, that Khafre's name was
correctly identified on the stela of Tuthmosis IV, and that the temple was the
temple of the Sphinx. Later on, Mariette's temple was recognized as the valley

Opposite: The Inventory
Stela, showing its generally
poor standard of execution.

temple of Khafre's pyramid complex and the true Sphinx temple was in due course excavated. The two temples, though differing internally, are externally very similar in size and shape and clearly belong together, so the association of Khafre with the Sphinx remains strong on the evidence of these temples and the finds Mariette made (and others after him) in the Khafre valley temple: among them, evident emplacements for other sphinx statues that may have been up to 8 m long.

Mariette also found at Giza, close to one of the small subsidiary pyramids on the east side of the Great Pyramid, an inscription that did much to convince some scholars that the Sphinx must be older than either Khafre or his predecessor Khufu. The small pyramid is attributed to Khufu's daughter Henutsen and it was in a temple (of Isis) by this pyramid that Mariette found in 1858 an inscription on a stela which claims that the temple was found by Khufu in a ruined state and rebuilt – which would mean that the original temple predated him. The stela is known as the 'Inventory Stela' because it mainly consists of a list of statues and other items that Khufu is said to have found when he set about repairing the temple.

According to the Inventory Stela, not only did Khufu find a ruined temple of Isis to restore, but also the Sphinx already in existence and similarly in need of repair.

> Long live . . . the King of Upper and Lower Egypt, Khufu, given life. . . . He found the House of Isis, Mistress of the Pyramid, by the side of the hollow of Hwran [the Sphinx] . . . and he built his pyramid beside the temple of this goddess and he built a pyramid for the King's Daughter Henutsen beside this temple. The place of Hwran Horemakhet is on the south side of the House of Isis, Mistress of the Pyramid. . . . He restored the statue, all covered in painting, of the Guardian of the Atmosphere, who guides the winds with his gaze. He replaced the back part of the nemes head-dress which was missing with gilded stone. . . . The figure of this god, cut in stone, is solid and will last to eternity, keeping its face looking always to the east . . .

About the missing back of the head-dress, the Inventory Stela implies that it was struck by a meteorite at some time and that Khufu repaired it according to available plans of the monument.

All this greatly impressed some scholars of the late nineteenth century and would no doubt impress us today if it were not for the fact that the Inventory Stela can now clearly be seen as the work of a very late period in Egyptian history: a period, what is more, when self-conscious archaism was the order of the day. The whole stela, in its form and in the style of its inscription and decoration belongs to Dyn. XXVI, the so-called Second Saite Dynasty between 664 and 524 BCE, when the monuments of the now remote past were often restored and reworked, the heroes of old were fondly remembered and artistic styles of former days were lovingly imitated. It was all rather like the Victorians' Gothic Revival. Saite presence at the Sphinx is attested by the finding of a broken

The Sphinx seen over the top of the Sphinx temple, with Khafre's pyramid behind it to the west.

granite statue of King Psammetichus II of about 590 BCE and a small limestone headless sphinx, north of the Sphinx temple, with the name of King Apries on it, of about 580 BCE.

The Inventory Stela is an anachronistic invention, a pious fraud in which a latter-day king borrows the name of Khufu to cloak his own operations at Giza in glory, and to promote the antiquity of the cult of Isis at Giza. (It also indicates, of course, that we should expect some of the repair work at the Sphinx to belong to Saite times.) The nineteenth-century scholars quickly saw through the general archaizing of the Inventory Stela, but some of them were inclined to regard it all the same as a late copy of a genuine Old Kingdom work. You can still hear this argument put forward today, but not by scholars. The evidence is all against it: the cult of Isis was little known in Dyn. IV times; the title 'Mistress of the Pyramid' would make no sense when Khufu was to be the first to build a pyramid at Giza; the temple in which the stela was found had clearly been extended into, and was built in part out of, Henutsen's own temple, probably in New Kingdom times to judge by some of the other finds later made in it; Henut means mistress and memory of Henutsen's name would have inspired the title later attributed to Isis. The Saite period saw a revival at Giza of the cults of Khufu, Djedefre, Khafre and Menkaure and the 'temple of Isis' was found after Mariette's time to have contained various pieces of statuary taken from local Old Kingdom tombs to deck it in appropriately traditional style. The stela offers various anachronistic titles for the gods whose statues it lists and the names Hwran and Horemakhet for the Sphinx were unknown before Dyn. XVIII. So the Inventory Stela is no evidence at all for the age of the Sphinx, though it planted in people's minds the notion that it might be older than the pyramids, a view which continues to this day among non-scholars.

After Mariette's time, later in the nineteenth century, excavations at the Sphinx were renewed by Gaston Maspero, the French Director-General of the Service of Antiquities in Egypt 1881–6 (and again 1880–1914). He was at first inclined to think that the Sphinx might be Egypt's oldest monument, of predynastic date, but later came round to the view that it must be the work of Khafre. Still, when he says that 'the Sphinx has not yet told us all its secrets', we must agree with him. He also said that he had the Sphinx cleared again of its sand covering to give tourists to Lower Egypt something to see. Maspero recalled that the local Arabs had always believed in a subterranean chamber beneath the Sphinx, as had Mariette, and he was struck by the number of representations on stelae found nearby of the Sphinx lying on a pedestal base. He thought that, while there was evidently no four-sided free-standing pedestal below the Sphinx, there might perhaps be a single cut face in front of it, which in turn might give access to a chamber. Funds were raised by popular subscription in France to search for the pedestal and work was duly begun, but progressed slowly. Caviglia's Roman staircase had not been rediscovered after a fortnight and so attention was transferred to the area immediately under the head, where the little shrine between the paws and the stela of Tuthmosis IV were soon turned up again. But really there had been no advance on the findings of Caviglia and Mariette when work was abandoned. Maspero judged that the hypothesis of a pedestal, with or without a chamber, had not been truly tested by the operations he had contracted. But his clearance certainly provided the growing numbers of tourists to Giza with an added attraction on top of the pyramids, as the numerous and varied photographs of the time clearly illustrate.

Excavation by the Egyptian Antiquities Service between 1907 and 1909 turned up material belonging to the New Kingdom pharaoh Amenophis II close to the Sphinx; and then the next major phase of archaeology at the Sphinx came in 1925, when a French engineer named Emile Baraize made a more determined effort than any before to keep out the sand and conserve the monument. He did not clear the sand away fully but he did build a massive wall to hold it back – a wall which it was necessary for the next excavation to demolish, with difficulty, fifteen years later. It was clear in 1925 that various repairs were needed to the Sphinx. The hole made by Perring and Howard Vyse needed to be plugged to prevent occasional rainwater from causing splitting of the rock. The neck was suffering serious erosion by wind-blown sand. It was thought that there was real danger of the head's being blown off in a severe wind storm. Accordingly, the head was now supported with cement extensions at the back and where the original lappets of the head-dress had long since been eroded away, following their original shape as far as was known and possible. From this moment, the Sphinx head was to look quite different from what previous generations had seen. Cracks were filled in the face and the hole in the top of the head (into which presumably some sort of crown had been fitted at one time) was protected with an iron plate. The large fissure across the haunches was filled with cement. Some of the repair blocks of previous restorations, found by Baraize to have fallen off, were replaced.

Baraize's excavations turned up several pieces of evidence of the continuing attention paid to the Sphinx in the later days of ancient Egyptian history. He found stelae of Roman and Greek times, a limestone slab from the days of the late New Kingdom pharaoh Ramesses II and indications of the presence of a temple from earlier in the New Kingdom. These took the form of temple foundation deposits (model vases and model copper instruments), with inscriptions mentioning Amenophis II as the beloved of Horemakhet, by which name the Sphinx was known during and after the New Kingdom. He found various private stelae of New Kingdom times and a series of miniature votive sphinxes in limestone and plaster, painted red. A New Kingdom mud-brick building whose remains he began to uncover had a limestone door-frame which referred to the Sphinx under the name of a god called Hwrna: this is an early appearance of the same name as is featured anachronistically on the Inventory Stela. Like Mariette, Baraize also found statue fragments that probably belonged to one of the box-like shrines built on to the Sphinx, most likely in the New Kingdom.

Baraize cleared the immediate area around the Sphinx, building walls to keep the sand from getting in again; he also made a partial clearance of the temple in front of the Sphinx. Ten years later, in 1936, Professor Selim Hassan began his

The Sphinx in its enclosure, photographed before the modern tourist road was paved through the site. The wider Sphinx enclosure can be seen behind the monument, while at the right are some of the tombs cut into its northern face.

extensive and important excavations at Giza. He used light railway tracks with hand-pushed trucks to take away the sand that, despite Baraize's most recent clearance, still swamped much of the site. Maspero had used the same 'Decauville' railway in a smaller way. Professor Selim had three tracks with twelve trucks each and was able to take out 1,300 cubic metres per day and dump it up to 1 km away. He reckoned that by the middle of 1937 his men had dealt with a quarter of a million cubic metres of sand and debris.

Selim Hassan started by demolishing Baraize's walls, which were substantial, and some late mud-brick structures on the site, after duly recording them. On 20 September 1936, he found a large stela of Amenophis II just to the north of the Sphinx and its immediate enclosure, and just beyond the reach of Baraize's previous work, where indications of a mud-brick temple of the time of Amenophis II had already been encountered. In the debris here, Professor Selim found many small votive figures of lions and sphinxes in bronze, faience and limestone. He went on to uncover fully the remains of the temple, a mud-brick structure with some parts in white limestone from Tura across the Nile. In the temple, which had evidently been begun by Amenophis II of Dyn. XVIII in about 1400 BCE but adapted by Dyn. XIX pharaohs like Seti I and Merneptah c. 1300–1200 BCE, many more votive pieces came to light: lions, sphinxes, hawks, small stelae and plaques. The entrance to the temple, itself a long hall with smaller side chambers, had been guarded with a pair of sphinxes.

The original Dyn. IV temple of the Sphinx was clearly lost beneath sand and debris by the time Amenophis II came to put up his temple there, well over a thousand years later: the foundations of his new temple were built over the west end of the northern passage of the old temple.

Many stelae were found around and about the Amenophis II Sphinx temple. Among them were numerous small versions with depictions of the human ear – the so-called 'ear tablets'. Similar pieces have been found in the temple of Ptah at Memphis. The idea was presumably to encourage the god to hear the pleas of the dedicators of these small stelae. They were to be the ears of the god, in this case Horemakhet, the Sphinx. Sometimes the god is shown hawk-headed, and in one case on a pedestal. Maspero had already drawn attention to finds like this and speculated about some sort of pedestal under the Sphinx, if only the side of one. A find from the Amenophis II temple at the Sphinx throws some interesting light on the Egyptian tradition of royal self-promotion. A stela tells of a youthful visit of Amenophis to the Sphinx and how – remembering it when he became king – he was moved to build his temple by the monument. The stela of his son Tuthmosis IV really only repeats this formula, going one better with the addition of the dream. It all goes to show that renewed interest in the Sphinx in their time was not just the accidental result of a nap in the noonday sun. The stela of Amenophis speaks of 'the pyramids of Horemakhet', which further suggests that the Sphinx was already seen as older and more important than the pyramids of Giza.

Indications of foreign interest in the Great Sphinx during the later days of ancient Egypt were detected close by the Amenophis II temple. To its west, a large number of buried pottery jars were found, containing cremations of the Roman period. A similar find was made elsewhere at Giza: people still wanted to be buried near the hallowed ancient monuments.

Selim Hassan went on to make an investigation of the original Sphinx temple in front of the Sphinx that Baraize had partially cleared ten years before, establishing its Dyn. IV credentials. By the end of 1936, Selim's clearance at the Sphinx had reached the western face of the enclosure, behind the Sphinx's hindquarters. He then worked eastward along the northern edge of the wider enclosure, where he found those rock-cut tombs facing south to the Sphinx's northern flank that we have already mentioned in connection with the dating of the Sphinx. They are mostly Old Kingdom tombs and their south openings are unusual. They can only have been cut after the creation of the wider Sphinx enclosure. As most of the tombs are of Dyn. IV date, they established for Professor Selim Hassan that the Sphinx enclosure was already cut (in part, at least) by that time during the Old Kingdom. Usually such tombs had openings to the north or east: some more could have been cut in the western cliff of the Sphinx enclosure to face east, but they were not. Selim Hassan concluded that they were not because they would have been too close to the hindquarters of the already carved Sphinx. In this way he arrived at a date no later than Dyn. IV for the carving of the Sphinx, in line with Egyptology's view that most likely Khafre caused the creation of the Sphinx and put his own face on it.

The sand between these tombs, facing south in the north face of the wider Sphinx enclosure, and the Sphinx body had never been cleared in modern times before Selim's excavation. In this area he found a statue of a priest of the lioness-headed goddess Sekhmet. Nearby a number of small votive stelae were found, one of them showing the Sphinx and pyramids in a unique style for ancient Egypt, in that a modern sort of perspective is reproduced with the pyramids partly obscured by the Sphinx in front of them and partly obscuring each other, while a statue in front of the Sphinx is realistically shown to be between its forelegs with its lower part obscured. Against this background of signal accuracy of representation, Selim Hassan drew attention to this stela's depiction of a collar around the Sphinx's neck and hawk plumage on its back and speculated that these were, at least in later times, real features of the Sphinx. A hawk hovers above the Sphinx on this stela and the inscription tells that it was made by the clever scribe Mentu-Hor and dedicated to 'Horemakhet, the Twice-great God, the Lord of Heaven'.

Other finds made in the same area between the north face tombs and the Sphinx ranged from Old Kingdom to late New Kingdom in date, as would be expected if the Sphinx enclosure was made in Old Kingdom times and went on in use till the New Kingdom, at which time sand invaded this part of the site. Nearer to the Sphinx, Selim Hassan found a mud-brick wall that had evidently been the place where stelae were set up. One of these stelae bore traces of brilliant colour in blue and yellow and Selim remarks that it would all have been quite a sight. In New Kingdom times, if not before, the Sphinx itself was highly painted, decorated perhaps with plumage and collar, and wore a tall plume on

In the foreground lie the remains of the temple of Amenophis II, to the north-east of the Sphinx.

top of its head, according to some of the votive plaques. To this day, a red powder is often encountered between and behind the repair blocks on the lower part of the Sphinx, the presumed remains of painting in earlier times (though it has been suggested that it might be the product of erosion).

In March of 1937 Selim discovered traces of yet another temple of the Sphinx to the north of the temple of Amenophis II, very ruined and probably robbed to build the latter. Again there were stelae, votive lions, sphinxes and hawks. This was an earlier New Kingdom temple, built by Tuthmosis I a century before the Amenophis II temple, in about 1500 BCE. It is to the reign of Tuthmosis I that the first ancient Egyptian record of the Great Sphinx belongs, using the name Horemakhet for the god of the monument. It is clear that it was in the early part of the New Kingdom that the cult of the Sphinx was quickened, leading over a period of about a hundred years to the building of the temple of Amenophis II (the original Sphinx temple being filled with sand and rubbish by then) and the restoration work of his son Tuthmosis IV.

Professor Selim speculated that the original identity of Khafre with the Sphinx was all but forgotten by New Kingdom times, leaving the Sphinx free to maintain under the name Horemakhet an entity of its own about which a cult could be developed. We shall explore the significance of the Horemakhet name in a later chapter.

On the stela of Tuthmosis IV, the Sphinx is known as Horemakhet and also as Kheperi-Re-Atum, the trinity of the Sun in the morning, the Sun of noon and the Sun of eventide. We saw at the beginning of this book how the theme of crawling infant, upstanding man and tottering crock reached down the centuries to be incorporated into the Greek Sphinx's riddle. Kheperi, Re and Atum all appear in the Pyramid Texts of the Old Kingdom, so the idea went back a long way by the time of Tuthmosis IV. The problematic mention on the same stela of Khafre suggests that the New Kingdom people who were developing the cult of the Sphinx in his own right as Horemakhet may still have remembered King Khafre as having something to do with the matter.

The Dyn. XIX pharaoh Seti I extended the temple of Amenophis II at the Sphinx in about 1300 BCE, and an inscription of his discovered there by Professor Selim calls the Sphinx both Horemakhet and Hwl. Hwl is evidently a variant of the Hwran name encountered on the Inventory Stela of about 600 BCE. Other variants include Hwrna, Hwran, Hwron, Horon. The hieroglyph used by the ancient Egyptians for both the sound of the letter r and the letter l was a couchant lion, rather like the Sphinx seen side-on but lion-headed, so all these variants are in fact quite close together in sound, and not so very far removed from the ancient Egyptian god's name that the Greeks called Horus, Egyptian Hor. Professor Selim concluded that a Canaanite divinity called Hwron, associated with a town in Palestine and attested by records from outside Egypt, was readily identified in New Kingdom times with the old Egyptian god Horus and venerated at Giza in the form of Horemakhet, the Sphinx. He noted that in several cases stelae had been dedicated to Hwrna-Horemakhet by people with un-Egyptian-sounding names, such as Yukh, for example. The Greeks spoke of a town called

Horonopolis and one of Professor Selim's stelae mentioned a 'place of Hwron' or 'Hwronia'. He noted that there were in his own day a couple of Arab villages near Giza called North and South Harronia, in his version. He concluded that a community with a large foreign component had imported a Canaanite deity into Egypt in New Kingdom times (when Egypt's empire sometimes extended into Palestine) and identified the import with the native Horus. In a final twist of the tale, he recalled that Abd al-Latif and al-Makrizi had both mentioned that the local Arabs of their day called the Sphinx Abul Hol, which seemed to mean Father of Terror in Arabic but which he now derived from the ancient Egyptian Per Hwl, House of Hwl or Hwron (etc.), the place of the Sphinx.

Finally Professor Selim was able to offer an explanation for the pedestal problem that had bothered Maspero and others who noted the stela depictions that appeared to show the Sphinx sitting on a raised base, a free-standing pedestal. Archaeology discovered no such pedestal beneath the Sphinx, which lies in an enclosure hollowed out of the rock to remove limestone, surrounded on three sides with the clean-cut faces of that enclosure. But in clearing the Sphinx temple, Selim was able to show that the rock in front of the paws had been cut down by about 2.5 m and the smooth face so created was incorporated into the western wall of the temple. From the entrance into the court of the temple, the view to the west seemed to show the Sphinx lying on top of a pedestal peeping over the top of the temple's back wall, the illusion completed by a concave cornice there that was actually reproduced in some of the stela depictions. That these stelae show a pedestal with the correctly observed detail of the cornice is a remarkable fact – for the Sphinx temple was largely if not entirely buried in sand by the time they were made. There must have been a public reminder available of what the Sphinx had looked like from the temple in former days, in the shape of pictures or descriptive records.

Professor Selim published an account of his work at the Sphinx in the late 1940s. Since then, the Sphinx has needed no large-scale clearance, but regular maintenance: not only to keep it clear of any more sand that might blow in but also to conserve its fabric as far as is possible. It has perhaps needed repair since the moment it was made, because of the poor quality of the bulk of the rock out of which it was carved. Moreover, the limestone is permeated with salts that are drawn out with moisture (condensed and absorbed during the night) by the heat of the day. At the surface the salts dry out and crystallize, forcing off flakes of stone.

Some of the blocks built on to the Sphinx body may be of Old Kingdom age, indicating repairs at an early date (or the necessity to part-build the monument from the start). We know that Tuthmosis IV, before he became king and allegedly on the prompting of his dream, cleared sand away from the old body in Dyn. XVIII. Professor Selim excavated mud-brick walls designed to keep the sand out, with bricks stamped with the name of Tuthmosis IV. It was probably Tuthmosis IV who ordered the first substantial repairs at the Sphinx, replacing any original masonry blocks that had fallen off and fitting new ones where severe erosion had taken place. He may have painted or repainted the monument, and perhaps installed a statue of his father, Amenophis II, between the forelegs, as well as the stela that tells the story of his dream and work of restoration: we recall that some of Selim Hassan's stelae show a statue in front of the Sphinx's chest. It is possible that there had been a statue of some sort at the Sphinx's breast from the start, whose original presence is now indicated only by the eroded bosses down the front of the monument – if so, it was no doubt already badly decayed by the time of Tuthmosis IV.

Ramesses II, who enjoyed a very long reign in the 1200s BCE, put up another two stelae of his own in the chapel in front of the Sphinx, and it is apparent that his reign saw further repairs there. We know that one of his many sons was a keen restorer of ancient monuments. A letter from an official of the time instructs a colleague to deliver eight labourers to extract stone for the Sphinx. The paws look as though they may have been the beneficiaries of this work, but most of their outer casing was probably fitted in Roman times. The sand-retaining walls were reinforced in the time of Hadrian, and the pavement of the Sphinx court was restored under Marcus Aurelius.

So it appears that repairs and maintenance have always been required at the Sphinx. Baraize in the 1920s put into effect the most extensive measures of modern time, especially visible in the head-dress extensions which some archaeologists now think unnecessary and ripe for removal. During the Second World War, the head was additionally supported under the chin with sandbags on top of a dry-stone pillar up the chest that gives a very novel effect to this familiar monument in photographs of the time.

Conservation and archaeology have gone on together at the Sphinx in recent years. In the late 1970s a thorough clearing of the Sphinx enclosure turned up more archaeological evidence pertinent to the dating of the monument. Dr Mark Lehner and Dr Zahi Hawass carefully examined all the debris of the clearance (and were even able to probe into the fissure at the Sphinx's hindquarters), identifying Old Kingdom pottery and hard hammer stones of the sort used in Old Kingdom times to smooth limestone. They concluded that this was material left behind by the people who made the Sphinx, during the Old Kingdom. They also located a 9-m long passage into the rock that starts in the fissure at the rear of the Sphinx, but all it contained was a pair of old shoes left over from Baraize's clearance. An aperture in the north side of the Sphinx that was photographed by Baraize in 1926 and subsequently blocked up has also been re-explored, similarly turning out to lead nowhere. Dr Hawass was able to reinvestigate the hole in the top of the Sphinx's back made by Perring and Howard Vyse in their search for ancient tunnels or chambers in the body of the monument, finding a boring rod left in when their drill became stuck, together with a fragment of the damaged back of the Sphinx's head-dress. Dr Hawass, who is the head of the Giza Antiquities Authority, has been at pains to point out that no other tunnels (or chambers) than the three mentioned above have ever been shown to exist in or under the Sphinx. We know when Perring and Howard Vyse made their hole and what they were looking for: the other two could have been made at any time after the carving of the Sphinx, perhaps in the same spirit of seeking secret chambers that motivated al-Mamun at the Great Pyramid, or for pious reasons during the Saite restoration.

Some people still want to believe that there are hidden chambers beneath the Sphinx, but their evidence for such is either dubious in the extreme (being based on the dreams of a 'psychic' and extravagant astronomical speculations) or reliant on the interpretation of remote sensing experiments in the Sphinx enclosure without validation by archaeological excavation. No artificially made tunnels or chambers have ever been discovered at the Sphinx as the result of remote sensing by seismometry, magnetometry, resistivity, acoustics or ground-penetrating radar. It is important to emphasize this point – physical probing of the anomalies turned up by the remote sensing experiments of the 1970s and '80s has at the most only revealed natural cavities that have been described by Dr Lehner as looking like the holes in a Swiss cheese.

The possibility of unknown chambers in or under the Sphinx is one of the remaining 'riddles' of the monument, though it might be thought an equally stubborn riddle that people so want to believe in that possibility. Another, of course, concerns the possibility that the Sphinx body at least might be older than the time of Khafre, perhaps by thousands and thousands of years. Geology has been said to support this idea. People with a taste for hidden chambers usually combine it with a predilection for the Sphinx's vast antiquity, though the two ideas do not have to run together.

There might be tunnels and chambers under the Sphinx, but the idea that the body of the monument – if not its head – could have been carved in about 7000 BCE or 10,000 BCE is rendered very unlikely by the detailed archaeology of the Sphinx enclosure in relation to the pyramid complexes of Giza, and utterly implausible by what archaeology reveals of the state of Egyptian culture in predynastic times and world culture at the end of the last ice age.

One of the stelae discovered
by Professor Selim Hassan
that show the Great Sphinx:
in this case with an
oversized statue in front.

EIGHT

THE SPHINX IN PICTURES

The earliest pictures of the Sphinx were produced by the ancient Egyptians themselves in New Kingdom times, when the Sphinx was already more than a thousand years old. Archaeological finds at the site of the Sphinx, particularly those made by Selim Hassan in the 1930s, include many stelae with depictions of the monument, showing considerable variation as to the details they record, or purport to record.

On some of the stelae, the Sphinx sits on a corniced pedestal, on others there is no pedestal. Sometimes a crown tops the head of the Sphinx: in some cases the combined Red and White Crowns of Lower and Upper Egypt, in others a tall plumed crown. Sometimes the beard is shown wedged like a king's beard, at other times curled at the tip like a god's (as is the case with the actual fragments of the beard). On some of the stelae, the Sphinx wears the plumage of a bird, and a collar or cape. On most of the stelae, the proportions of the Sphinx are shown more in accordance with the standard design of sphinxes after the Great Sphinx, but it is interesting to note that the Dream Stela itself depicts the proportions of head and body a little closer to the real Sphinx than the rest do; this stela of Tuthmosis IV between the Sphinx's paws shows no crown on its two Sphinx representations and the beard is of the divine pattern. But on the Dream Stela, no statue is shown before the Sphinx's breast, though many of the others do show it there. One of the most interesting of these is that of the scribe Mentu-Hor which uses unconventional artistic means, by the standards of the ancient Egyptians, to suggest that the statue is between the Sphinx's forelegs, by hiding the lower part of the statue's legs behind the outstretched limb of the Sphinx. In a similarly bold way, two pyramids are shown behind the Sphinx, part-hidden by its body, and one part-obscuring the other. This sort of perspective drawing is very unusual in Egyptian art and suggests that on this occasion a more than usually naturalistic effect was sought, which inspires confidence in the potential accuracy of details like the presence of the statue and the collar about the neck.

Some two-and-a-half thousand years after Mentu-Hor, the German traveller Johannes Helferich visited Giza and left us an account of the Sphinx which, though it contains that fanciful material about the ancient priests' getting inside the Sphinx's head to address the multitude, does circumstantially suggest that he was reasonably familiar

The Sphinx and pyramids, on the stela of Mentu-Hor (after Selim Hassan).

The Giza pyramids and Sphinx according to Sandys in the seventeenth century.

The Sphinx according to the *Description de l'Egypte* at the end of the eighteenth century.

with the site. The woodcut he had made for publication in 1579 would suggest the opposite: this Sphinx is blatantly female and about all that has come through of the real situation of the monument at Giza at the time is that the breast is shown buried in the sand and, perhaps, that the hair resembles the damaged head-dress of the Great Sphinx. We recall that Helferich thought the Sphinx was an image of Isis.

The illustrator of George Sandys' *Relations of a Journey begun in 1610* made a much better job of depicting the Sphinx. Sandys noted that 'Pliny gave it a belly' though only its head was visible to him, and he must have made a pretty detailed sketch of it in the field, for the woodcut in his book is really remarkably apt in showing the erosion of the neck, with knobbly protuberances, and the damage to the head-dress, with grooves and notches. What is more, this illustration of Sandys' book largely avoids the cultural contamination with the classical style that spoils many of the renditions of Egyptian art made before the end of the eighteenth century.

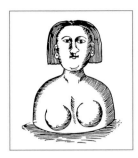

The Sphinx according to Helferich, 1579.

The picture of the Sphinx in Richard Pococke's account of his Egyptian travels, published in 1743, does not altogether escape the classical influence. Erosion and damage are fairly accurately recorded, but the nose of the monument – gone for several centuries by Pococke's time – is shown intact and the mouth is utterly un-Egyptian in character, rather primly self-satisfied in fact. The Danish marine architect Frederick Norden published the story of his travels in 1755, with a Sphinx drawing in more recognizably ancient Egyptian spirit. The erosion of the face and the damaged nose are recorded in Norden's picture and something of the George Washington set of the head is captured, with its slight backward tilt, but the eyes, lips and chin are still not right.

The Sphinx according to Pococke, 1743.

With the magnificent *Description de l'Egypte* that was published over a number of years in the early part of the nineteenth century, the first really accurate depictions of the Sphinx became available to world scholarship – in a limited way, for the volumes were necessarily very expensive and printed in small numbers. Napoleon's team had done their work well and their efforts in the field were well served by those who brought out the volumes of the *Description* back in France after Napoleon's downfall. The engravings of the Sphinx vividly portray the damaged state of the face and the head-dress and the erosion of the neck as Napoleon's engineers and savants found the monument. At the front, sand came up to the shoulders and nothing of the breast was visible (until the engineers dug down, possibly just uncovering the Tuthmosis IV stela before abandoning work); but the whole ridge of the back was visible, and at the hindquarters the sands fell away to reveal something of the rump of the Sphinx. What was entirely new in depictions of the Sphinx was that the whole setting of the Giza Plateau was accurately recorded about it, with correct perspective in the placing and rendering of the pyramids behind it. No doubt the artists who made their sketches on site could avail themselves of the most up-to-date cameras and other drawing aids.

The Sphinx according to Norden, 1755.

When Howard Vyse published his account of *Operations carried on at the Pyramids of Gizeh* in three volumes in the early 1840s, the first photograph of the Sphinx had not yet been taken. Howard Vyse's picture of the Sphinx under excavation by Caviglia shows the sand dune around the Sphinx quite parlously opened up in front of the breast and round the left shoulder, revealing the front paws and the chapel between the forelegs. The Dream Stela is quite well depicted, with something of its graphic design conveyed, while the jumbled masonry behind it and the column of blocks suggest evidence for the original presence of a statue and the support plate of the beard. But the distance from enclosure floor to chin is vastly exaggerated and the disproportion of head and body quite marked.

The first photographs of the Sphinx were taken in 1849 by Maxime Du Camp and published in 1852 in one of the earliest books to be extensively illustrated with real photographic prints made from negatives – in this case calotype paper negatives. Du Camp travelled with Flaubert a year or two before *Madame Bovary*, and both writers were bowled over by the Sphinx. 'No drawing I have seen conveys a proper idea of it,' wrote Flaubert, 'the best thing is an excellent photograph that Max took.' In the better of Du Camp's two photographs, the benefits of the first modern sand-clearances are still to be seen, but the Dream Stela has apparently gone under again. In the background is the pyramid of Menkaure with one of its subsidiaries. Khafre's pyramid is out of frame to the right, and his

The Sphinx under excavation, about 1820.

The Sphinx by Maxime Du Camp, 1849. From the Photographic Collection of the New York Public Library.

The Sphinx at the extreme right of a photograph by Hammerschmidt, 1858.

The Sphinx by Zangaki,
before 1880.

The Sphinx by Sebah, in the
second half of the
nineteenth century.

causeway is entirely invisible under the sands. The featureless and too-light sky has resulted from the colour-blind quality of the early photographic processes.

Thousands of photographs were taken of the Sphinx as the age of photography got under way, by amateurs as well as professionals as the business of photography in the field became simpler and more reliable after about 1880. Before that, there was a ready market for prints of Egyptian antiquities sold by professional photographers like Beato, Bonfils, Hammerschmidt, Lekegian, Sebah and Zangaki. Their photographs chart chiefly the swamping and clearance of the sand about the monument.

A striking picture by Hammerschmidt, in which foreground trees grow out of half-submerged ruins on the slope of the Giza Plateau, shows the Sphinx head peeping out of the sand below the Great Pyramid of Khufu: it was taken in 1858, at about the time that Mariette was excavating at the Sphinx. Despite Mariette's work, the sands soon invaded the breast area of the monument again and photographs from the 1860s show no front paws, no chapel, no stela – all this was once more buried under a sand drift. One of Zangaki's photographs shows picturesque camels at the Sphinx's breast, sitting on a sandbank that hides the forelegs, chapel and stela below, with the photographer's travelling darkroom drawn up alongside the upper right flank of the monument. A picture by Sebah, taken from the north-east, with Menkaure's pyramid in the background, shows

The Sphinx by an unknown nineteenth-century photographer.

The Sphinx seen over the valley temple of Khafre, by Sebah.

particularly clearly the great fissure at the hindquarters and the severe gouge in the left-hand side of the top of the head. Another, by an unknown photographer, also shows this deep (and inadvertently rather characterful) cut in the top of the head, with a sentinel figure sitting above the uraeus: the pyramid to the right of the picture is that of Khafre. A second photograph taken by Sebah shows the Sphinx's head with the Khufu pyramid behind it and the valley temple of Khafre in the foreground, first excavated by Mariette: the plain granite pillars and lintels of the temple interior are clearly seen, together with some of the massive (and highly eroded) limestone blocks of the core construction of this building. Though cleared by Mariette, sand is seen in this photograph to be reinvading the interior. A picture by Fiorillo of 1882 shows members of the British Army disporting themselves on and around the Sphinx in the year when the British under Sir Garnet Wolseley asserted Britain's imperial power in Egypt.

It was partly to give tourists something extra to see in Lower Egypt (which, despite the pyramids, could not rival Upper Egypt for spectacular ruins) that Maspero undertook further excavations at the Sphinx in 1885. After that, the Sphinx remained on fuller view than before. A photograph by Lekegian documents the erosion of the southern flank of the Sphinx, with the cavernous fissure of the haunches at the left, and shows the ancient masonry work that was added to build up the eroded body of the monument. Another photograph of the time shows the Dream Stela covered over with a dark cloth (its upper part at least) to protect the design at the top of the inscription, if not all of the inscription itself. Masonry lies about between the paws and in front of the little altar discovered by Caviglia: presumably remains (afterwards relaid) of the paving of Roman times. A tiny figure in his black djellaba sits at the neck in the shade of the massive head, giving an unusually good idea of the colossal scale of the monument.

Baraize's work from 1925 into the early '30s achieved a more complete clearance of the immediate Sphinx enclosure than had been made before in modern times. A photograph from the late '20s shows, most strikingly, the Roman-period paving of the area in front of the Sphinx. The Sphinx's head (now favoured with the cement extensions of the head-dress) is framed between the Khafre and Menkaure pyramids like Horus on the Horizon. This photograph was taken with a wide-angle lens that has exaggerated the size of the paws in relation to the chest and head, but it has made it possible to see very clearly the eroded nature of the south wall, in particular, of the immediate Sphinx enclosure and the way, behind the Sphinx, that the strata rise to the north (they also rise to the west). On top of the north face of the immediate Sphinx enclosure (to the

The Sphinx by Fiorillo, 1882.

The Great Sphinx in
modern times.

The Sphinx by Lekegian, showing the scale of the head against a standing human figure and the characteristic erosion of the Sphinx body. Note the fissure at the haunches, before it was part-filled with cement.

The Sphinx, with the Dream
Stela under cover, by an
unknown late nineteenth-
century photographer.

right in the photograph) Baraize's extra walling can be seen: it was removal of this walling in the area at the bottom right of this photograph that revealed how the south-west corner of the temple of Amenophis II overhung the corridor leading to the Sphinx from the original Sphinx temple (beneath our feet in this photograph and cleared later on by Baraize and then by Selim Hassan).

To add to the questionable effect of the cement head-dress extensions added by Baraize, the Second World War saw the building of a pier up the Sphinx's breast, topped with sandbags, to support the head against, one supposes, the threat of bomb blast. This all had the appearance of a huge beard that, taken with the cement extensions, rather unexpectedly produced an oddly plausible, if bastard, piece of new ancient Egyptian art. The wartime photograph also shows the location before the recent road was made up to the Great Pyramid. Just over the Sphinx's left shoulder can be seen the end of an ancient mud-brick wall: beyond it is the continuing western face of the wider Sphinx enclosure. At the extreme right are some of the tombs cut into the north face of the Sphinx enclosure that Professor Selim Hassan held to indicate that the enclosure (and therefore the Sphinx) were not cut out after Old Kingdom times.

A modern colour photograph shows the present state of the Sphinx, lying in its highly eroded state in its immediate deep-cut enclosure, with the pyramid of Khafre to the left (with some of its casing still in place at the top) and the pyramid of Khufu to the right. The built-on elements of the monument, including the tail

The Sphinx as revealed by the clearances (and restorations) of Baraize in the late 1920s. Photo: Lehnert and Landrock.

The Sphinx buttressed against war damage in the 1940s. Photo: E. Sved.

curling up at the haunches and the box at bottom left-centre that is probably a New Kingdom shrine-base (for a statue of Osiris) contrast with the very worn state of the living rock of the body. Over the fully clad foreleg at bottom right, the top of the Dream Stela of Tuthmosis IV can be seen. (Above that in the distance at the foot of the Great Pyramid we can see the museum housing the wooden boat of Khufu found nearby.) The erosion of the southern and western walls of the Sphinx enclosure is clear at bottom left: in the corner between the two walls there is the notch created where the enclosure cuts into the ditch alongside the Khafre causeway (which runs up to the Khafre pyramid from bottom left at the top of the enclosure wall); the presence of this notch, filled with pieces of granite, indicated to Professor Selim that the enclosure had been cut after the ditch of the causeway and that the notch had had to be plugged to prevent rainwater from running into the enclosure and round the lower body of the Sphinx.

But what did the Sphinx look like when it was first made, and the years had not yet taken their toll of erosion and damage – with the beard (and its support plate) in place, with the uraeus cobra intact on its brow, with the head-dress gathered together in a queue on the back of the body, with the lappets of the head-dress descending over the shoulders, but without perhaps any statue yet before its breast and without the Dream Stela in its little chapel between the paws? How much was originally built on to the living rock with additional masonry blocks, or perhaps added in plaster, we cannot say. The two foremost scholars of the Sphinx in our day have disagreed about that: Dr Zahi Hawass has suggested that most if not all of the body was clad from the first; Dr Mark Lehner thinks it was mostly carved from the living rock to begin with and only required cladding after hundreds of years of neglect and erosion. Our reconstruction shows few details of masonry, therefore, without implying that none at all was present at the start, if not a good deal. The Sphinx temple in front of (and below the level of) the monument itself may never have seen much use to judge by its not quite finished state, and so it is possible that the Sphinx, too, was never completed and was neglected within a short time. Some three hundred years after Khafre's death, during the time of social collapse that Egyptologists call the First Intermediate Period, the signs are that his valley temple was ransacked and his statues there deliberately smashed – it is unlikely that the Sphinx would have escaped the attentions of the wreckers at the same time, when the monuments of Giza were attacked in general. The beard would have been an easy target and the vandals may well have forced off some of any cladding blocks that were part of the original design. Egyptologists believe that it is from this time, in about 2200 BCE, that the decline of the monument dates. The sands would have quickly swamped the neglected Sphinx, and under them the process of erosion would have got to work on the lion's body, while the desert winds scoured the neck and picked out the weak lines in the human head and face. So that by the time of Tuthmosis IV, the Sphinx was ripe for restoration, as it has been on at least three occasions since, including our own day.

Such, at least, is the view of the Egyptologists about the creation and decay of the Great Sphinx, its restoration and subsequent further decline. But there are other interpretations of the Sphinx's history and vicissitudes and they continue to be developed and aired by their proponents.

A sketch of the Great Sphinx as it might have appeared in about 2500 BCE.

The Sphinx seen from behind,
facing east to the sunrise.

NINE

THE ALTERNATIVE SPHINX

According to the Egyptologists, the Great Sphinx is the product of ancient Egypt's Old Kingdom and most likely of King Khafre in about 2500 BCE. As a result of his extensive work at Giza, Professor Selim Hassan was able to establish that the original excavation of the Sphinx enclosure could not have taken place after Dyn. IV, since the south-facing tombs cut into its northern side were of that date and could only have been made after the enclosure was created; at the same time he noted that the south-west corner of the Sphinx enclosure cuts into the trench running along the north side of Khafre's causeway, which must therefore have been there before the enclosure was excavated. Indeed, the trench was blocked to prevent rainwater from emptying into the amphitheatre of the Sphinx. These observations make for a narrow band of time into which the creation of the enclosure can be put by Egyptologists. On the one hand, the demarcation of Khufu's and Khafre's complexes had already been made; on the other, the enclosure was excavated before the end of Dyn. IV. The fact that a head of very obviously Old Kingdom character (indeed closely resembling the Dyn. IV sculptures of Khafre, Djedefre and Menkaure) tops the monument goes to show that the knoll left by the extraction of stone in the enclosure was not long neglected (if at all) but was carved into the Sphinx during Dyn. IV.

Selim Hassan was able to show how the New Kingdom notion of a pedestal under the Sphinx had come about, when the view of the Sphinx from the court of the temple in front of it was half-remembered. It was easy for first the ancient Egyptians, then the Christian Egyptians and then the Arabs to speculate about chambers in a pedestal under the Sphinx; and once the idea of hidden chambers was abroad, it was bound to persist with or without the pedestal.

It became clear in the nineteenth century that the ancient Egyptians of New Kingdom and later times had no precise knowledge of the Sphinx's origins. Tuthmosis IV may have heard something in connection with Khafre, but he already regarded the Sphinx as an entity in its own right, the divine Horemakhet, rather than the figure of a particular ancient king. Since the gods descended from time out of mind, it was natural to think of the Sphinx as immemorially old. By the time of the Inventory Stela at around 600 BCE, the Sphinx was readily regarded as older than Khufu's pyramid. Pliny's remark about the Sphinx in the early years of our Common Era are based on the version the Egyptians had long adopted by his time: that the Sphinx was the god Harmachis (the Greek version of Horemakhet); but he didn't fall for the folklore he had heard about the transport of the whole monument to Giza from elsewhere.

Priestly records and popular lore probably kept alive a dim memory of the complexity of the internal arrangements of the Great Pyramid after the end of the Old Kingdom – stray mentions in Middle Kingdom texts suggest as much. In Herodotus' day, in the middle of the fifth century BCE, the locals were talking of secret shafts and chambers under the Great Pyramid, 'which Cheops [Khufu] meant as vaults for his own use, built on a sort of island surrounded by water brought in by canal from the Nile'. This conjures up so extravagantly romantic an image, like something from *The Phantom of the Opera*, that one could wish it were true. But in fact, deep beneath the Great Pyramid, there is simply an unfinished rock-cut burial chamber, quite dry – in it, interestingly, one can see, because it is unfinished, how the ancient masons blocked out their work in sections. (A similar situation is to be seen at the back of the Sphinx.) At least Herodotus' informants were clear that the Great Pyramid was the tomb of Khufu.

Eight centuries after Herodotus, a new dimension was added to the concept of hidden chambers under the pyramids in the cursory remarks of Ammianus Marcellinus about 'underground galleries . . . to save the ancient wisdom from being lost in the flood'. Ammianus Marcellinus was not a Christian, for all his reference to the flood, but an heir of late pagan philosophy who had absorbed the idea of the Egyptians' 'ancient wisdom'. Horapollon, in the next century, also promoted the idea of the arcane knowledge of the ancient Egyptians, expressed in the mysterious hieroglyphs.

And al-Mamun was not just after earthly treasure when he employed his men to break into the Great Pyramid in the ninth century CE. He encouraged his men with the lure of gold and gemstones within and, according to some accounts, smuggled in a treasure to pacify them when nothing was found. But al-Mamun was a patron of science who founded universities in the Muslim world and made Baghdad into a centre of learning, with an astronomical observatory. Al-Mamun sponsored the translation into Arabic of the Greek manual of astronomy called the *Megiste Syntaxis*, *Almagest* in Arabic, written by Ptolemy of Alexandria in about 140 CE. It was the rumour of secret chambers inside the Great Pyramid, containing (among other wonders) astronomical charts of great learning, that really inspired al-Mamun to break into it. It appears that in reality he found nothing in the pyramid, despite some stories of a jewel-decked statue in the sarcophagus. Perhaps in search of chambers even more hidden than the ones they had succeeded in penetrating, al-Mamun's men took up part of the floor in the burial chamber and even dug short tunnels into the walls of the King's and Queen's Chambers, finding nothing.

The rumours that told of hidden chambers in the pyramids were matched by others that told of passages under the Sphinx. Al-Kodai and al-Makrizi both related stories of the Christian Egyptians that told of a chamber under the Sphinx from which three passages radiated to the Giza pyramids, each entrance guarded by a magic statue. Such stories do incorporate elements derived from the robbing of genuine tombs of the ancient Egyptians, but obviously need have no basis in fact where the Sphinx is concerned: they are just stories, like the ones about secret passages from the cathedrals and castles of our own towns.

The Giza locals never let go of their belief in secret chambers inside or under the Sphinx. And European travellers to Egypt in Renaissance times, with Horapollon et al. in mind, were ready to absorb the idea. We saw that Helferich in the second half of the sixteenth century could assert as if he had been in it that a hidden passage permitted entry into the head so that priests might gull the public 'as if the statue itself had spoken'. We saw too that the local Arabs at the time of Napoleon's expedition to Egypt thought that his savants were trying to find treasures inside the Sphinx and, indeed, had actually found the doorway into it just as work had had to be abandoned. When Maspero was overseeing excavations at the Sphinx in the late nineteenth century, the locals revived the secret chamber legend and concluded that the archaeologists were searching for a magic onyx cup belonging to King Solomon.

As we have seen, no chambers or passages under or inside the Sphinx, except for the three mentioned earlier, have ever been located. Egyptologists of the twentieth century, while not closing their minds to the possibility of such features, had other scholarly matters to pursue, and Professor Selim's account of the Sphinx remained the basis for thinking about the monument. The idea of secret chambers was kept alive, not in the minds of Egyptologists, but in the dreams of an American psychic of the 1930s named Edgar Cayce.

Cayce could not be described as an educated man – apparently he was almost illiterate. But in his role as 'The Sleeping Prophet' he attracted a large following of believers. In the way of such people, he was credited with powers of prediction and healing. He also went in for remembering past lives. One of his dreams cast him among the survivors of the destruction of Atlantis who, he said, arrived in Egypt in 10,500 BCE and proceeded to build the Great Pyramid and the Sphinx. (This dating seems needlessly timid on Cayce's part when one recalls that Madame Blavatsky had more robustly declared the Sphinx to be eighty thousand years old – and her grounds for saying that must have been at least as good as Cayce's.) The Sleeping Prophet further claimed that records of the ancient wisdom of the Atlanteans were buried in chambers by the Great Pyramid and Sphinx, hidden through the millennia but intended for rediscovery pretty soon: before the end of the twentieth century, in fact. Their rediscovery would preface a cataclysm like the one that had destroyed Atlantis and, it seems almost needless to say, would see the Second Coming into the bargain. Much of Europe confidently expected the close of the first millennium of the Christian Era to witness the

end of the world, but in vain: Cayce was among those who have looked
forward to a great deal of trouble for us all at the close of the second
millennium. He thought the Atlantean 'Hall of Records' would be opened in
1998 – which promises limited sales for those of us who write about these
matters, if he is right, though fortunes have already been made by some
continuators of his notions.

Atlantis is the literary invention of the Greek philosopher Plato, in the
fourth century BCE. He described an island, west of the Pillars of Hercules (by
which the Greeks referred to the Strait of Gibraltar), whose people ruled parts
of Europe and Africa in prehistoric times until, when they tried to conquer the
whole world, they were defeated by the Athenians and then overwhelmed by
the sea. It seems that it was through his own family that Plato probably derived
the inspiration (but not the details) for his story. Solon, a distant relative of
Plato's, had visited Egypt in about 590 BCE and brought back the tale of an
island people who had been destroyed in a day by a dire catastrophe that saw
them submerged under the sea. It is very likely that the Egyptians had passed
on to Solon their memory of the sudden decline of the great trading empire of
the Minoans on Crete, who flourished before 1500 BCE. Mixed in with the
story of the collapse of the Minoans was very likely a memory of the
destruction of the island of Thera by volcanic eruption at roughly the same
time. (No Egyptian records of any of this have survived to us.) A garbled
account would have been created of cataclysm, tidal wave, submergence and
the disappearance of a once-powerful trading force. Plato's interest in the story,
despite the seemingly precise details he gives of the size and location of the
island, was not historical, but literary. He quite possibly made up the name of
the island himself, to relate it to the Atlas of Greek legend, the Titan who held
up the whole world, after whom the Atlas Mountains of North Africa were
named. He put his Atlantis out into the western ocean beyond the known
world for added impact. The purpose of Plato's story of Atlantis, put into the
mouth of a character in two of his philosophical dialogues, was to point up the
problematical aspects of Athenian imperialism in his own time. It is perhaps
superfluous to point out that none of the details of Plato's story (an island in
the Atlantic, ruling parts of Africa and Europe, defeated by the Athenians
thousands and thousands of years ago) fits in with anything we know of
history, prehistory and geology.

But Plato had created a vivid myth that was revived in Renaissance times when
the New World of the Americas was at first identified by some with legendary
Atlantis. Our knowledge of the Atlantic Ocean bottom and the processes of
continental formation and drift makes it certain that there was never any large,
populated island out in the Atlantic beyond the Strait of Gibraltar. Rational
comment on Plato's Atlantis must recognize the nature of the use he wanted to
make of the tale and of the possible elements of real Mediterranean prehistory
that had come down to him. Plato's submerged Atlantis, it should be noted, had
nothing to do with the Greek story of Deaucalion's Flood, or Noah's Flood, or
the Mesopotamian story of a great flood or any of the other flood stories of the

world: flood stories are inevitable in most human traditions and do not amount to proof of a single great inundation at one particular time in the past, for which there is no geological basis.

Cayce seems not to have envisaged his Atlantean Hall of Records as being in or under the Great Pyramid. His utterances, like those of Nostradamus before him, are not grammatically constructed and are therefore comfortably obscure for those who want to build free interpretations on them. But he seems to associate the chamber with the Sphinx in some way and this has been sufficient to motivate a search for underground passages and rooms beneath the Sphinx enclosure. In the late 1970s, resistivity scans suggested to American investigators that there were anomalies in the bedrock beneath the rear paws and in front of the front paws of the monument. Anomalies might mean cavities, which might mean artificially created cavities: chambers or passages. Further work was done in 1978, part funded by the Edgar Cayce Foundation, using a resistivity survey to locate such anomalies. The method relies on the fact that buried features lead to variations in the resistance of the ground to electric current. Changes resulting from similar features can also register as fluctuations in the magnetic field in the ground under survey. Both methods have been tried at the Sphinx. The anomalies detected in 1977 and 1978 proved to relate to natural features of the limestone bedrock of the Sphinx location: drilling holes revealed no artificial cavities where they occurred. The limestone of the Giza Plateau is known to contain some natural cavities and fissures. Limestone is a sedimentary rock, laid down in beds, but with joints within the beds that can be opened up by solution: although limestone is not usually very soluble, not by pure water at least, it can be rotted by rainwater in which there is in solution a minute proportion of atmospheric carbon dioxide. In arid conditions limestone is very resistant to erosion except by physical means like wind-blown sand, but it is very susceptible to chemical weathering, especially by solution, in humid conditions. Dew is causing serious erosion at the Sphinx today. People who want to build with limestone like to find joints opened up by solution in the beds as it makes the process of quarrying that much easier. Giza was an excellent place to quarry limestone, to build the pyramids: that is how most Egyptologists think the excavation of the Sphinx enclosure came to be undertaken, before the knoll of largely poor quality rock left over suggested the carving of the Sphinx itself.

In winter 1992/3, supporters of the Edgar Cayce Foundation contributed to further geological survey work at the Sphinx, detecting an anomaly that appeared to some to suggest the presence, under the front paws of the Sphinx, of a cavity rectangular in shape (9 m × 12 m at 5 m depth) that might be man-made. Further anomalies were located along the side of the Sphinx, where acoustic testing in 1982 had similarly suggested the possibility of a cavity. To date, these possible cavities have not been confirmed by any sort of archaeological investigation and their artificiality (indeed existence) has not been demonstrated, because the Egyptian authorities put a stop to work that they judged to be undertaken not for scientific purposes but for reasons of 'propaganda' as Dr Zahi Hawass has put it. Funding by people associated with the commemoration of a dead sleeping prophet does not automatically disqualify the work done as unscientific, but it certainly inspires no confidence in the aims of that work. The Egyptian people, moreover, might quite naturally conclude that a notion that deprived their own ancestors of the authorship of the Sphinx and the Great Pyramid, and gave it to the fabulous Atlanteans, was something of a gratuitous insult to their history. We can go further and say that the idea of an Atlantean supercivilization of 10,500 BCE, replete with however much 'ancient wisdom', diminishes the true achievement of the whole human race in its painful progress to whatever real civilization we have managed to secure for ourselves over the last five thousand years. 'Propaganda' was not therefore an inappropriate word to use in connection with some of the researches carried out at Giza in the 1990s. Meanwhile, it remains likely that detected anomalies represent naturally formed depositional and erosional features of the rock around the Sphinx.

There may, of course, be cavities and fissures, even man-made chambers, under the Sphinx but, if there are, they must be scientifically investigated by archaeologists if they are to tell us anything valuable about the making of the monument. Finding just suggestions of their possible presence as a result of enthusiasm for the claims of a 1930s psychic does not warrant speculation that they and the Sphinx were carved at Giza in 10,500 BCE.

Another 'alternative' line of enquiry about the age of the Sphinx (which also turns out to favour the 10,500 BCE dating) has been proposed in recent years by people who have pondered the astronomical alignments through time of the whole pyramid field from Abu Rawash north of Giza to Dahshur to the south. We have seen that the Sphinx faces sunrise at the equinoxes, due east. The Giza pyramids (though not so much the earlier ones at Saqqara and Dahshur) are very precisely orientated with the cardinal points of the compass. The entrance shaft and the northern King's Chamber shaft of the Great Pyramid point to the polar region of the sky. Various people have commented on these and many more alignments found on the ground and inside the pyramids, particularly the Great Pyramid, and astronomical implications were first noted in the nineteenth century. Laborious calculations made it possible then to work out some of the alignments of past times, to check what particular stars might have been sighted up, say, the Grand Gallery of the Great Pyramid. Computers made this work much easier to perform from the 1960s on, and the arrival of graphic computer displays now means that whole night skies of the past can be wheeled across our view again, to see how they looked in relation to the monuments of the people of past times.

All discussion about the age of the Sphinx in the light of its astronomical alignments is inevitably, and rightly, linked to the question of the astronomical alignments of the pyramids at Giza and elsewhere. Egyptologists believe that the Sphinx and the Giza pyramids are of roughly the same age, and they put their time of construction at about 2500 BCE. Most of the people who think that the Sphinx is much older than that also think that the grand plan of the pyramids at least, if not its full implementation, also goes back to very remote times. Some appear to think that the entire Great Pyramid may be as old as their old Sphinx, others that its ground plan (and, who knows, maybe blueprints for its interior too) go back to their early Sphinx date. Yet others may include the Khafre pyramid, even Menkaure's, in their very old bracket, with or without the rest of the buildings in each pyramid complex. So we must in the end review some of the astronomical theories about the pyramids, too, when we finally judge the ideas about the Sphinx's age in the light of astronomy.

If we first consider the Sphinx by itself, we note immediately that it faces due east to the equinoctial sunrises. It is clearly in some way a solar monument. All the year round it gazes towards the rising Sun and twice a year it looks directly at the sunrise. A priest or anybody else who stood on the plateau above and behind it could look straight along its body and see the Sun come up over its head at the spring and autumn equinoxes. (The summer and winter solstices constitute a fan of sunrise positions at whose apex the Sphinx gazes directly at the equinoxes.) Looked at from the reverse point of view, from in front, the Sphinx stands guard at the edge of the Giza necropolis with the Sun setting straight behind it (and the pyramids) in the west.

Sphinxes in general were placed by the ancient Egyptians to act as guardians of important places, sacred places like temples and necropolises. We have seen that Khafre's valley temple, next door to the Sphinx temple, was evidently guarded by sphinx statues, and that the Great Sphinx was known in later times as Horemakhet, Horus on the Horizon. This name alludes to the Egyptians' ancient sky-god Horus (closely associated with the kings of Egypt) in the particular form of the Sun's orb lying on the eastern horizon at sunrise, to which the Sphinx directs his gaze, or on the western horizon behind the Sphinx at sunset, or traversing the whole wide sky between the two horizons. The Sphinx greeted the rising Sun of the daytime world, perhaps indeed from the start embodied the very deity of the Sun in a king's guise, and at the same time stood guardian at the entrance to the underworld, the royal tomb-field in which the dead lay in darkness like the solar orb below the horizon after sunset in the west.

Since the time of the Maidum pyramid, the provision of temples on the east–west axis of the pyramids points to the solar component in beliefs about the royal dead, even though the pyramid interiors remained (mostly) on a north–south axis that probably goes back to the stellar orientation of the Dyn. III step pyramids. Where religion was concerned, the Egyptians were never absolutist and would not abandon a good old idea because a good new idea had come along: they were even able to sustain simultaneously several formally quite contradictory ideas, like many religious people. So a dead king might spend eternity sailing from horizon to horizon with Re in his sun boat at the same time as dwelling with the circumpolar stars, that never set with the passing of the nights and seasons.

The Sphinx always looks to the Sun but through the ages the background of stars against which the Sun rises and sets has moved with a phenomenon called by astronomers the precession of the equinoxes. The Earth circles the Sun and spins on its own axis as it circles, with the Moon in orbit around it. You might expect the Earth's axis of spin to be perpendicular to the plane of its orbit around the Sun, but it is not, thanks largely to the pull of the Moon on the Earth's equatorial bulge as it circles the spinning Earth at an angle to the plane of the solar system. And so the Earth's axis is at an angle of 23½° to the perpendicular of the plane of its orbit around the Sun. It is the Earth's yearly circling of the Sun on its tilted axis that gives rise to the Sun's apparent path among the stars in the course of a year. This path is called the ecliptic because it is the line near which eclipses of the Sun and Moon occur. The constellations of the zodiac lie along this line: they are the background, in the form of a continuous belt of stars, to the Sun's annual path. Because it is spinning, the Earth's axis does not become perpendicular to the Moon's orbit but rather it precesses, like a wobbling toy top with a red line painted around it, its poles very slowly tracing circles and its equator very slowly tipping to and fro.

If we ignore for a moment this very slow precession, we can picture the Earth tilted on its axis, spinning round once daily, orbiting around the Sun in 365¼ days: the tilt means that in winter the northern latitudes lean away from the Sun, and in summer lean towards it, giving us the pattern of the seasons. In winter, there are few hours of daylight in the north since the sunshine falls on only a small segment of the tilted-away globe; in summer, there are more daylight hours since the Sun lights up the bigger area tilted towards it. At the spring and autumn equinoxes, the lengths of the daylight and the dark are equal, with the Sun directly over the equator.

It takes nearly twenty-six thousand years for the Earth's wobbling axis to trace a complete circle of the poles, about thirteen thousand years for the axis to swing from any one direction to its extreme opposite. This means that the pole star we look to today, Polaris, will be displaced by Vega in about another thirteen thousand years; four-and-a-half thousand years ago at the time of the building of the Great Pyramid, the pole star was Thuban. In thirteen thousand years' time the Northern Hemisphere will enjoy its longest days in December and its shortest in June.

One of the effects of precession in terms of astronomical observation is that the moment of sunrise at any particular time of the year takes place against a slowly changing (over twenty-six thousand years) background of stars. The background of the Sun's yearly course is made up of those stars and constellations that lie in a band along the plane of the ecliptic: we picture twelve constellations lying on this continuous band, the twelve signs of the zodiac. The Greeks called these constellations the zodiac because most of them are in animal form: Greek zodia, for little animals. The zodiac was not invented by the Greeks but by the Babylonians, and the oldest record of the zodiacal signs as such is a horoscope of 419 BCE, though the constellations we still know as the lion, the bull and the scorpion were first mentioned in

Mesopotamian texts of 1000 BCE and possibly date back to even earlier times in Sumer. But the recognition of the apparent path of the Sun through the stars and the full development of the zodiac were not accomplished until the fifth century BCE.

Precession was first noted by the Greek astronomer Hipparchus in about 120 BCE, by comparing measurements of star positions made by his Greek predecessors with those of his own day, but it was not until the time of Newton in the seventeenth century that the Earth's motion was well enough understood to explain the mechanism of precession.

Precession means that the Sphinx has watched the Sun rise against a background of slowly shifting signs of the zodiac through the millennia. Modern computer techniques make it relatively easy for us to see just what constellations were on the skyline at any desired date of sunrise. Much has been made of the fact that, in 10,500 BCE, it was the zodiacal constellation of Leo that lay on the horizon at sunrise at the vernal equinox. Presumably, this date of 10,500 BCE cannot be credited with absolutely mandatory precision, for each of our present-day signs of the zodiac takes up over two thousand years of the precessionary cycle. Still, the proponents of the theory do quote 10,500 BCE as the all-important year. Leo is one of the few signs of our zodiac that looks anything at all like the thing it is named after, one of the few constellations anywhere in the sky of which that much could be said. Leo does indeed resemble a couchant lion or sphinx seen side-on and many people have suggested that the ancient Egyptians recognized this constellation and related it in some way to their Sphinx. The argument goes on to say that the Sphinx was plainly associated with the sun-god Re both in his name as Horemakhet Kheperi-Re-Atum and in his eastward gazing orientation towards the equinoctial sunrise. So it comes down to this, for the moment: the Sphinx is a solar monument, the Sphinx faces the Sun, the Sphinx's shape is a lot like our constellation Leo, the lion, and in around 10,500 BCE at the spring equinox the Sun rose out of our Leo.

The authors of this proposition have further elaborated their scenario to use the position of the Sun somewhat before sunrise, below the horizon and below the hindquarters of Leo in spring of 10,500 BCE, to speculate about a hint from the past for us to look for a hidden chamber thirty metres or so beneath the rump of the Giza Sphinx. There are many problems with this notion, not the least being that nowhere in the wide world let alone in Egypt have there been found any traces of a culture of 10,500 BCE capable of carving the Giza Sphinx, by possessing the organization, ideology and technological resources to do it; not surprisingly no remotely comparable piece of work, large or small, exists anywhere in the world that dates to 10,500 BCE. But there are detailed objections too. Notwithstanding the resemblance of zodiacal Leo to a couchant lion or sphinx, there is no evidence that the ancient Egyptians ever recognized the constellation of Leo until very late times indeed, when they were subject to Babylonian influence in these matters. And by very late times, we mean only a few centuries BCE. Even if

The pyramids of Giza, seen
from the south, to reveal
the offset position of
Menkaure's pyramid (in
front here) with respect to
Khafre's and Khufu's
monuments.

the Sphinx was made by non-Egyptians, pre-Egyptians, people from Atlantis or people from outer space (the last refuge of the superman idea), it would be very odd to think that a prominent monument inspired by a constellation not at all unlike a lion (once the resemblance has been pointed out) would not have caused the historical Egyptians to include a single recognizable rendition of Leo among their star maps. And yet they did not.

The first star charts of the ancient Egyptians that we possess come from coffins of Dyn. X of the First Intermediate Period, at about 2150 BCE, after the close of the Old Kingdom. These coffin texts and drawings describe a system of sky division not into twelve zodiacal constellations around the plane of the ecliptic but instead into thirty-six star configurations lying somewhat south of the ecliptic plane. None of these configurations has anything to do with the Babylonian, Greek and modern signs of the zodiac. Besides these thirty-six configurations, the ancient Egyptians also marked out in the rest of the sky about twenty-five constellations, among them a crocodile, a hippopotamus, a falcon-headed god and a lion. But this lion cannot be matched to the couchant lion of our Leo and in general the ancient Egyptians' representations of their constellations are from the first so inconsistent with each other and with the stars we see that it has only been possible to identify three with any confidence. They are our Orion, which the Egyptians associated with their god Osiris; our Sirius and their Sopdet in a star grouping pictured as a recumbent cow; and our Ursa Major, which they saw as the foreleg of a bull (not our Taurus).

The first appearance in Egypt of the signs of our own zodiac comes in the so-called Zodiac of Dendara which was carved at a very late date in Egyptian history, after the Greek conquest, more than two thousand years later than the Giza pyramids. The Dendara Zodiac combines ancient Egyptian star configurations with the zodiacal constellations of the Babylonians and Greeks. There is nothing to suggest that the Egyptians entertained any of the signs of the zodiac, including Leo and Taurus, before the last few centuries BCE. And it comes hard to be required to believe, as some recent speculative writers have asked us to do, that any shadowy 'brotherhood' of scientist-priests, keeping alive the ancient wisdom of the makers of the Sphinx, was unable to sneak a single representation of the allegedly all-important constellation of Leo into the amateurish star maps of the Egyptians.

So to try and date the Sphinx by noting that, had it existed in 10,500 BCE, it would have regarded the sunrise of the vernal equinox in a constellation first attested nine to ten thousand years later, seems too tall an order to take seriously. This, on the face of it, extravagant notion of Sphinx dating has, however, been buttressed by arguments concerning the astronomical alignments of the Dyn. IV pyramids along the edge of the Western Desert opposite modern Cairo.

It was noted in the last century that the entrance shafts of many pyramids point up at an angle towards the Pole Star; and calculations were made to determine what pole stars before our present Polaris might have been sighted, at various estimated dates of construction, up the entrance corridor of the Great

Pyramid. If you cared to speculate that the Great Pyramid was built in about 3400 BCE, you could plump for alpha Draconis; if you judged that it was made in about 2500 BCE, there was Thuban as the candidate. In the 1960s, similar thinking was applied with real sophistication of both Egyptology and astronomy to one of those mysterious shafts that emanate from the King's Chamber (and also the Queen's Chamber) of Khufu's monument. Alexander Badawy and Virginia Trimble showed that in about 2500 BCE the southern shaft that exits from the King's Chamber, up at an angle through the masonry of the pyramid, would have pointed to the stars of Orion's belt as this constellation crossed the celestial meridian. Thanks to precession, the stars of Orion now culminate a bit higher in the sky than they would have done four-and-a-half thousand years ago. Since Orion, as Osiris, is a known constellation of the ancient Egyptians and Osiris was the god of the underworld and of resurrection, it was informed speculation to conjecture that the southern shaft of the King's Chamber played some part in the beliefs of Khufu's time about the fate of the dead king in the afterlife. (Orion's annual reappearance in the night sky, after seventy days of invisibility, at about the time of the summer solstice, may have contributed to the resurrection myth of Osiris, along with the more or less simultaneous inundation of the Nile.) The northern shaft of the Great Pyramid's King's Chamber is aimed, like the pyramid's entrance corridor, at the polar region of the sky, whose stars never dip out of sight and were accordingly known to the Egyptians as 'those that know no tiredness' or 'no destruction' – another fitting stellar destination for a dead king. Caution obliges us to repeat that, though the Great Pyramid contains these shafts, it carries no texts whatsoever to tell us anything about the beliefs of the time; the later pyramids with texts on their walls concerning, for example, Osiris or the polar stars, have no shafts!

Recent speculative writers have taken up the sort of ideas that were handled soberly by Trimble and Badawy and vastly extended their scope. Some of the speculation is suggestive: the alignment of the southern shaft of the Queen's Chamber with the bright star Sirius (identified with Isis, consort of Osiris) at culmination in c. 2500 BCE is not implausible alongside the alignment of the King's Chamber southern shaft with Orion at that date. But where the dating of the Sphinx is concerned, far-fetched theorizing about the topography of the Dyn. IV pyramids at and near Giza has been called in to support the date arrived at by computing the pre-dawn sky of the spring equinox of 10,500 BCE.

The new speculators say, to cut a long story short for the moment, that the Giza pyramids were positioned so as to reflect on Earth the arrangement of the stars of Orion's belt, that these three pyramids were part of a larger plan to reflect the entire constellation of Orion on the ground and that the most precise match of the pyramid field below and Orion above occurred at that very dawn in 10,500 BCE when the Sun was coming up in Leo.

They say that some, at least, of the stars of Orion can be identified with the Giza pyramids plus the ruined pyramid of Djedefre at Abu Rawash and

Sunset behind the pyramids
at Giza.

the pyramid of obscure attribution at Zawyet el-Aryan. We shall judge the
plausibility of this claim later. They claim that the position of their Orion on
the ground in relation to the nearby course of the Nile closely mimics the
positional relationship between Orion in the sky and the Milky Way. They
have taken up an earlier suggestion that the ancient Egyptians (or their
Atlantean mentors in this case), having equated the Nile on Earth with the
'Winding Waterway' of Heaven, the Milky Way, constructed their
mythology (even their history) on the basis of celestial movements:
apparently so as to transmit some arcane message of doom to our own
times, according to these recent speculators. The Egyptians, be it said, also
regarded the Milky Way as the grains of wheat dropped by the goddess Isis
while fleeing the murderer of her husband Osiris; additionally, a plausible
case has been made for the Milky Way as the inspiration for depictions of
the sky-goddess Nut arched over the world and swallowing the Sun at
sunset, to give birth to him again at dawn. Certainly the Nile and the Milky
Way were obvious correlates for the Egyptians, in the same way as the
Italians have called the Milky Way the Strada di Roma and the English have
called it Watling Street, but the Nile was not the only simile of the Milky
Way for them.

Enthusiasts for the 10,500 BCE dating of the Sphinx set great store by the
fact that at that date, indeed at the very moment of sunrise at the vernal
equinox, just as the Sun rose in Leo, so a north–south line through the pyramids
of Giza pointed exactly to the celestial meridian with Orion straddling it at the
same angle as their pyramid Orion on the ground straddled their north–south
line, while the Nile flowed south to meet the Milky Way going straight up the

sky. But, granted for the sake of argument that the Egyptians or even their supposed Atlantean forerunners had planned to replicate Orion on the ground in relation to the Nile, it is not obvious that they would absolutely insist on seeing this pattern of the stars cross the meridian exactly in line with a north–south arrow drawn through the Giza pyramid field. Before looking into the proposition in detail, it is not unthinkable that the ancient Egyptians of the Old Kingdom might have mapped out Orion (their Osiris) on the ground in the same relation to the Nile as Orion in the sky to the Milky Way. (After looking into it in detail, it *is* unthinkable, as we shall see.) If the work was done successfully (as the Old Kingdom Egyptians were perfectly capable of doing), then the resemblance would have been striking and they would have had their little bit of Heaven on Earth. If in 2500 BCE one had stood at Giza looking south down the river and called to mind the pattern of the pyramids around one, it would only have been necessary at the right time of the year to turn one's head a little on looking up to see the same pattern in the sky. The very particular alignment of Orion on the celestial meridian with a north–south line through the pyramids in 10,500 BCE is only demanded if you want to believe that your Orion on the ground was the brainchild of people much older and more advanced than the ancient Egyptians, who planned the whole thing, including the Sphinx, to communicate their 'ancient wisdom' to later ages, by means of improbable astronomical-topographical correlations discovered only by yourself.

As it happens, none of this matters, since – when we come to look into it – the pattern of the pyramids on the ground does not match the stars of Orion. It was the Giza group of pyramids that sparked the idea in the first place, for the Menkaure pyramid is smaller than the other two and offset from the line of Khafre's and Khufu's pyramids in a superficially similar way to the lesser magnitude and offset position of Mintaka with respect to Al Nilam and Al Nitak of Orion's belt. Be warned: astronomical photographs of Orion do not leave one with an accurate idea of the visual appearance of Orion's belt. One published photograph, with pronounced optical artefacts as a result of overexposure and flare, makes the three stars of the belt look positively pyramid-like. It is very salutary to take a look at Orion for oneself. Then the first impression that strikes one is that the three stars look much too far apart to replicate the Giza pyramids, unless one imagines that they represent only the tiny tips of the pyramids, with the bulk of the monuments invisible around them; if you see them that way, then the rest of the stars of Orion are obviously too close to represent other pyramids on the ground. Further, the lesser magnitude of Mintaka is scarcely evident in normal observation. It soon becomes apparent that there are far more stars in Orion than pyramids on the ground. The exponents of the 'in Earth as in Heaven' notion of the pyramids try to match up Saiph with Djedefre's wrecked pyramid at Abu Rawash, and Bellatrix with the unfinished pyramid at Zawyet el-Aryan. Take a map of Giza and its environs which shows the position of these pyramids and scale it with an accurate diagram of Orion and you will find that, when the tips of the Giza

Pyramids and stars. How the stars of Orion fail to correspond with the topography of the pyramids when Orion's Belt is matched with the Giza trio. Circled stars are those with no pyramid equivalents at all, even if we admit Betelgeuse and Rigel (or alternatively Bellatrix and Saiph) despite the too-great distances of Zawyet el-Aryan and Abu Rawash. Correspondence between the Nile and the Milky Way can only ever remain approximate and subjective.

pyramids are lined up with the stars of Orion's belt, the Abu Rawash pyramid falls too far to the north and the Zawyet el-Aryan pyramid too far to the south. Moreover, the whole geometry of Orion must be greatly distorted to fit in Saiph and Bellatrix at all. It seems that the Atlanteans, for all their 'ancient wisdom' could not replicate Orion on Earth, or that the ancient Egyptians, for all their practice in surveying and land management, could not do it either, if it ever crossed their minds to do so. What we know of their achievements tells us that, had they wished to do it, they certainly could have done so, so it seems they did not wish it.

The situation with this theory is worse than that. The inescapable bright star Betelgeuse altogether misses a terrestrial counterpart and Rigel is also unaccounted for – the accurate placement of a counterpart of the former would have involved building a pyramid down in the Nile Valley, something the Egyptians never did. I suppose there is no telling what the Atlanteans might have done. In fact, a better looking match of Orion in the sky and the pyramids on Earth than the one proposed by the recent speculative writers is obtained if you try to equate Abu Rawash with Rigel and Zawyet el-Aryan with Betelgeuse, but the geometry is still awry, the distances are still a long way out, Saiph and Bellatrix have no matching pyramids and now Saiph would require a pyramid to have been built down in the Valley. On any scheme, the Orion nebula, below the belt, also lacks a terrestrial twin and at least seven other visible stars in Orion have no earthly representatives. Supporters of the theory are apt to say, weakly, that perhaps the missing structures have been destroyed or have got lost under the desert sand, or even more weakly that perhaps the grand plan was never completed.

On the other hand, the situation on the ground includes several important features associated with the pyramids for which there are no celestial counterparts. In the heavens, there are no subsidiary pyramids, no valley temples (no mortuary temples either) and, perhaps most strikingly, no Sphinx. If the Sphinx is older than the pyramids (older in execution if not planning) and the cores of its temple and of the valley temple attributed to Khafre are as old as the Sphinx, then it is odd on this theory that there are no stars in Orion to represent these features, especially the Sphinx itself. Perhaps having a constellation all of its own (albeit one for which there is no evidence in ancient Egypt or anywhere else till thousands of years after 10,500 BCE) is to be considered more than enough.

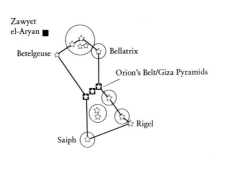

Zawyet el-Aryan ■

Betelgeuse ☆

Bellatrix

Orion's Belt/Giza Pyramids

Rigel

Saiph

■ Abu Rawash

Faced with the failure of the star-correlation theory to match the overall structure of Orion with the monuments around Giza, we must conclude that even the apparent similarity (such as it is) between the belt stars and the three Giza pyramids is just fortuitous. As we have seen, in real life it is not as impressive as it can be made to look on paper. And after all, only three points are involved – it is not as though the resemblance took in a dozen items in a complex pattern (which it conspicuously fails to do). You build one pyramid, then put another next to it: you have a line between them. When you come to build a third, it would really only be significant if you continued the first line. The second pyramid appears to have been shifted during construction in any case, and the third was enlarged. It was the lie of the land and the need to keep clear of each other's north–south sight lines and causeways that determined the placing of the pyramids – all that and sheer chance, too, most likely.

With the collapse of the idea that the pyramid field by the Nile was made to replicate Orion by the Milky Way, we can reject the culmination of Orion at dawn in 10,500 BCE as any sort of supporting evidence for the astronomical dating of the Sphinx, or for there being a subtly signposted chamber beneath it. Granted the Sun rose and blotted out the stars just after our Leo was to be seen a little sphinx-like on the eastern horizon at the spring equinox of 10,500 BCE (and for some years thereabouts): when you have said that, you have said all there is to say about it. Except to remind ourselves that in all the archaeological record of the world, there was no-one about with the necessary organization and technology to carve the Sphinx at that time and the Egyptians themselves would not know the constellation of Leo for another ten thousand years.

TEN

THE REAL AGE OF THE SPHINX

The Alternative Sphinxes of the psychics and the amateur astronomers (in so far as they can be distinguished) pose no threat to the Egyptologists' dating of the monument. The only serious reason to reconsider the matter of the Sphinx's age has come from a reputable geologist. The ultimate impetus for his work on the Sphinx may have derived from an unorthodox source, but his observations must be taken seriously by Egyptology.

Naturally geologists have long taken an interest in the Sphinx and the Giza Plateau as a whole, and the basic geology of the situation is well established. Dr K.L. Gauri of the University of Louisville in Kentucky worked out the sequence of rock members in the Sphinx and its enclosure in the mid-1980s, alongside the archaeological investigations of Dr Mark Lehner and Dr Zahi Hawass. Three rock members are represented at the monument. There is a bottom level of hard but brittle limestone, largely hidden under the lower cladding of the Sphinx body but partly seen in the enclosure walls and floor, that was formed many millions of years ago by sedimentation in shoal-water. Above that, the slightly younger middle member, which accounts for the bulk of the body of the Sphinx, is composed of seven separate beds which all have the interesting characteristic of passing from worse to better quality of rock from bottom to top, though the overall quality of the middle member is poor – which is why the Sphinx gives a general impression of serious erosion and damage. Joints in the limestone deposition, running criss-cross in the locality of the Sphinx, have in the past caused dislodgement of blocks of the body core and account for the large fissure at the rear of the monument. The top member of the Sphinx site turns into a rather pure and hard limestone above the neck, which makes for the finer preservation of the facial detail, give or take some wind erosion and the physical damage inflicted by the pious medieval sheikh. The stone of the head is not found elsewhere on the Giza Plateau today, probably because its outcrop was entirely quarried away by the necropolis builders with the exception of the knoll they wished to carve into the king's likeness. The lower part of this top member is not such good rock, and the neck is badly eroded, very evidently by wind-blown sand. All the levels of rock within the Sphinx and its enclosure slope up from east to west and at the same time down from north to south.

Opposite: Between the Sphinx's forepaws, the Dream Stela still stands before the badly eroded breast of the monument, under the much better preserved head.

The erosional circumstances of the Sphinx today were explored by the team of Egyptologists and geologists in the 1980s. The phenomenon of overnight condensation and absorption by capillary action was noted, with evaporation in the morning sun that leads to crystallization of salts within the rock's pores and spalling off of surface flakes as a result of the expansion of the crystals. It was also noted that condensation on the bedrock of the Sphinx and its enclosure could take place beneath a sand cover, leading to a situation in which the sand might be perfectly dry at the surface but wet through only a few centimetres beneath, while the rock itself could be soaked in water at some depth underneath the wet sand. This circumstance was judged to encourage the migration of salts from the depths of the bedrock towards the surface.

So both the geological structure and the erosional plight (at least in modern times) of the Sphinx were understood by geologists in the later 1980s. Egyptologists such as Dr Lehner concluded that erosional processes essentially similar to today's could account for the decay of the Sphinx between the end of the Old Kingdom and the early centuries of the New Kingdom, when they judged that the first major restoration of the Sphinx was undertaken.

A novel interpretation of the geological situation of the Sphinx was proposed by Dr Robert Schoch, associate professor of science and mathematics at Boston University's College of Basic Studies. He was introduced to the study of the Sphinx by another of those speculative writers on the ancient world, who sincerely believes that the Egyptologists have got it all wrong and, indeed, that the entire scholarly consensus view of the origins and evolution of civilization is misguided and misleading. For people who take such a stand, any indication of a great age for the Sphinx – going far beyond anything that could be remotely acceptable to Egyptologists, or archaeologists in general – would come as a godsend. One big facer like that would be enough, in their eyes, to overthrow the whole scheme so carefully and painstakingly put together over the past two hundred years. If the Sphinx could be shown to have been heavily eroded by running water, then, they say, it would have to have survived much wetter times than today, wetter than Old Kingdom times, wetter than any times that Egypt has known since as long ago as at least 5000 BCE, and the longer ago the better. So the theory goes.

A first thought among the alternative thinkers was that the Nile flooding

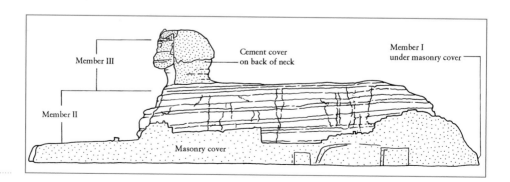

The composition of the Sphinx (after Lehner).

might have washed around the Sphinx in some satisfyingly remote epoch, but this idea had to be given up when it became clear that to erode the monument up to the neck floods of twenty metres or more would have been required over the Nile Valley. To perpetrate erosion on the core blocks of the mortuary temple of Khafre, up the Giza Plateau, would have taken floods of thirty metres or so. Even the most hardened alternative thinkers seem to have baulked at that. If erosion by water is your choice, it has to be rainwater.

Dr Schoch was not the first geologist to conclude that the Sphinx site had been subject to rainfall erosion. One geologist even resurrected Mariette's nineteenth-century notion that the Sphinx might be an old naturally eroded rock formation minimally dressed up to look like a man-made carving. But Dr Schoch rightly emphasized that the excavated enclosure in which the Sphinx stands proves the monument to have been artificially carved in the first place and then eroded – he thinks by rainwater.

Dr Schoch first saw the site, from the viewing platform for visitors to the Sphinx, in 1990. Work on site in winter 1992/3, alongside seismographic work by others that produced some of those readings suggestive of cavities in the bedrock, led him to believe that the Sphinx and its enclosure walls showed unmistakable signs of erosion by rainwater run-off, in much wetter times than today or during the Old Kingdom, between 7000 and 5000 BCE. Date of erosion does not of itself confirm date of carving, so the Sphinx might be older than Dr Schoch's estimate of the time-span of its erosion. Between about 5000 BCE and 10,000 BCE, Egypt's climate fluctuated between relatively wetter and drier periods, so there were wetter times than today's in which rain erosion might have taken place if the Sphinx's body was already carved. It should also be noted that even in Old Kingdom times up to about 2300 BCE, as is evidenced by plant and animal species depicted in the tomb paintings, the weather of Egypt was wetter than it has been since. But even now, winter rains pose something of a threat in Egypt – I remember seeing the side of a modern mud-brick house in Luxor taken out entirely by collapse after heavy rains. The ditch alongside Khafre's causeway evidently needed to be blocked in Old Kingdom times against the possibility that rainwater drainage could run down into the newly cut Sphinx enclosure, according to Professor Selim. It did rain in the Old Kingdom, and more than today. But Dr Schoch concluded that only the heavier rains before 5000 BCE could have produced the erosion pattern of the Sphinx and its enclosure walls. Egyptologists, of course, can see no cultural context at all in which the Sphinx could have been carved before 5000 BCE, or 3000 BCE for that matter, and several good reasons for putting its carving at about 2500 BCE. Before about 10,000 BCE, conditions were cold and dry in Egypt, so erosion of a pre-existent Sphinx is hard to imagine before that time – indeed, the pre-existence of the Sphinx before 10,000 BCE is itself an idea all but impossible to entertain.

Dr Schoch made his ideas accessible to the world of Egyptology in an article in the summer 1992 issue of the American magazine *KMT* (which takes its title from one of the ancient Egyptian names for Egypt, Kemet, with inserted vowels, meaning the 'black land' – the fertile soil watered by the Nile). He began by

The Sphinx seen from the
back, showing the tail
curling up to the right and
the right hind paw: note
how much is missing at the
back of the head and on
top of the shoulders and
back.

observing that the Sphinx body and the walls of the enclosure exhibit a pattern of weathering commonly associated with exposure to rainwater run-off, showing a rolling and undulating vertical profile with many vertical and sloping channels where joints in the bedrock have been opened up. He·contrasted this situation at the Sphinx with the state of weathering seen at other rock-cut features of the Giza Plateau (such as various Old Kingdom tombs) where erosion by wind-blown sand has picked out areas of poorer quality rock to leave the anciently cut façades and doorways otherwise not markedly damaged, and certainly not displaying the rounded and undulating weathering of parts of the Sphinx. These observations, as we shall see, naturally led on to arguments about precisely what levels of the limestone beds of Giza could be equated with what others in different parts of the necropolis: for the beds do not lie horizontally all over the whole site, but slope down from north to south and west to east; moreover, ancient quarrying has left them discontinuous over the area. Thus it is not always easy to decide that, say, a certain Old Kingdom tomb away from the Sphinx is cut in the same rock as the body of the beast. When they are not of the same rock, comparison of their states of erosion is more complicated than simply saying that one is evidently eroded by the wind since Old Kingdom times and the other must be eroded by water since seven thousand or more years ago.

In his *KMT* article Dr Schoch took the view that the serious erosion going on at the Sphinx today is a comparatively recent phenomenon, of perhaps the past two hundred years, associated with changes in the water-table and with pollution. He noted that erosion by condensation of dew and subsequent evaporation, bringing crystallization in the pores of the rock and spalling off of surface flakes, is evidenced in the interiors of some of the rock-cut tombs of Giza, but he concluded that this process at the Sphinx today could not account for the highly rounded weathering on the body and the enclosure walls that spoke to him of the action of rainwater over a long period. Heavy and frequent rain he judged not to have fallen since well before Egypt's dynastic history began in about 3100 BCE. He pointed to certain mud-brick tombs at Saqqara of the Archaic Period (Dyns I and II) that show no signs of erosion by exposure to rains to point up his conclusion that his rain-weathered Sphinx must be older than the beginnings of Egyptian civilization.

Dr Schoch noted that there is some evidence for a period of heavier (if sporadic) rains between about 4000 BCE and 3000 BCE and that, as we have seen, even in Old Kingdom times until about 2300 BCE, conditions were less arid in Egypt than they have been since; but he did not want to assign the better part of his rainwater weathering of the Sphinx to these periods since he judged the degree of erosion to demand a long period of heavy and regular rainfall since the carving of the monument. In a note at the end of his *KMT* article, he acknowledged the observation that burial in wet sand might have contributed to the erosion if it could be shown to have occurred, but again he clearly thought this mechanism inadequate to explain the very great erosion of the body.

In wishing to push back the date of the carving (and the commencement of erosion) into the wetter period before 5000 BCE, Dr Schoch was fortified by the findings of the seismic research conducted at the Sphinx at the same time as his own work. Data collected by detecting the reflected and refracted effects of sledge-hammering a steel plate on the floor of the Sphinx enclosure suggested to him and his seismographer colleagues that there is deep subsurface dissolution of the limestone bedrock beneath the floor of the enclosure, indicative again of long exposure at some time in the past (since cutting) to heavy rainfall.

Dr Schoch further noted that the limestone core blocks of the Sphinx temple and of the valley temple of Khafre were cut from rock removed from the Sphinx enclosure, and that they show a similar pattern of erosion to the body of the Sphinx and the Sphinx enclosure walls. He went so far as to think that the granite casing applied to these core blocks was cut to fit their highly eroded surfaces. In this way, he arrived at a two-stage theory of construction history for these temples: in his view they were originally made, like the Sphinx, thousands of years before Khafre came on site to find them badly eroded and ready for restoration with new granite facings. (Dr Schoch acknowledged that the head of the Sphinx is certainly an Old Kingdom carving, if not of Khafre himself, but he thought Khafre or another Dyn. IV king might have ordered an original lion's head to be recarved in his own image.) Egyptologists were bound to be tickled at the thought that the ancient Egyptians might have gone to the trouble of laboriously carving hard granite to fit the randomly eroded surfaces of much softer limestone blocks that could easily have been dressed to take the granite facings, even assuming for the sake of argument that they had found the temples already old and in need of repair.

As with the temples, so with the Sphinx. Dr Schoch suggested that Khafre or some other Old Kingdom ruler had found a monument badly in need of restoration and proceeded to clad much of it in repair blocks as long ago as 2500 BCE. It was his understanding that Egyptologists, in particular Dr Mark Lehner as a result of the Sphinx investigations of the 1980s, had decided that few if any of the repair blocks of the Sphinx were of Old Kingdom date – so that, once again, Dr Schoch found himself going against orthodox Egyptological thinking. But in fact, the Egyptologists had concluded that parts at least of the Sphinx, for instance its right hind paw and maybe the slope of its back behind the head-dress, were from the start built on to the core of living rock. Dr Zahi Hawass has been prepared to think that the original construction work went further than that, but Dr Lehner has concluded that most of the add-on work at the Sphinx belongs to New Kingdom and later times.

The seismic work around the Sphinx gave Dr Schoch an additional line of reasoning in discussion of a possible date for the original carving of the monument. Seismography suggested that subsurface erosion goes less deep behind the rump of the Sphinx to the west than it does on the northern, southern and eastern sides. This in turn suggested either that the rump of the Sphinx was not carved as early as the rest or that it was originally only just freed from the rock without a floor surface behind it, which was subsequently cut out by Khafre or another in Old Kingdom times. Professor Selim Hassan had speculated that the Sphinx was originally made to be seen from the front, though of course he did not doubt that it was carved in Old Kingdom times. Indeed he thought that its flank could never have been seen from the south because of the original obstacle of Khafre's covered causeway. (Higher ground to the north largely prevented any distant view from that perspective.) Dr Schoch proposed that the floor surface behind the Sphinx was not exposed to the elements until about 2500 BCE and that, since the other three sides of the enclosure floor evidence 50–100 per cent more subsurface erosion, then they may have been exposed at some date between 7000 and 5000 BCE. The date in question might be an even older one, since most probably erosion would proceed more slowly at greater depth, thanks to the protection of the rock above.

To Dr Schoch's great credit, he saw that there was with his theory from the start the great problem of identifying any plausible Egyptological or wider archaeological milieu for any sphinx-carving before 5000 BCE. Unlike the arch-speculators who have wanted to take the Sphinx out of all known archaeological context, giving it over to Atlanteans or some other unevidenced supercivilization of the remote past, Dr Schoch sought some plausible excuse for its existence at the dates he entertained. He wondered whether the remains that have been found of pre-neolithic peoples in Egypt, with their flint technologies and rock-art depictions of the animals they hunted, may represent only marginal bands living on the fringes of a more sophisticated population whose own superior remains have disappeared under the alluvium of the shifting Nile or the waters of the Mediterranean. But absence of available evidence where we are able to look is never proof of evidence that might be available elsewhere, so Dr Schoch next appealed to the finds made at archaeological sites such as Jericho, with its 9-m-high stone tower and impressive wall and rock-cut ditch, at about 8000 BCE. In the light of Jericho, he concluded that the Sphinx 'would not have been a totally isolated phenomenon in the neolithic world'. However, there is certainly no trace of an Egyptian neolithic at this date on any site we know of: farming is not evidenced anywhere in Egypt until 5000 BCE at the earliest. There was no settled living in permanently established and defended sites like Jericho, with sizeable populations able to undertake communal works. And it is difficult to see why the exponents of some outside farming economy like that of Jericho might have travelled into a late palaeolithic Egypt inhabited by hunter-gatherer bands to carve the Sphinx, an object of sophisticated ideological import rather than a practical matter like a defensive tower.

At the end of his original *KMT* article, Dr Schoch raised the possibility that the carving of the Sphinx might be datable by measurement of isotope production at its surface as a result of cosmic ray bombardment since the carved rock was exposed. Radiocarbon dating might possibly be carried out on the mortar between some of the built-on blocks of the Sphinx, as it has been on the pyramids. As with the pyramids, it might give a slightly too early date for the work, since mortar may contain organic material (wood, in fact) that was already a century or two old when it was used to make the mortar. But in any case, such a dating would only apply to the fitting (or refitting) of the repair blocks. Much of that work almost certainly occurred in New Kingdom and later times; and, if some of it was done in Dyn. IV, its dating would still not establish the date of the original carving of the monument. Dating by means of cosmic ray isotope production at the carved surface is therefore an attractive idea at first glance, but it seems likely that the continual erosion of the Sphinx body has removed the raw material for such a dating method: the head is clearly Dyn. IV, from the neck down the erosion is heavy; only the lowest member of the rock might afford datable material. Whether satisfactory date determinations can be made on the Sphinx in this way remains to be seen.

Dr Schoch concluded his *KMT* article by modestly admitting that he was prepared to be proved wrong about his tentative conclusions, but for all he had heard so far he remained convinced that the Egyptologists' account did not hold up. Egyptologists, however, were bound to feel that he had not paid sufficient regard to their detailed knowledge of their own subject of study. Egyptologically, everything about the Sphinx points to a Dyn. IV age for the monument: only a geological opinion suggests otherwise. The Egyptologists' case is a detailed one and it does hold up – it is the geological interpretation that does not fit.

The first reply in the pages of *KMT* to Dr Schoch's theory came not from an Egyptologist, but from a professor of geology. Professor James A. Harrell of the University of Toledo, Ohio, answered Dr Schoch in the issue of summer 1994. He emphasized that, while weathering patterns manifested at the Sphinx can indeed be produced by rainfall, they can also result from periodic wetting of limestone not in the form of running rainwater but rather in the form of a saturated sand cover. We have seen that even today condensation can wet sand and underlying bedrock to some depth beneath a dry top surface. Dr Harrell suggested that in the past the wetting of the sand could also have been caused by rainfall in the wetter days of the Old Kingdom (until about 2300 BCE) or by river floodwater. In this century, floodwater could reach almost to the Sphinx enclosure at times, and capillary action can carry moisture up to two metres upwards into sand and limestone. The Old Kingdom tombs which Dr Schoch said belonged to the same strata as the Sphinx and yet were very differently weathered were, Dr Harrell emphasized, higher – and consequently drier – up on the Giza Plateau, away from Nile flood or from burial in rain-wetted sand. Down in the Sphinx enclosure and on the terrace where the temples stood, the limestone could have stayed wet for months at a time after heavy rain or flooding, and with nightly condensation to top up the water content. The vertically undulating erosion of the Sphinx body and enclosure walls which Dr Schoch identified as classically the product of rainwater erosion, Dr Harrell attributed to accelerated weathering – under sometimes wet sand cover – of the marly layers, in particular, of rock member two, resulting from the expansion of clays during periods of wetness and precipitation of salts during periods of drying.

Interestingly, Dr Harrell noted that even in today's dry climate in Egypt, heavy rains still penetrate the sands of Giza faster than their water can evaporate; the lie of the land, moreover, directs the run-off of rainwater towards the Sphinx from the area of the Great Pyramid of Khufu and of the Khafre pyramid. I wonder, in fact, whether the pyramids of Khufu and Khafre at Giza did not act as water catchments (rather like the obsolete arrangements on the east side of the Rock of Gibraltar) in Old Kingdom times. Their smooth casings (now robbed away) angled up on their four sides offered a catchment area nearly twice the size of their base areas, so that any heavy rains that fell would have been chuted down to their bases in some quantity, much of it to pour down towards the Sphinx by virtue of the lie of the land around them. Sitting in its quarried enclosure, swamped in sand as a result of neglect after the closure of the Old Kingdom, the Sphinx would often have been wet even in the relatively arid times that set in after 2300 BCE. So would the walls of its enclosure, and so would the Sphinx temple and Khafre's valley temple on the terrace in front of the Sphinx (these temples being largely lost under the sands by the time of Tuthmosis IV).

Dr Harrell went on to meet some of Dr Schoch's detailed points. Whereas Dr Schoch called in the evidence of the preservation of the mud-brick Dyns I and II tombs at Saqqara to indicate that they must postdate the heavily weathered Sphinx, Dr Harrell pointed out that these early tombs are in fact pretty badly decayed and were in any case in a high and dry situation up on the desert plateau. About the notion that the granite casings of the Sphinx and valley temples had been carved to fit on to already eroded limestone core blocks, he cautioned that much of this casing has been refitted during modern restorations and the Old Kingdom builders liked anyway (for obvious reasons) to leave the unseen backs of blocks unfinished. He called for more fieldwork to determine exactly what rock levels in the Sphinx and its enclosure correlate with what levels seen among the Old Kingdom tombs of Giza – in any case these are mostly at higher elevations and were never buried in wet sand.

Dr Harrell thought that the seismic evidence held by Dr Schoch to indicate differing periods of exposure for the rear and front areas of the Sphinx enclosure might in fact only reflect differing rock qualities – the result of coral reef formations detected at a greater depth in front of the Sphinx in line with the west to east downward slope of all the beds.

In the same (summer 1994) issue of *KMT*, Dr Schoch was able to reply to these observations. He said that it was not proved that the Sphinx enclosure was filled with wet sand in the past, when Nile flood levels were lower than they are today, and not proved that condensation could wet the sand and bedrock below the surface of a sand infill. (But such was indeed Dr Gauri's personal experience at the site and we must regard it as very likely that the Sphinx enclosure has often been filled with sand since Old Kingdom days: it is in fact very difficult to keep the sand out, as has been discovered several times since Caviglia made the first attempts to shift some of it at the start of the last century.)

Dr Schoch referred in general terms to some Old Kingdom tombs to the south of the Sphinx on the eastern edge of the plateau that might be expected also to have been covered in wet sand on Dr Harrell's theory, but which do not show the same sort of erosion as the Sphinx. He stated his view that the wet sand theory could not in any case account for the opening up of various crevasses, fissures and cracks in the Sphinx body and the walls of its enclosure that looked to him like typically water-weathered features. He remained convinced that the backs of the granite casings had been painstakingly carved to fit the eroded limestone core blocks, and rejected Dr Harrell's explanation of the differential results of seismography at the front and back of the Sphinx enclosure floor. He noted in particular that severe erosion could be demonstrated at the top of the Sphinx enclosure walls (creating quite a sloped-back edge), where the rock is of better quality than the rest – the opposite of what you would expect on the hypothesis of erosion by wet sand cover, but fitting in well with his theory of erosion by rainwater run-off.

Dr Harrell replied in the fall 1994 issue. He repeated that the Old Kingdom tombs that do not show the same sort of weathering as the Sphinx are indeed at a higher elevation than the Sphinx and its related monuments and carved from better rock. Even so, he claimed that there is evidence elsewhere at Giza of the same sort of undulating weathering as is seen at the Sphinx, albeit less pronounced (on account of elevation and rock quality). He met Dr Schoch's point about the sloped-back erosion of the top of the Sphinx's southern and western enclosure walls by attributing this slope mostly to the original design of the enclosure, with deliberate battering of the top of the walls (seen elsewhere at Giza, he said), augmented by mechanical damage over the centuries as robbery, restoration, sand clearance, tourism ancient and modern and so on all took place.

The fact that the fissures and cracks in the Sphinx limestone beds look like water-eroded features and could not, as Dr Schoch objected, be produced by burial in wet sand was not a problem for Dr Harrell. He had never said that they played a role in his hypothesis: he attributed them to the enlargement of old joints in the limestone beds through dissolution by circulating subsurface waters, before ever the Sphinx was carved. Such fissures, he said, are a common feature of limestones in Egypt and have no bearing on the Sphinx's date of carving.

Whereas Dr Schoch had stood by his belief that the seismic evidence indicated greater weathering in front of the Sphinx than at the rear, thereby deriving an estimate of the age of carving of the front at least of the Sphinx, Dr Harrell in turn stood by his hypothesis of a coral reef feature as an explanation of the seismic reading.

In general, Dr Harrell emphasized the obvious propensity of the Sphinx limestone to weather badly: his wet sand theory (which allows for wetting by floodwater, by rain and by condensation) suggested one cause of this weathering and the current situation of daily flaking as a result of dew constituted another. He did not attribute the modern situation entirely to pollution, either: so that it probably operated in the past as well as in the present. He concluded that most of the weathering of the Sphinx body occurred in the eleven hundred years between its carving and the extensive fitting of restoration blocks by Tuthmosis IV. All in all he judged that four thousand five hundred years was ample time to encompass the weathering seen at the Sphinx today, and it seemed ludicrous to him to think that many more thousands of years were required.

Dr Schoch was able to reply in the same issue. He still could not see that the Sphinx enclosure was ever likely to have been filled with wet sand and still could not believe that wet sand could in any case produce the weathering pattern observed. He objected that Dr Harrell's idea of mechanical damage to the enclosure walls could not account for the scalloped weathering of vertical fissures in these walls, which in his view could only have been produced by rainwater run-off. He again stood by his seismic interpretation, and branded Dr Harrell's characterization of the Sphinx limestone's propensity for erosion as only an assertion and not a fact, especially when the different erosion of the same limestone in other parts of the necropolis was taken into account. Dr Schoch ended by appealing for more fieldwork at Giza to try to settle the matter.

A communication from another *KMT* correspondent, G.B. Johnson of Logan, Ohio, built upon Dr Harrell's wet sand theory by emphasizing the corrosive capacity of salts contained in the sands of Egypt. In his view it is the leaching of salts out of wet sand that is the cause of the erosion of the Sphinx body and enclosure walls. Mr Johnson supplied a photograph of two pottery dishes from Abu Rawash, one of which was found inverted on the sand and the other upturned and filled with sand – the latter was heavily corroded whereas the former was pristine.

In the same issue of fall 1994, Dr Mark Lehner contributed a substantial article in defence of Egyptology's dating of the Sphinx versus Dr Schoch's new interpretation. Dr Lehner is himself an interesting example of personal progress in the study of Egyptology. As a very young man his interest in the Sphinx and pyramids was fired by the ideas of Edgar Cayce, but study in Egypt soon turned him into a professional Egyptologist. From 1979 he was director of the Sphinx Mapping Project of the American Research Center in Egypt, which produced a complete photogrammetric record of the Sphinx and made possible the computer replication of the monument. In the course of all his work at Giza, Dr Lehner has come to know the Sphinx like the back of his hand and is, with Dr Zahi Hawass, at the forefront of Egyptological study of the monument. We note that the great Flinders Petrie, who put the study of the pyramids on a sound basis along with so much else in Egyptology, himself started out at Giza to test the theories of a nineteenth-century crackpot.

Dr Lehner noted that until his *KMT* article, Dr Schoch had previously pointed in a video programme to the tomb of Debehen, near the south-east corner of the Khafre pyramid, as an example of an Old Kingdom tomb not eroded like the Sphinx and therefore not as old as the Sphinx (though Dr Lehner disputed that Debehen's tomb belonged to the same rock stratum as the Sphinx's body); now here Dr Schoch was in *KMT* vaguely mentioning (without naming) tombs in the eastern part of the escarpment at Giza in the same role. Dr Lehner could not see that these tombs, whichever they were, could belong to the same limestone levels as the body of the Sphinx: they were likely to be cut into the better rock that, at the location of the Sphinx, forms only the lowest part of the monument. He complained that Schoch had also not identified the early dynastic mud-brick tombs of Saqqara whose relatively good state of preservation he attributed to their being younger than the Sphinx. Dr Lehner cautioned that many such tombs were only excavated in the twentieth century, their ruins having previously been protected under the rubble of later structures and the dry sands of the desert plateau. For Dr Lehner there was thus no point in comparing their state of erosion with the Sphinx's, especially if Dr Schoch was not naming the Dyn. I or II tombs in question.

With regard to Dr Schoch's idea of a two-stage construction history for the Khafre and Sphinx temples, Dr Lehner pointed out that the standard building method of the Old Kingdom (whether for pyramids, tombs or temples) always involved both core and casing to produce the end product: consequently the limestone cores of the Khafre and Sphinx temples 'do not and never did represent finished architecture'. But the use of such huge core blocks as those of the Khafre valley temple and the Sphinx temple is only seen elsewhere at Khafre's mortuary temple up by his pyramid and at Menkaure's unfinished mortuary temple, by the third pyramid of Giza. Menkaure's temple is instructive because we can see there work in progress, as it were, work abandoned before completion. It is clear that the softer limestone core blocks were being cut back to fit the harder granite casings. The same procedure would have been adopted at the temples by the Sphinx: it would have been quite impractical to think of cutting the hard granite to fit the roughed-out shape of the core blocks. Even allowing for the moment that the core blocks were eroded before the casings were fitted, we can see that it would still only have made sense to dress the soft limestone rather than think of working on the hard granite. Dr Lehner's article was accompanied by

The eastern wall of Khafre's valley temple under current restoration; note the granite cladding blocks in place at the base and the areas of severe erosion of the limestone core blocks exposed above the granite casing, comparable with the erosion of the Sphinx's body.

photographs taken at the Khafre valley temple in 1909 and again in the 1990s to show that, in only eighty or so years, some of the limestone core blocks lacking granite casing have visibly eroded since exposure by excavation; at the same time limestone core blocks whose granite casings have always remained in place to protect them are shown in a photograph to be well preserved after four-and-a-half thousand years, and not to display the first-stage weathering that Dr Schoch thinks had afflicted both the temples long before (in his view) they were cased in granite in Dyn. IV. This observation of Dr Lehner's obviously weakens Dr Schoch's contention that the Sphinx too was already in need of extensive cladding in the time of Khafre, just as he or another Old Kingdom ruler found the temples in need of repair, according to Dr Schoch. The evidence shows that, unprotected, the limestone of the temples and the body of the Sphinx is all too prone to erosion over even short periods of time.

The question of the sloped-back southern and western walls of the Sphinx enclosure was also dealt with by Dr Lehner, who included photographs to show that they were clearly cut at a slope from the first – a slope well evidenced in places where they are scarcely eroded at all. Rainwater did not, therefore, account for the slope. The western end of the enclosure particularly interested Dr Lehner since Dr Schoch had proposed that this face, behind the Sphinx's hindquarters, was indeed cut back during Dyn. IV, exposing the floor of the enclosure at the back of the Sphinx for the first time – at a date much later than the exposure of the floor at the eastern end of the monument. It was on the different seismic readings obtained at the back and front of the Sphinx that Dr Schoch had based his estimate of the likely carving date of the Sphinx body. He had also used the notion of a Dyn. IV cutting of the western enclosure wall to meet Professor Selim Hassan's argument about the notch where the channel alongside Khafre's causeway would run into the Sphinx enclosure, unless blocked as it is by pieces of granite. Professor Selim argued that the Sphinx enclosure and therefore the Sphinx too must have been carved out after the completion of Khafre's causeway because the ancient builders would never have cut the causeway's ditch to empty into the Sphinx. Dr Schoch had proposed a two-stage carving of the enclosure of the Sphinx, with the back extension only cut in Khafre's time, after the building of his causeway whose ditch had not broken into the enclosure until that backwards extension. In this way, it had been possible for Dr Schoch to argue that the Sphinx (and its enclosure minus the back extension) long predated the creation of the causeway and its ditch, and the blocking of the ditch had only become necessary when the rear of the Sphinx enclosure was cut back to the west during Dyn. IV. But Dr Schoch had also instanced the western, back wall of the Sphinx enclosure as a classic case of rainwater erosion: indeed its undulating profile with heavily rounded cracks shows exactly the pattern of erosion that Dr Schoch had attributed without hesitation to erosion by rainwater run-off. Dr Lehner was able to highlight the contradiction contained in, on the one hand, pointing to the weathering here as evidence of long exposure to heavy rainfall long before Dyn. IV and, on the other, maintaining that the wall in question was only cut back during Dyn. IV.

Dr Lehner ended his *KMT* article with evidently heartfelt words expressing a feeling that many an archaeologist and historian might share when experts from other fields, particularly the natural sciences, take it upon themselves to contradict their well-founded opinions: 'Professor Schoch does not take *our* word about the Sphinx and Egyptian history simply because we are Egyptologists. He should not expect us to take *his* interpretations and correlations for true simply because he is a geologist and stratigrapher.'

Since the cases made by Schoch, Harrell and Lehner, the correspondence pages of *KMT* have gone on with letters from all sorts of interested parties, and the question of the Sphinx's age has been aired in other journals. Dr Mark Lehner and Dr Zahi Hawass contributed articles to the September/October 1994 issue of *Archaeology* that further developed their own ideas about the Sphinx's age and history, and objected to Dr Schoch's proposals. They made the apt point that no other Old Kingdom mortuary complex has produced more evidence of large statuary than Khafre's – the gigantic carving of the Sphinx finds its likeliest context with Khafre on this count alone. Both of Khafre's temples (the mortuary and valley buildings) were originally decked with many large statues of Khafre himself and his valley temple shows the emplacements of other very large sphinx statues, more than 8 m long. The *Archaeology* articles went on to marshal archaeological evidence for the dating of the carving of the Sphinx. The western end of the Sphinx enclosure, behind the lion's rump, was never finished (like other details of the enclosure and the Sphinx temple too): a shelf at the back was left with numerous lumps and channels in it that resemble the unfinished floor of the abandoned first burial chamber of Khufu beneath the Great Pyramid. In the infill of these features, Dr Lehner and Dr Hawass found half of a typical Dyn. IV jar and stone hammers with traces of copper on them, clearly used in the cutting out of the floor of the enclosure at this point. Dr Schoch, it is true, also believes that the western end of the enclosure was only cut down in Dyn. IV times, but has not explained why its wall is so vividly eroded in the pattern that he attributes to rainwater erosion much earlier than the days of Dyn. IV. Dr Lehner and Dr Hawass see no reason to think that the rear end of the enclosure was cut any later than the rest: it is simply unfinished, in a way often encountered at Egyptian monuments. It is worth remembering that the extensive use of copper tools is not evidenced before the sixth millennium BCE in the ancient world, and not before the fourth in Egypt.

Another piece of archaeological evidence for the date of the Sphinx presented itself to the writers of the *Archaeology* articles at the north-west corner of the Sphinx temple, where the southern corner of the later temple of Amenophis II juts out over the passage to the enclosure of the Sphinx. When the Amenophis II temple was built in New Kingdom times, the Sphinx temple and the Sphinx enclosure were swamped in sand, so that the new temple was built high over them. A mound of sand was left under the corner of the New Kingdom temple by modern excavators and at the base of that mound Lehner and Hawass found three large blocks left there on their way to the corner of the Sphinx temple – another example of unfinished work on the part of the Old Kingdom builders.

One block was found to be resting on Dyn. IV pottery and the other two had under them traces of the sort of clay the Egyptians used as a lubricant in moving blocks. Again, this evidence clearly points to building work on the Sphinx complex during Dyn. IV. Interestingly, Drs Lehner and Hawass believe that the Sphinx itself may never have been finished either, let alone the Sphinx temple and enclosure. In that case, the very large fissure from flank to flank across the haunches of the beast may well have been left open when work on the Khafre complex was abandoned to start work on Menkaure's pyramid and temples.

Contra Schoch, Lehner and Hawass propose that the erosional processes going on today, with flaking off of the harder layers of the middle member and crumbling of the softer ones, also went on in the past and that the fissures attributed by Schoch to rain erosion were opened up long ago by subsurface groundwater, as Professor Harrell proposed. They object to his identification of the rock in which tombs like Debehen's were cut with the rock of the Sphinx body, thus rejecting his conclusion that these tombs are necessarily much younger than the Sphinx. They again counter Schoch's idea of a two-stage construction of the temples by the Sphinx, noting that where granite casing has remained always in place against the limestone core, the latter is not eroded like the Sphinx body and the exposed limestone temple blocks.

The latest substantial word to date on the geology of the Sphinx has come from Dr K.L. Gauri and colleagues, in the journal *Geoarchaeology* in 1995. Their article reviews the layering of the Sphinx rock and the way the whole series is dipped from west to east and north to south: they say that the same dipping process, which went on in the Eocene (over forty million years ago), also caused the joints in the limestone beds; and that these joints were opened up below ground into cavities and channels prior to the Pliocene, more than seven million years ago, as a result of limestone dissolution by hydraulically circulated underground water. Such cavities, like the large one that carries across the Sphinx's lower back into the northern enclosure wall, were exposed when the Sphinx was carved. (Similar fissures and cracks are found in various tombs at Giza and in the underground shafts of the Great Pyramid.)

Dr Gauri and his colleagues from the University of Louisville describe the ongoing erosion of the Sphinx today as a common form of stone disintegration in desert areas, where extremes of temperature create condensation. They emphasize that the size of the pores within the limestone plays an important part in the process – the small pores seen in the lower parts of each of the middle levels of the body are less able to accommodate the expansion of salt crystals within them than larger pores towards the tops of the levels, suffering more damage and producing the effect of vertically undulating erosion seen on the body and parts of the enclosure walls. They assert that similar undulating erosional profiles can be found on the cut surfaces of other Old Kingdom features on the Giza Plateau, if not to the same extent as at the Sphinx: for example, in the area of ancient quarrying between the Sphinx and the tomb of Khentkawes. The different states of erosion seen all over the necropolis they attribute to the differing qualities of the rock and the differing circumstances of weathering in the various places. They show a photograph of a recently cut limestone repair block left out for only one winter that displays a flaked top surface, rounded top edges and bits that have fallen off. Significantly, they attribute the rounded weathering of the cracks and fissures that Dr Schoch put down to rainwater erosion to the fact that a greater surface is presented at and into the cracks for the weathering process to work on.

It seems fair to say, then, in the light of the geological observations of other professionals like Harrell, Gauri et al., that Dr Schoch's conclusions about the erosion of the Sphinx do not have the force of inevitability with which he set them forth. The erosional features of the monument do not compel us to think that the Sphinx must have been carved in much wetter times long before the Old Kingdom; they are capable of other explanations which do not disdain the knowledge and experience of the Egyptologists. The Egyptologists have good reason to date the making of the Sphinx to Khafre's reign in Egypt's Old Kingdom and there are no archaeological reasons to consider an older date, or an authorship by non-Egyptian agencies from Jericho or Atlantis. Geological expertise urges that the Sphinx may have been eroded by rainwater since 7000 BCE or by wet sand and condensation since 2500 BCE – Egyptological expertise urges that it must have been the latter.

The Egyptological reasoning that ascribes the carving of the Sphinx to Dyn. IV of the Old Kingdom embraces much more than the immediate archaeological situation of the monument at Giza, highly persuasive as this is on its own account. It also encompasses the religious motivation behind the creation of the Sphinx, in the context of the ancient Egyptians' sun-cult and their beliefs about the afterlife of their kings. Egyptology is thus able to make rational headway with an explanation for the making of the Great Sphinx. Dr Schoch was only able to appeal to people like the tower-builders of Jericho as potential makers of the Sphinx, without saying why they might have wished to do such a thing. The less inhibited speculators have proposed fantastic cosmic messages about the end of the world from the supermen of Atlantis as reasons for the making of the Sphinx in 10,500 BCE: well, I suppose it would have to be something like that to motivate the otherwise rather pointless creation of a one-off large lion statue at the end of the ice age. If we want to form a more sensible idea of the reasons for which the Sphinx was made, we need to know something about the world that gave birth to it.

ELEVEN

THE WORLD OF THE GREAT SPHINX

We have seen that arguments based on its state of erosion cannot overthrow all the good archaeological and Egyptological reasons for thinking that the Sphinx was carved during Dyn. IV and almost certainly as part of King Khafre's pyramid complex. Certainly this was pre-eminently the dynasty of grandeur, with the biggest and best built of all the pyramids of Egypt: it is fitting that the largest piece of Egyptian sculpture (bigger even than the Abu Simbel carvings of the New Kingdom) should belong with those pyramids.

To hope to try and understand why the Sphinx was made and what it meant to its creators, we need to recognize the nature of the Dyn. IV world in which it was created. It was a world in which much that went on – as must be the case with all human societies – would be perfectly comprehensible to us today in terms of our own ambitions, squabbles, hopes and fears; at the same time, much about it is inevitably quite alien and surprising. Its social order, its religion, its art, its 'scientific' knowledge, its technical accomplishments, are all things quite unlike their equivalents in the developed world today. The very categories of these things did not exist – religion, art and 'scientific' knowledge were all bound up together and woven into the character of the social order. That we have to put 'scientific' into inverted commas already demonstrates that we are dealing with a very different world. And yet it was one in which our occasional glimpses into the human motivations of the time reveal people operating essentially according to the same imperatives as do we ourselves.

The social structure of the Old Kingdom during Dyn. IV was of a character that has only faint echoes in the world today. The autocracy of the Russian tsars, who cast themselves as boss of all that went on in their vast realm, has been perhaps the nearest approach to it. But the tsars were only God's agents on Earth. The Japanese emperors may have been held to descend from gods, to be indeed in some way divine, but their real political power was severely curtailed. The Egyptian kings of Dyn. IV were real gods (as real as any others) and they really did hold the reins of total power; the bureaucracy, even the provincial bureaucracy, was not large and all lines of delegation led directly to the king.

The king was indeed the kingpin of the whole society. One of his designations

Opposite: The throne base of one of Khafre's statues from his valley temple, with the oval cartouche containing his name at the top.

Khafre's most complete
statue, showing the lions'
heads and forelegs on the
sides of the throne.

made him the 'good god', the incarnation of Horus, an ancient sky-god pictured
as a falcon or falcon-headed man who came to be closely associated with the
sun-god Re under the name Re-Horakhty. Originally a god of the Delta, this
Horus was the hawk who flew highest, whose eyes were the Sun and Moon.
When this god was syncretized with the sun-god of Heliopolis, Re-Horakhty was
pictured as a man with a hawk's head surmounted by the solar disc, with an
encircling serpent around it: the uraeus of the royal head-dress (seen on the

Sphinx) was the cobra that spat forth the flame of the Sun, pointing up the identification of the kings with the sun-god. Re-Horakhty was the sun-god in all the vigour of sunrise on the eastern horizon. The statue of Khafre from his valley temple beside the Sphinx shows the back of his head enfolded in the protecting wings of the falcon of Horus; the sides of his throne, meanwhile, have the heads, forelegs and paws of lions, also closely associated with the Sun. Two originally distinct conceptions seem to have been brought together under the name Horus: Horus the falcon sky-god and Horus the son of Osiris and Isis. The identification of dead kings with Osiris, god of death and resurrection, is first positively attested about two hundred years later than Dyn. IV, in the so-called Pyramid Texts inscribed in pyramids of Dyn. V and Dyn. VI kings, but it is likely that such beliefs began in earlier days, and the identity of the living king of Egypt with Horus fitted well with the notion of his dead father's identity with Osiris, father of Horus and king of the afterlife. Once again, it must be remembered that the ancient Egyptians were used to maintaining simultaneously various beliefs that we might think mutually contradictory. So the king might be Horus son of Osiris, and the son (if not incarnation) of Re-Horakhty, and the son of his natural father all at the same time. (The New Testament's account of the parentage and lineage of Jesus comes close to a similar indistinction.) The dead kings of Egypt might in the same way be at one with Re, and Osiris, and the pole stars.

The Egyptian kings were the first of the god-kings of history, who reached the end of their line in western civilization, albeit in a debased form, with the pagan Roman emperors. The contemporary rulers of the Mesopotamian city-states never achieved the elevated status of their Egyptian counterparts. It was perhaps the geographical isolation of ancient Egypt, especially of Upper Egypt, that lent itself to such centralized and divinely sanctioned rule. If no man is a hero to his valet, then we may assume that the Egyptians for practical purposes were able to distinguish between the king as a god and the king as a man, but there is no doubt that the ideology of kingship was strong and far-reaching in Dyn. IV times, though it weakened as the Old Kingdom headed for collapse in about 2200 BCE.

In any case, the notion that the king was a god, whose birth and rule were part of the divine fabric of the cosmos, prevented the institution of kingship from being conceived of merely as a despotism. Since the cosmos was itself a righteous process for the ancient Egyptians, then so must be the earthly rule of the king. The essential righteousness of things was called 'Maat' by the Egyptians, a word of great scope that embraced good order and good practice along with goodness and justice. The king must of his nature rule with Maat, with responsibility for the good order of all things. The father of Khufu, Snofru of the early days of Dyn. IV, was called 'Lord of Maat' and the requirements of Maat for all of human life were discussed in some detail in a text of Dyn. V, only a little later than Khufu and Khafre.

For all that, real life was bound to fall short of Maat on many occasions – the royal succession, for instance, could be a rough ride in practice, however divine the paternity of the candidates. Khufu's eldest son seems to have been

The profile of Khafre, with light falling on the high cheek.

dispossessed by Djedefre, the old king's son by a secondary queen, though he went on piously enough to complete their father's pyramid complex – the name of Djedefre occurs on one of the ceiling blocks of the pit containing the magnificent funerary boat beside Khufu's monument.

The king was, then, a god because of his all-important role in a divinely ordered world. Under the king, the apparatus of the state was administered during Dyn. IV times by a court of officials who were close to the king, very likely his relatives. The king's sons by his various wives, even if not themselves in line of succession, were important officers of the state. Such a son of Khafre served into the succeeding dynasty. Royal wives and daughters did not usually wield political power but they were accorded high honour on account of their importance to the royal succession. Ankh-haf was a son-in-law of Khufu's who was clearly an important personage of his time – the fine portrait bust from his tomb at Giza reveals the character of the man very forcibly. Hemon, most likely the overall architect of the Great Pyramid, was Khufu's cousin and Master of Works, and again his statue is a striking realization of self-confident resourcefulness.

Memphis was the seat of king and government in Old Kingdom Egypt. No doubt it was the biggest town in the country, stretching for miles along the west bank of the river, somewhat to the south of present-day Cairo. To the north and on the opposite side of the Nile was the town of Heliopolis (which the ancient Egyptians called Iunu), where the cult of the sun-god was centred. There were other important ancient Egyptian towns (and religious foundations) at Hierakonpolis (Nekhen), Abydos (Abedju) and Edfu (Mesen), and probably in the Delta too, though evidence for these is harder to find.

Opposite: The profile of the Sphinx with similar light on the cheek: the fundamental resemblance to Khafre's statue is clear.

The head of Khafre's
famous statue, enfolded in
the wings of Horus.

The only surviving
depiction of Khufu, builder
of the Great Pyramid – a
tiny ivory statuette in the
Cairo Museum.

Snofru in a relief from one
of his pyramid complexes.

The town pattern was one of mud-brick houses in narrow streets, with a thick town wall round the whole community. The entire population of ancient Egypt in Dyn. IV times is unlikely to have exceeded two million. Provincial government was not at all independent of the power of the king at Memphis, at least not during Dyn. IV. It resided in the temples of the provincial towns, which linked it back to the divine central authority of the king. Egypt has been called a country run by priests, but we could better describe it as a country where the priesthood was part of the apparatus of government. It was this system that made recruitment for large-scale public works, in particular pyramid building, easy to put into effect over the whole country. Taxes were paid in kind: in the provision of labour for the king's works. Temple lands might be exempt from tax, but private landowners paid their taxes in the form of the contribution of labour from their estates.

The building and administration of the pyramids constituted the centrepiece of the whole economic system. Social organization for the purposes of irrigation farming had called into being a nation of peasants directed by an upper class of nobles and priests with the necessary assistance of a middle class of bureaucrats, scribes and craft specialists. But the benign circumstances of farming in Egypt, with an annual Nile flood that did the work of fertilization without requiring too much human intervention, left this farming-based society with time on its hands for a substantial season. And in that season, the workforce was available for public works: building pyramids, the manifestation of the king's power and glory in this world and the next, was an ideal occupation. It used up the labour that was otherwise going spare, it kept up the necessary organization of craft specialists, it supported the country's workforce in kind, it maintained national *esprit de corps*, it reinforced the central ideology of kingship ruling over a divinely ordered land. This is perhaps why the building of the pyramids appears to have been always a rolling project, one job being finished off (or abandoned) as another began, even though some of the reigns of Dyn. IV were long ones. Snofru, Khufu and Khafre all ruled for more than twenty years, Menkaure for eighteen, Djedefre for eight and Shepseskaf at the end of the dynasty for only five years.

The work on the pyramids was not slave labour, although enforced toil – in an ancient version of the labour camp – was a sanction used against those who evaded their taxes in the form of work on government projects. Nor probably was the workforce on the pyramids as large as later writers like Herodotus were led to think. Current estimates allow for perhaps a regular contingent of about ten thousand, supplemented during the period of Nile inundation by about fifty thousand more. The living quarters of the regular workers were on site, and traces of these workmen's huts have been found beside the pyramids at Giza, along with their storehouses and even bakeries.

The technology available to the builders of the pyramid complexes (which were the only structures of the time built entirely of stone) depended, of course, on the brute strength of men and beasts (oxen most often) to perform the physically demanding part of the work. There was no machinery as we would

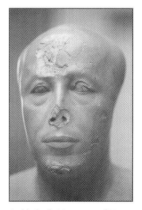

Ankh-haf. Museum of Fine Arts, Boston.

understand the word, no wheels or rotating pulleys in use at this time. Two thousand years after the building of the Giza pyramids, Herodotus was told in Egypt that the ancients had possessed lifting machines to raise the blocks of the pyramids, and this probably reflected the use of counterweighted balances, but we cannot be sure that such devices existed in the Old Kingdom times. The core blocks of the pyramids were quarried on site and probably dragged on sledges or over rollers, or perhaps rolled themselves in barrel-like cradles, up ramps to the scene of building operations. Either huge ramps of mud-brick and sand were continually raised and extended to get blocks up on to the ever-rising top levels of the pyramid under construction, or smaller ramps ran up each side of the pyramid as it rose. Ropes, cradles and levers were used to manoeuvre the blocks into position. Copper tools were used to cut softish stones like the limestone of the core blocks (as well as to cut wood) and, with the additional use of an abrasive of quartz sand, to saw harder stones too. Hammer stones and chisels of very hard stone were used on granite and diorite, which could be split by water-swollen wooden wedges and quarried by heating the rock with fire, quenching it with water and pounding it with heavy mauls of hard stone. Finer limestones than those available on site, and granite casings, were brought to Giza on the Nile flood, on board barges.

The builders of the pyramids had available to them various means for levelling their constructions and achieving perpendicular work. Water-filled trenches allowed the determination of level bases for the monuments and plumb-lines (which are attested in the archaeological record) assisted the vertical alignment of building work. The very accurate compass orientation of Khufu's and Khafre's pyramids could have been achieved by the construction of a dead level artificial horizon over which the rising and setting points of convenient stars could be sighted (from a fixed point) and marked by use of the plumb-line. Bisection of the line between rising and setting points, from the same fixed point, established the direction of true north.

Contrary to the notions of some of the recent speculative writers, the Egyptians were not the most sophisticated star-gazers of the ancient world. That distinction goes to the Mesopotamians, who in turn influenced the Greeks in their pioneering of scientific astronomy. All ancient peoples, especially in clement climates where star-gazing was neither an uncomfortable nor frequently unrewarding activity, watched the skies. As they still do today, the patterns and movements of the heavenly bodies inspired feelings of both awe and curiosity. Awe might feed the religious propensities of the observer; curiosity divorced from awe might eventually lead to conclusions of a scientific character, as it did with the ancient Greeks. In a pre-scientific cultural context, curiosity might equally promote myth-making.

The Egyptians were a pre-scientific people, with an ingrained capacity for religious thinking and a lively creativity where their myths were involved. A significant part of their religion was much concerned with the sky and its denizens: the fixed stars (which nonetheless wheel in the night sky, some rising and setting and disappearing for a season and others forever circling the pole),

Ancient Egyptian sculptors making a sphinx. From a New Kingdom tomb.

the daily and annually moving Sun, the waxing and waning Moon and (to a lesser extent) the wandering planets. This is why the high priest at Heliopolis was called 'Chief of Astronomers'. The sun-god Re was the supreme expression of the ancient Egyptians' religious attitude towards the sky. And it may well be, as some authors have proposed, that the stars in all their complexity were the starting points for many of the mythological stories of the Egyptians. Orion, as we saw, was identified with Osiris and the period of invisibility of this constellation followed by its reappearance in the night sky at about the time of inundation paralleled the mythological details of the murder and resurrection of Osiris, attended by his devoted wife Isis, who was identified with the nearby star Sirius. It is perhaps interesting to note that the layout of the constellation of Orion bears a reasonably strong resemblance to the smiting pose of the Egyptian kings depicted on the Narmer Palette and then on countless reliefs throughout Egyptian history: however, Osiris himself was not portrayed in this way, but as a tightly shrouded mummy.

But the ancient Egyptians were a very practical people and the skies also held out to them the promise of a system of time-keeping and a calendar by which their agricultural round could be regulated. They succeeded, evidently in predynastic times, in counting the number of days in the year by accurately observing (presumably with permanently established markers) the position of the solstices. They arrived at the number 365 for the days of the year and experience must have soon forced upon them the realization that the number must be slightly larger than that, but not by a whole day. They never did adopt the leap year concept to deal with the approximately six hours extra length of the year.

Alongside the 365–day year, the predynastic Egyptians also developed a lunar calendar, which demands a twelve-month year with twenty-nine or thirty days a month. But any purely lunar calendar (averaging 354 days) fails to match the 365-day solar calendar, so a specially added thirteenth month of eleven days had to be introduced every two or three years to keep the two systems in step. All this arises, of course, from the accidental rates of the Earth's rotation and orbit of the Sun, and the Moon's orbit of the Earth; in fact, there are now fewer days in the year than there were millions of years ago and the Moon is further away from the Earth than it was, but the changes are not significant within the time-span of human history.

The ancient Egyptians used a further celestial phenomenon for calendrical purposes: the heliacal rising of Sirius (rising just before the Sun blotted out the stars), heralding the season of inundation with the first month of the first season of the new year. Out of these solar, lunar and stellar approaches to calendar making, there arose in Old Kingdom times a system of twelve months of thirty days each, to which five special days were added at the beginning of the year to make it up to 365. This was the beginning of our own calendar, which has since refined the system to take account of those six extra hours or so of the solar year. It was precisely because the ancient Egyptians did not adjust their calendar for this descrepancy that their civil years and natural years got out of step, affording us one method (by means of 'Sothic dating', as discussed in Chapter Three) to work out the true dates in our terms of the recorded events of Egyptian history.

An Old Kingdom scribe, on display in the Cairo Museum before a relief showing at the left a noble and his wife and at the right workers on his estate.

As we saw when we reviewed attempts to date the Sphinx by far-fetched astronomical alignments of the remote past, no Egyptian system of constellations is evidenced at all in Old Kingdom times. Some hundreds of years after Khufu and Khafre, the lids of certain Middle Kingdom coffins do demonstrate the Egyptians' alternative to our zodiac, in a belt of stars south of the ecliptic where our own zodiacal constellations are pictured. Among Egyptian star groups, only Orion and a constellation involving Sirius can be positively identified with our own star patterns, together with another ancient Egyptian constellation that they saw in our Ursa Major. Even in New Kingdom times, a thousand and more years after the Giza pyramids, when there are a number of star maps with constellations in the form of animals and gods, no more matches can be identified. This is, as we have emphasized, an important point to note in considering speculations about the Sphinx as Leo – there is no evidence for Leo in Egyptian star depictions until the Babylonian–Greek zodiac was brought to Egypt in the last few centuries BCE.

The practical character of the Egyptians' approach to what we might broadly call 'scientific' matters is well seen in their mathematical methods. They needed mathematics in the course of their daily lives particularly in connection with the measurement of land, the assessment of crop yield and taxes in kind, and such

Opposite: Hieroglyphs of one of the Pyramid Texts in the pyramid of Wenis.

engineering projects as pyramid building. In Old Kingdom times, they had established standard measurements for area and for length: in building the Great Pyramid, for example, they used a standard measurement of length that we call the cubit, being the forearm from fingertips to elbow, about 52.4 cm. The Great Pyramid was built to be 280 cubits high with its final burial chamber at $20 \times 10 \times 11$ cubits; the Sphinx body was evidently 100 cubits long. The Old Kingdom (and later) Egyptians added and subtracted as we do, but their methods of multiplication and division were by refined approximation, doubling and doubling (or halving and halving) to get close to the desired figure and then adding or subtracting smaller multiples or singles until you were as near as possible, if not spot on. Such methods led to close approximations for much of the time, with remainders, but as the object in view was always some practical application rather than theoretical mathematical enquiry, it all worked well enough. Lots of us still arrive at quick and sufficiently accurate approximations by exactly the same means. Their fractions were cumbersome, being mostly confined to one-over-something which required, say, $\frac{15}{16}$ to be arrived at as $\frac{1}{2} + \frac{1}{4} + \frac{1}{8} + \frac{1}{16}$. There is no documentary evidence (and it would be unlikely in the extreme in the light of the above) that the Egyptians ever understood *pi* except by purely rule-of-thumb experience: rolling a drum will facilitate a rough and ready estimate of the relationship between its diameter and circumference. Some authors have made much of the supposed presence of *pi* in the relationship between the base perimeter measurement of the Great Pyramid and its (inferred) original height. This relationship may be illusory or accidental or the result of a drum-rolling acquaintance with *pi*. The other Dyn. IV and later Old Kingdom pyramids do not evince this feature. To claim that *pi* in the Great Pyramid means that the Egyptians (or their Atlantean inspirers) knew the Earth was a sphere (and even, with the addition of a suitable if arbitrary enlargement factor, knew the size of it) has no basis in anything we learn, from their various cosmogonies, about their ideas of the origin and layout of the Earth.

Another area in which the Old Kingdom Egyptians display a sometimes 'scientific' sort of attitude is their medicine. There is a medical text on papyrus, which itself probably dates to the seventeenth century BCE, that is considered on grounds of its language (in terms of vocabulary, grammar and syntax) to be derived from an original of Old Kingdom or even early dynastic times. Its approach to medical problems is surprisingly empirical at times, especially with regard to broken bones and how to treat them, where its tone is positively Hippocratic in its disregard for supernatural considerations. It is also important because it notes that the beat of the heart can be picked up all over the body and is a good sign of the general health of the patient. There is no notion of the pulse-rate as such, much less of the circulation of the blood, but this is sound empirical observation and reasoning. Mummification, with its extraction of the visceral organs and the brain, must have taught the ancient Egyptians a certain amount about the body, but it is worth remembering that, while the heart and liver were preserved (in their own containers) for burial, the brain was discarded. Evidently the ancient Egyptians, in common with other peoples of antiquity, had no recognition of the brain's importance as the directing organ of the body.

In later periods, the Egyptians believed that all people (and not just kings and nobles) could survive death and enjoy the blessings of the afterlife, unless judgement went so badly against them that they suffered the total extinction of 'repeated death'. They believed, moreover, that every individual was made up of a number of psychic components whose nuances are not always very clear to us. The akh, the ka, the ba, the shadow, in all as many as eleven distinct entities or forces, made up the individual man or woman in this world and the next. We should remember in this connection that our own culture has been used to distinguishing body, mind and soul in a not dissimilar way. In the days of the Old Kingdom, the full elaboration of later times was not yet in place and the 'democratization' that eventually extended a personal afterlife to all had not necessarily yet occurred. Of course, kings with their assured place in the divinely ordered cosmos were equally assured of their life after death. As rulers in this world and sons of Re, they would go on as rulers in the next and sail with Re in his sun boat by day and by night or dwell with the polar stars. Later on in Dyn. V and in Dyn. VI, dead kings were certainly also associated with Osiris in the afterworld, but we cannot be certain that these beliefs were to the fore in the times of Khufu and Khafre. The cult of Osiris, together with his consort Isis, is not much attested before the Pyramid Texts of Dyns V and VI, inscribed on the walls of the chambers of pyramids belonging to Kings Wenis, Teti and later rulers. The Pyramid Texts are really a collection of spells intended to promote the dead king's interests in the next world, often of a rather barbarous tone that does suggest that parts of them already went back some way in Egyptian history before they were first written down on the walls of these late Old Kingdom royal tombs. A small sampling is sufficient to indicate that tone.

> The sky is dark.
> The stars are dimmed.
> The celestial expanses tremble.
> The planets are stilled.
> They have seen the King appearing in power,
> As a god who lives off his fathers.
> The King is the bull of the sky
> Who conquers at will,
> Who lives on the being of every god,
> Who eats their entrails.
> The King it is who eats their magic,
> And swallows their spirits.
> Their big ones are for his breakfast,
> Their middle-sized ones are for his dinner,
> Their little ones are for his supper.
> See, their souls are in the King's belly,
> Their spirits are in his possession,
> As the leftovers of his meal of the gods,
> Which is cooked for the King out of their bones.

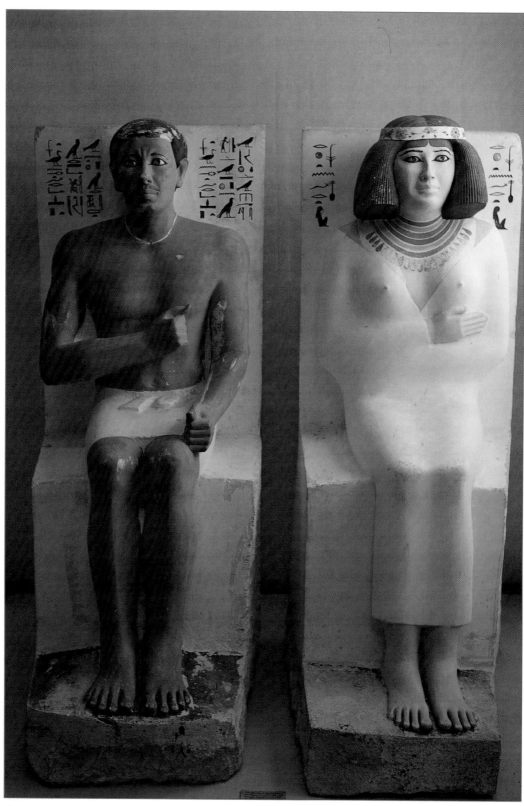

Rehotep and Nofret. Cairo
Museum.

Geese in a painting from
Itet's tomb at Maidum.
Cairo Museum.

The Egyptians were not exponents of abstract thought. Their religious
conceptions were realized in vividly concrete terms and the artistic means by
which they gave shape to their ideas were essentially naturalistic, in keeping with
their practical temperament. Their art was achieved within the limitations of
certain conventional formulae, of perspective for example, but there is no art
without fruitful limitations. Their artistic imagination produced such fanciful
reorganizations of nature as, to take the subject of our study here, the sphinx
hybrid of man and animal, but the components of these reorderings are
themselves entirely naturalistic. The tomb paintings and sculptures of the Old
Kingdom are products of the very highest order among the artistic creations of
mankind. Look at the geese painted on the walls of Princess Itet's tomb at
Maidum, in about 2600 BCE, or those sculpted heads of men like Ankh-haf and
Hemon, at the startlingly realistic statues of Rehotep and his wife Nofret, also
from Maidum, and at the royal sculptures of Djedefre, Khafre and Menkaure.
The same sure hand and eye is seen in the design and making of the furniture
from the tomb of Khufu's mother Queen Hetepheres: armchair, bed, chest,
bedroom canopy (for mosquito netting, one imagines), carrying chair.

Because Old Kingdom Egypt had been unified out of originally separate
kingdoms, themselves amalgams of previously independent settlements, the
religion of Dyn. IV times centred upon different deities in different towns and
localities, with different creation myths and different hierarchies of gods. What
the creation myths often had in common was the idea, natural enough to people
who observed each year's Nile flood and the subsequent ebb that revealed newly
fertilized earth, that the world had emerged from oceanic chaos as a mound of
dry ground upon which the creator god spontaneously manifested himself at the
'first time'. That god in the cosmogony of Heliopolis (known from sources later
than the Old Kingdom) was Atum, the All, who made everything else out of
himself, including the other gods like Geb (earth) and Nut (sky) and so on, even
the sun-god Re. (In the sophisticated theologies of the priests of later times, a
sort of monotheism was evolved in which all the gods were but manifestations of
the single divine force: Atum, Re, Re-Horakhty-Atum, Amun-Re or whatever
name the god went by.) Old Atum was himself a solar deity, who much later
became identified with the setting sun, and among his sacred animals was the
lion, though he was always depicted as a god in human form, a god with a
human face.

At Memphis, the capital city of unified Egypt, the creator god was Ptah. A text
known to Egyptologists as the Memphite Theology has been thought to go back

to an Old Kingdom original and therefore accurately to reflect the most official version of the creation story in the days of Khufu, Khafre and the Sphinx. In the Memphite Theology, Ptah created the world, in his capacity as the heart and tongue of the gods, the mind and word of God as we might say, by thinking it up and uttering it into existence. If this idea really goes back to the times of Dyn. IV, then it reveals a sophistication of thought to go with the assurance of the art of the time.

Though the settlements of Egypt all harboured local gods (who sometimes went on to become nationally popular for one reason or another), some of the deities of the Egyptians were from the start of a universal character, reflecting their association with features of the natural world encountered by all. Geb was the earth-god, Nut the goddess of the sky, Shu the god of the air, Tefnut the goddess of the dew, Re the sun-god, Nun the ocean, Hapi the Nile, Osiris the vegetation. Orion and Sirius were similarly noticed everywhere. But information about the religious beliefs of the Egyptians of Dyn. IV is exiguous, so we must be careful not to assume that particular beliefs about particular gods that are attested in later times must necessarily go back to early times: Osiris and Isis are a case in point, as we have seen.

The Egyptians thought of the created world as a great oval of earth floating upon the ocean, with the Nile flowing out of the sea in the south and back into it in the north; the sky they sometimes thought to possess the same topography as the earth below, with a celestial river of its own. In the night sky, the Milky Way constituted an obvious parallel to the Nile on earth and, with the exception of the unsetting circumpolar stars, the entire stellar array was observed over the year to wheel nightly into the underworld below the horizon. As we might expect, the underworld in turn was thought to resemble heaven and earth in its topography, with its own nether Nile. This was the Egyptians' Duat, the place to which – at least according to later beliefs – the dead resorted. It would not be surprising, from all we know of their undogmatic and unexclusive attitude to religious belief, if the Egyptians thought the Duat was somehow both in the sky and in the underworld. Certainly, dead kings were identified with the never-setting polar stars as well as with the Sun. The sun-god Re crossed over the land of the living by day and traversed the underworld by night: paintings later than the Old Kingdom show Re being swallowed by the sky-goddess Nut at dusk (her body spangled with stars to represent the night sky) and being born from her at dawn. It is clear that the cult of the sun-god Re was advancing in the years between Khufu and Khafre: Djedefre and Khafre are the first kings to incorporate the name of Re into their own; in Dyns V and VI the pre-eminence of Re became well established. These kings were sons of the sun-god and incarnations of the sky-god Horus, who merged with Re in the divine manifestation called Re-Horakhty, Re-Horus of the Horizon: the Sun rising in glory and crossing the daytime heavens of this world. In death, part of the essence of these kings became one with the sun-god and travelled through the night sky of the underworld with him. Thus, in life and in death, these kings were identified with the sun-god.

Many of the gods of ancient Egypt possessed animal attributes in themselves that intrigued, if not shocked, the Greeks and are apt to convey to us a suggestion of primitiveness of the sort that we associate with ethnographic museums. These gods not only had their sacred animals but were in some way part animal themselves. What recommended the animal world to the Egyptians for its capacity to realize the divine was its unchanging nature. What they wanted above all to believe about the world, about life, was that everything was somehow eternal. What they valued was the unchanging. Unlike the messily evolving world of human affairs, the animals were always the same from generation to generation, looking the same and doing the same things. Though they were reluctant to acknowledge that the human world changes with the generations and within every lifetime, events forced them to admit it. At the end of the Old Kingdom, for example, change – and change what's more very much for the worse – could not be denied. But the animals went on always the same, their lives forever the perfect expression of their natures. When their natures held some significance for human reflection, as was the case with the soaring falcon, the powerful bull, the unmatched lion (among many others), then the eternal realization of their natures provided a vivid intimation of divinity to the ancient Egyptian mind.

The lion, as we have seen, had long been a motif of Egyptian art before the image of its body was hybridized with the image of a royal head to make the Sphinx: so had been the falcon. And in fact that earliest hybridization of the lion known from the archaeological record involves not a human head but the head and wings of a falcon – the 'griffin' seen on the late predynastic Oxford Palette. It may well be that the sphinx idea arose in the first place as a lion-bodied transformation of Horus. Certainly the Horus element in the sphinx never went away, despite the dominance of the human-faced and wingless version of the icon that was initiated with the Great Sphinx of Giza. In the sphinx imagery of the later Old Kingdom rulers Sahure and Pepi I, the hawk component reappears, and the very name of the Great Sphinx in New Kingdom times – Horemakhet – emphasizes the Horus aspect of its cult. Some of Professor Selim Hassan's New Kingdom stelae found by the Sphinx show a hawk version of the image, and in one case a stela's depiction of the Sphinx is named simply Horus. Perhaps it was the decision to give the Great Sphinx a particular king's human features that inaugurated the classic sphinx hybridization of lion and man in Dyn. IV times, disguising but certainly not rejecting the Horus element in the sphinx idea. A human head on the lion's body was in line with the iconography of Atum, the venerable creator god of Heliopolis, who was always pictured with a human face though one of his sacred animals was a lion. In this way, the Sphinx might function at one and the same time as an embodiment of Horus, the god of Egyptian kingship, and of Atum, the primal solar deity, given the face of a real king of Egypt. That king was most likely Khafre, who built the pyramid complex of which the Sphinx forms an integral part. Alternatively, it is just possible that Khafre's successor Menkaure finally put his own features on the monument as part of his completion work on site before moving on to his own complex. At all events, the Great Sphinx is a monument to the cult of divine kingship in ancient

A depiction on a Late Period sarcophagus of part of the Duat, with guardian sphinxes at each end of the oval enclosing an image of the falcon-headed god. Cairo Museum.

Egypt in intimate association with the celestial deity most comprehensively named as Re-Horakhty-Atum: the sun-god and sky-god merged as a manifestation of the First Creator, Atum, the All. Eleven hundred years after the carving of the Sphinx, the Dream Stela could still invoke Atum-Horemakhet.

Dr Mark Lehner has advanced strictly archaeological reasons to think that the Sphinx from the start represented not just an earthly king like Khafre (even when kingship was itself divine) but a god in his own right. Dr Lehner takes up earlier Egyptological opinion that the beard of the Sphinx is of the 'divine beard' pattern (tightly plaited and curled up at the tip) never seen on royal statuary in Old Kingdom times but featured in relief depictions of the gods from Dyn. V. On the basis of long study of the Sphinx, he concludes that the detailed similarity of the rock layers in the beard fragments and in the body of the monument demonstrate that the beard was not an addition but rather a part of the original execution of the Sphinx design, supported by a wedge of stone going back to the breast of the monument, fragments of which were found by Caviglia. (This conclusion, incidentally, tends to militate against any notion that the Sphinx's head was recarved during Dyn. IV out of an older lion's head.) To go by his divine beard, the Sphinx would appear to have represented something more than just a particular king from the first. The Sphinx temple in front of the monument has all the appearance, moreover, of a solar temple with its unroofed open court and sanctuaries to the east and to the west, suggesting a place where offerings were made to a solar deity whose face regarded the sunrise and behind whom the Sun set over the pyramids in the west. (Later sphinxes, it should be noted, were not representations of great gods but of particular kings and queens, however divinely ordained, and very rarely sport the divine beard.)

The evidence of the beard supports the view that the Great Sphinx was originally an image of the god Atum (or Re-Horakhty-Atum), given the requisitely human features of the king who ordered the carving of the monument as part of his funerary complex – in line with the human-faced iconography of Atum rather than the hawk-headed imagery of Re. The word which the Egyptians used for sphinxes in general from Middle Kingdom times, Shesepankh (which almost certainly lies behind the Greek word sphinx), means 'living image of . . .' and the entity whose image the Great Sphinx ultimately represented may well have been Atum of Heliopolis, with his strong solar and leonine associations but always human face. Professor Selim Hassan believed that the Sphinx entity is mentioned in the Pyramid Texts under the name of Rwty, a deity very close to Atum as a 'son' or manifestation of the great god. In Rwty, the lion element of the sphinx idea claims our attention, for Rwty was a lion-figured god in whom the theme of the divine guardian was realized. (In general, the ancient Egyptians associated the lion with the guardianship of places of entry and exit, whether in the banal context of door-bolts and water-spouts or in the transcendental situation of temples and tombs.) We need to be careful in extrapolating from the Pyramid Texts to the earlier time of Khafre, but plainly they do reflect some of the beliefs of earlier times. They speak of the dead king as 'taken to Rwty and presented to

Son et lumière at Giza, with laser projections of sphinxes that once stood in these positions in front of Khafre's valley temple beside the temple of the Great Sphinx.

Atum'. Rwty is sometimes written with two lion signs as determinatives, recalling the pairs of lions or sphinxes placed to stand guard at temple doorways, as in the case of Khafre's mortuary and valley temples and in numerous later instances: indeed Rwty was the name by which such sphinxes were sometimes identified. Rwty seems to have been considered in both a dual and a single manifestation. The New Kingdom 'Book of what is in the Underworld' (often called 'Book of the Dead') invokes 'Atum . . . who shines as Rwty'. And another magical formula from this source declares, 'Oh Atum, I was rendered shining before Rwty, the Great God, who opens the doors of Geb'; in other words, who guards the portals of the underworld (Geb being the earth-god).

Rwty, then, was a lion deity, closely associated with the sun-god. So was Aker, another dual divinity that later came to be regarded as a single entity. Because of their role at the gates of the other world, the world that is not the everyday world of life as we live it between sunrise and sunset, these gods were sometimes called the Lions of Yesterday and Tomorrow – surely one of the most poetic religious expressions ever uttered by the human race. 'I was yesterday, I know tomorrow.' They were seen as the guardians of the sunset and sunrise portals of the underworld, pictured as two mountains, on the eastern and western horizons. The great pylon gates of Egyptian temples represented these mountains. Temples were places where this world and the other world met, and they were often guarded by pairs of sphinxes. Aker was credited with a chthonic aspect too: earthquakes were the trembling of Aker's bones. And he was sometimes conceived to be the phallus of Re or Osiris, to symbolize the resurrection power of these great gods. In New Kingdom times, sphinxes are shown in company with the sun-god in his day and night boats; supporting the solar boat in the tomb of Ramesses IV, they are named Fair Entrance and Fair Exit (of the underworld). It has even been suggested that the man with two lions on the predynastic knife handle from Gebel el-Arak already represented the sun-god between the lions of yesterday and tomorrow.

Professor Selim noted that in the New Kingdom 'Book of what is in the Underworld' the fifth division of the Duat was called by the same name as one of the names of the Giza necropolis – Rostaw. He speculated that the Giza tomb-field was originally seen as the counterpart in this world of the underworld of the dead, as the link between this world and the other world, the entrance to the beyond. Rostaw means ramp and hauling place, tempting us to derive it from the long causeways up which the dead kings' bodies were drawn to their pyramid tombs, or from the entrance corridors through which the coffins were introduced into the tombs. Among scenes from New Kingdom tombs that illustrate the Duat, Aker is depicted as two lions in sphinx form in association with a pyramid-like structure, in a way that reminded Professor Selim of the Giza necropolis. He thought that mentions of 'The Highland of Aker' in the Middle Kingdom coffin texts similarly referred back to Giza. On this view, the place of the dead along the Giza Plateau was the earthly outpost of the underworld, its analogue and point of entrance. It was natural, at a time when the sun-cult was in the ascendant, to guard the Giza tomb-field with an imposing monument that at one and the same time represented: the sun-god in the guise of his sacred animal; the guardian

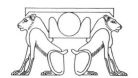

The two lions of the horizon, from the papyrus of Ani (after James).

lion-deity that was a manifestation of the sun-god; the dead king who was one with the Sun and ruled with him in the underworld beyond the sunset; and the living king too, incarnation of Horus, gazing to the sunrise of Re-Horakhty.

All these shades of meaning and more that we cannot now glimpse may have been attached to the Sphinx, including ones that after all this time might seem mutually inconsistent or contradictory to us. We must always remember that the Egyptians sought a multiplicity of insights into the divine and not a single doctrine. Work on the funerary monuments of the royal dead was, moreover, an ever ongoing process, over all the years of every reign. We cannot know precisely when during the long reign of Khafre it was decided to carve the Sphinx and build its temple, or to give the face of Khafre (or Menkaure) to the monument. The Sphinx temple, like the Khafre valley temple, may well have been built (with blocks extracted from the Sphinx enclosure) before attention was turned to carving the Sphinx itself. The head of the Sphinx may have been carved before the body, which might help to account for the different scales of the human head and lion body; on the other hand, if it was carved after the body, the same might be said. The Sphinx temple was never quite completed nor in places were the walls of the enclosure: quite possibly the Sphinx itself was never finished. How much of the entire complex was planned from the start is impossible to say. Khafre would certainly have wanted a causeway and valley temple like his predecessors, but the Sphinx and its temple may well have come late in his reign, in response to the growing cult of the sun-god. At his death, Menkaure – to judge by precedents – would have tidied up and moved on as quickly as he could to his own pyramid complex. If the Great Pyramid is anything to go by, plans probably changed more than once as Khafre's complex grew. If in the end it was Menkaure's head (or face at least – the face is slightly out of kilter with the head) that was put upon the Sphinx, then it is interesting to note that there are large statues of Menkaure from his pyramid complex wherein a similar disproportion of large body to small head is to be seen as with the Sphinx. In its damaged state, it is difficult to assess the resemblances of the Sphinx's face to Khafre's (or Menkaure's) on their statues. The bland, flat light of the *son et lumière* show at Giza can help here: the missing nose can seem to be magically restored at moments and then, I think, the resemblance to Khafre's statuary is strong.

What is clear is that the lion image was for the ancient Egyptians an expression of divine and royal power, as was that of the falcon. Lions and sphinxes were the guardians of sacred places, where this world interacted with the other world: they were the guardians of the Duat. All this was why King Khafre caused the carving of the Great Sphinx down by the valley temple of his pyramid, at the approach to the necropolis of Giza. It is in the context of Old Kingdom religion that we find the origin and meaning of the Sphinx – and not, needless to say, in fantastic speculations about Atlanteans and the night skies of twelve thousand years ago.

The image of Rwty and Aker, of Re-Horakhty-Atum, of Horus and of Khafre himself was to stand guard forever at the entrance to the sunset home of the dead, gazing at every day's new sunrise.

TWELVE

AFTER THE OLD KINGDOM

In the minds of the ancient Egyptians of Khafre's time, there may have been no distinction to be made between the Sphinx as dead king, as sun-god, as sun-god in the form of the living king, as guardian of the necropolis and more. The Giza Sphinx may not have been quite the first sphinx sculpture (on the other hand it may have been), but it was certainly *sui generis* in size alone – Cyril Aldred called it more a landmark than a work of art – and perhaps also in its representation of a great divinity in its own right, albeit with the face of a particular king. Subsequent royal sphinxes may show kings as embodiments of the sun-god but they are first and foremost images of those kings. With some exceptions, there are no divine beards on them.

A variant of the sphinx motif is in evidence from Dyn. IV onwards. Fragments of what was possibly a standing sphinx, though the head is missing, were found at the Giza tomb of Queen Khentkawes, who bridges Dyns IV and V. The Dyn. V king Sahure was depicted at Abusir (south of Giza) as a triumphant, standing lion with hawk's plumage and, in all probability, a hawk's head. This evidence, taken together with the winged and hawk-headed 'sphinx' of the predynastic Oxford Palette, indicates that the Horus element in the sphinx idea was strong from the beginning: it resurfaced in much later times and wings became an essential ingredient of the Greeks' version of the sphinx.

The remains of Old Kingdom sphinxes are few and far between, but there are two examples that have been attributed to the reign of Merenre of Dyn. VI, at about 2250 BCE, that look to future developments of the sphinx icon. One is in Moscow and is interesting because it displays the lion's mane around the human face that we associate with Middle Kingdom and later sphinxes. The other, a tiny version in the Royal Museum of Scotland, holds pots in offering to a deity; the deity is, significantly, Re-Horakhty. Here already the emphasis is less on the king as an incarnation of the great god and more on his priestly role towards the god. A fragment of the base of a sphinx belonging to the Dyn. VI king Pepi I and a version of Sahure's winged and trampling sphinx relief in a pyramid temple of Pepi II attest to the continuity of the icon in the closing decades of the Old Kingdom.

Perhaps the oldest sphinx statue, after the Great Sphinx itself, of what we might call the standard pattern (recumbent, lion-bodied to the paws, and fully

Opposite: A sphinx of Tutankhamun at Karnak.

Reconstructed sphinx fragments at the Cairo Museum, closely resembling the Louvre sphinx (p. 190) of Amenemhet II: both were probably modelled on the Great Sphinx and at one time stood guard together at Tanis.

human-headed like the Giza Sphinx) belongs to the Middle Kingdom's Dyn. XII and to a ruler known as Amenemhet II, of about 1900 BCE. In the past, this sphinx was believed to have been made for the late Old Kingdom king Pepi I (of around 2270 BCE) and subsequently appropriated by several successive rulers, including that great appropriator of other king's monuments, Ramesses II of about 1200 BCE, and moved to the place of its discovery in the Delta. It now seems certain that this sphinx in the Louvre is a Middle Kingdom piece, but Professor Selim Hassan believed that many an Old Kingdom sphinx might have been taken over and reinscribed by later rulers, disguising the Old Kingdom origins of these examples, after the period of political collapse called the First Intermediate Period, between the Old and Middle Kingdoms. Seen from the front, the Louvre sphinx of Amenemhet II looks essentially similar to the Great Sphinx of Giza – even the facial details are handled in a manner that strongly resembles the Khafre monument, though the head is bigger in relation to the body. The shoulders look more powerful than those on the Giza Sphinx, even allowing for the heavy erosion of these areas on the latter, so that altogether a better balance is achieved between lion's body and king's head. The beard, though broken off at about half its length, was not of the divine pattern.

There is a particular Middle Kingdom sphinx design, prefigured in the Merenre sphinx with lion's mane, in which only the face is human, and all other details are

Head of a female sphinx of
the Middle Kingdom.
Brooklyn Museum of Art.

The imposing sphinx of
Amenemhet II in the
Louvre Museum.

completely leonine. In place of the nemes head-dress of the Great Sphinx and the
Amenemhet sphinx, these so-called 'Tanis' sphinxes (after their place of discovery
in the Delta) have the ears, manes and heads of lions. Their human faces often bear
a strong resemblance to the portrait statuary of Amenemhet III, who reigned in the
second half of the nineteenth century BCE, though similarly hyperleonine but less
grim-faced sphinxes probably belong to other Middle Kingdom rulers. A less
overwhelmingly leonine form from the Middle Kingdom wears a sort of shoulder
cape not seen on earlier sphinxes. Another development of the Middle Kingdom is
the occasional provision of human hands, in place of the forepaws, to hold offering
vessels – reinforcing the inference that these sphinxes, while they represent divine
kings (a bit less securely divine perhaps than their Old Kingdom predecessors), do
not directly figure the sun-god but rather show the king in a suppliant, priestly role
towards the god. There is a beautiful head from a female sphinx, which was taken
off to adorn a Roman emperor's villa at Tivoli, that we may take to represent the
beginnings of the feminine version of the sphinx in Middle Kingdom times, unless
we accept the debatable female sphinx from Abu Rawash that might just predate
the Great Sphinx of Giza. A largely headless sphinx in Vienna that was evidently
female, with curled ends to its wig extensions, also dates to the time of Amenemhet
III. A piece of jewellery of the reign of Senwosret III, in the form of a plaque for the
breast, shows two standing 'sphinxes' with falcon heads, tall crowns and wings

A sphinx of Amenemhet III.
Cairo Museum.

Standing falcon-headed
sphinxes on a pectoral from
the time of Senwosret III.
Cairo Museum.

lying on their lion bodies. Winged sphinxes also figure on some magic wands in
ivory of Middle Kingdom date. Evidently the Horus theme retained its vigour
through Middle Kingdom times.

The Middle Kingdom was followed in about 1640 BCE by another time of
turmoil, the Second Intermediate Period, which saw the seizure of power in Lower
Egypt of the Hyksos kings, invaders from the east, who assumed the powers and
pretensions of the former kings of Egypt, adopting the pomp and titles of the

The Hyksos sphinx mauling a captive. British Museum.

native rulers at the same time as frequently sporting distinctly foreign-sounding names like Staan and Khian. One of them, called Apopi, took over some of the Tanis sphinxes and put his name on them, which is why they have also been called Hyksos sphinxes in the past. A tiny ivory sphinx carving of the Hyksos period seems to show a Hyksos king mauling a (possibly native Egyptian) victim.

The Hyksos were expelled from Egypt in about 1550 BCE by the Dyn. XVIII kings of Thebes whose coming to power ushered in what Egyptology calls the New Kingdom. An axe-blade from the tomb of the first king of the new dynasty shows a sphinx on both faces: one with human arms, the other hawk-headed and winged. The new rulers originated in the south, well away from the Old Kingdom capital of Memphis, and put their faith in their local god Amun over and above the old gods Atum, Ptah and Re. When they consolidated their power over the whole of Egypt, they amalgamated their god with Re to inaugurate the long-lasting high god Amun-Re whose pre-eminence was to endure into Greek and Roman times in Egypt. The New Kingdom pharaohs looked to the past glories of Egypt to sanction their rule, and it was in this spirit that the Great Sphinx was rediscovered by them in the early years of Dyn. XVIII. The first mention of the name Horemakhet occurs in the time of Tuthmosis I, third king of the dynasty at around 1500 BCE, who built a small temple to the north of the Sphinx. Coincidentally, perhaps, the large alabaster sphinx (8 m long and 4 m high, second only to the Giza Sphinx) found on the ancient site of Memphis in 1912, and thought by some to belong to the reign of Tuthmosis I, wears the divine beard like the Great Sphinx. The Memphis sphinx is the most important example of this rare pattern after the Great Sphinx – if it was carved for Tuthmosis I and not for some later New Kingdom pharaoh, it is tempting to see in the detail of its beard (and perhaps in the size of the whole piece) an echo of

The sphinx of Memphis.

reawakened interest in the deity represented by the Great Sphinx and called, from New Kingdom times onwards, Horemakhet: Horus on the Horizon, a name very close in meaning to the old Horakhty, but emphasizing perhaps the discrete entity of this particular embodiment of the sun-god at Giza.

But it was to be nearly a century after Tuthmosis I that Amenophis II and his son Tuthmosis IV restored the Great Sphinx to its past glory, building a new temple for the Sphinx and undertaking the first clearance and restoration of the monument since its neglect began at the end of the Old Kingdom. Before their work the Sphinx in about 1400 BCE must have looked not unlike the sight that greeted European travellers such as Helferich and Sandys, and the soldiery and savants of Napoleon, before the first modern clearances that began with Caviglia. (But without the facial damage done by the pious sheikh – though the beard was perhaps already broken off and in need of repair in New Kingdom times). The Sphinx temple had disappeared under the drifting sands, so that Amenophis II could build his own sphinx temple over the north-west corner of the old Sphinx one. The enclosure itself would have been full of sand, under which the body of the monument had been eroding since the end of the Old Kingdom. Much of the lion body of the Sphinx would have been invisible, only the top of its back and haunches likely to be on view. The Sphinx would have

The axe-blade of Ahmose, with winged and hawk-headed sphinx.

Standing sphinxes
trampling on the enemies
of the king of Egypt on an
end panel of a painted box
from the tomb of
Tutankhamun. Cairo
Museum.

Akhenaten as a sphinx raising his arms into the rays of the Aten sun disc. Museum of Fine Arts, Boston.

been essentially that human head sticking up out of the sand that was again all there was to be seen of the monument in our era, until the permanent sand clearance of modern times. Dr Lehner has speculated that the name Horemakhet may have been given to the Sphinx in New Kingdom times precisely because the head was then seen to be sitting on the sand in front of the large Khufu and Khafre pyramids like the Sun on the horizon between two mountains – we recall the mountains identified with the dual lions of Aker.

It is possible that a certain amount of robbing of the Sphinx site for re-usable materials went on in Middle Kingdom times, but most of it probably occurred during the New Kingdom, and, ironically, perhaps in the course of the efforts of Tuthmosis IV to restore the monument in accordance with the dream he claimed on his stela to have inspired him. That very stela, set up in front of the Sphinx's breast, may have been made out of a lintel from one of Khafre's temples: the space between the socket holes that remain on it fits three doorways of those temples, including the one at the entrance from the causeway into the mortuary temple of the pyramid, to which Dr Lehner thinks it probably belonged. He also notes that the restoration blocks of the Sphinx that he attributes to the first phase of restoration, carried out by Tuthmosis IV, are of the same thickness as the walls of the structure that originally covered in the Khafre causeway, which suggests the possibility that this was where the workmen of Tuthmosis took the material to repair the body of the Sphinx. But Dr Zahi Hawass believes that new blocks were cut to match the dimensions of the built-on components of the Sphinx's original areas of cladding.

Professor Selim Hassan found many New Kingdom stelae in the general area of the Sphinx, some of them dating back to the time of Amenophis II. Some, but not all, of them show a statue in front of the Sphinx's breast, though the details of its appearance differ on different stelae. Dr Lehner thinks that a statue of Amenophis II probably was set up in front of the Sphinx. The boxes that are clearly visible built on to the lower part of the Sphinx at several points are likely to have served as the bases of shrines for other statues (of gods like Osiris) that were attached to the Sphinx at various times during the New Kingdom. It may be that the Sphinx was painted in the time of Amenophis II and Tuthmosis IV, if not before: traces of colour are still just visible on the face and turn up between the restoration blocks and among the remains of the chapel built to house the stela in front of the monument. Certainly the monument was painted during still later restoration work, for some of the second layer of repair blocks carry traces of paint.

If, as is most likely, the divine beard was already broken by New Kingdom times, then no doubt Tuthmosis repaired this feature, using the original pieces (which show the same strata as the rock of the body). But Dr Lehner thinks the fragment of the cobra uraeus from the Sphinx's brow found by Caviglia and now in the British Museum was probably a repair piece, the original having eroded by the time of the first New Kingdom restoration.

Tuthmosis IV rounded off his restoration of the Sphinx by building great mud-brick walls around the enclosure, continuing them above the level of the top surface, to try to keep out the ever-encroaching sands of the western desert. Emile Baraize removed the best part of these walls in the 1920s, but left enough on the northern side for Professor Selim later to find stamp marks of Tuthmosis IV on some of the bricks.

The pharaohs who followed Tuthmosis IV went on favouring the site of the Sphinx, which was called Setepet, 'the select', 'the sacred place of the first time' as the Dream Stela puts it. Khafre's part in its carving seems to have been dimly remembered, to go by the tantalizing mention on the Dream Stela, but the Sphinx's aspect as a solar deity in its own right, divorced from its embodiment of the divinity of a particular king, led quite naturally to the assumption that it must be incomparably old, going back to the beginning of time. Its old temple was lost, there was a new one with a viewing platform and staircase, and a royal lodge was built on to what still remained above the sand of the Khafre valley temple. Tutankhamun built a rest house (a small mud-brick affair) behind that temple, to facilitate his own participation in the glory of the sacred place of the Sphinx during his brief reign in the 1320s: Ramesses II took that over some decades later. We know from a message sent between two officials that repairs were conducted on the Sphinx at some point during his long reign. Stone was drawn from a local quarry, perhaps to carry out secondary repairs to the paws of the monument. Two stelae were set up by Ramesses II in the chapel in front of the Sphinx: Caviglia found them.

Depictions of the Great Sphinx on the New Kingdom stelae found around the site, besides sometimes showing the statue in front of it and sometimes not, also sometimes show a tall crown on the head of the monument, a wide collar round its neck, hawk's plumage on its body and folded wings. Whether any or all of these features were from time to time added to the Sphinx is not certain: details might have been painted on to it, and the hole in the top of the head must have served to fix the crown. Certainly, greater variations than before were becoming apparent in the sphinx pattern as instanced in other examples of sphinx carving.

An unusually large number of sphinx figures have come down to us from the reign of Amenophis III in the first half of the fourteenth century BCE – he was

A tiny sphinx of Amenophis III in blue faience. Photo by courtesy of Sotheby's, New York.

Ram-headed sphinxes at Karnak.

the son of Tuthmosis IV and grandfather or father of Tutankhamun. These sphinxes range from the tiny, like an example in faience with human arms and hands holding offering pots in the New York Metropolitan Museum of Art, to the monumental, of which the most impressive are the two red granite sphinxes now on the bank of the Neva in St Petersburg, crowned with the tall White Crown of Upper Egypt. Another sphinx of Amenophis III, in the Egyptian Museum in Cairo, is notable for its wig in place of the nemes head-dress, its possession of a divine beard and the carving on its flanks of wings, which remind

A crocodile sphinx of ancient Thebes, with the Colossi of Memnon in the distance.

us again of the Horus element in the sphinx idea and look back (over a period of fifteen hundred years) to the Oxford Palette and forward to the winged sphinxes of later times and places.

Amenophis III ruled at the time of Egypt's greatest involvement in the affairs of the wider world of the ancient Near East, as an imperial power with allies and clients in foreign lands. The sphinx motif first appears in the art of Mesopotamia at about this time: it seems likely that it was adopted from the Egyptians, who had already exported a few small sphinx statues to foreign temples in Syria and

Palestine as far back as Middle Kingdom times. The Mesopotamian sphinxes of *c.* 1500 BCE always have wings, initiating the pattern seen in the Near Eastern and Greek sphinxes thereafter, but whether the Egyptians themselves or the Mesopotamians popularized this design it is not possible to say. From the Canaanite city of Megiddo comes a winged female sphinx of this time; while a sphinx with the head of Amenophis III's chief queen, Tiy, from the Sudan stands in a very 'Asiatic' sort of pose, reminiscent of Mesopotamian statuary.

The sphinx image reached the Greek world at about the same time or a little earlier, occurring in the archaeological record in Crete and Cyprus, and at Mycenaean sites on the mainland. 'Griffins' are to be seen in frescoes at Knossos and Pylos and the insides of silver cups from Cyprus exhibit sphinxes with sometimes human and sometimes bird heads; a sarcophagus shows winged sphinxes on their way to the characteristic pattern seen in the early classical Greek period – seated on their haunches with front legs arranged more like a cat's, and wings curving upwards rather than straight or bent down. After these early manifestations, the sphinx disappeared from the Greek world with the Dark Age that settled on the East Mediterranean in about 1200 BCE. It was to be about five hundred years before it reappeared in Greek art.

In New Kingdom Egypt, further variations on the sphinx pattern were pioneered. The temple of the god Khons at Karnak is approached by rows of criosphinxes, whose lion bodies are mated with the heads of rams; a casket from the tomb of Tutankhamun shows a sphinx with ram's horns. All this reflects the importance in New Kingdom times of the iconography associated with the Theban god Amun, whose sacred animal the ram was. The guardian role of the criosphinxes is apparent in the way that small figures of the king are tucked under the protective overhang of the rams' heads. From the mortuary temple of Amenophis III at Thebes came a crocodile-tailed sphinx, whose headless remains are still lying in the field where it was found: a similar crocodile sphinx is depicted in a drawing of the time of Queen Hatshepsut.

When sphinxes are equipped in the New Kingdom with human hands, they now have human arms too. Even the heretic pharaoh Akhenaten (son of Amenophis III), who tried to overthrow all the old gods of Egypt save for the sun-god in his manifestation as the solar disc, had himself portrayed as a sphinx with human arms and hands raised into the rays of the Sun.

In general, New Kingdom sphinxes are more slender and cat-like than their forerunners. The hitherto rare occurrence of female sphinxes is augmented with more frequent depictions. Queen Hatshepsut of about 1465 BCE preferred sphinxes that showed her in a kingly way, albeit with her own feminine face: a painted limestone example follows the Tanis pattern with lion's mane and ears, but a red granite sphinx of hers is in the Giza style; her terraced mortuary temple at Deir el-Bahari, on the other side of the river from Luxor, had an approach avenue of sphinxes, and more of them up on its terraces, reminding us of the guardian role of these figures.

But some of the female sphinxes of the imperial New Kingdom display quite novel and exotic features. Several show a distinctly lioness body, with teats along

Opposite: A lion-maned sphinx of Queen Hatshepsut. Cairo Museum.

An exotic-looking female sphinx with the teats of a lioness, on a New Kingdom throne base in the Egyptian Museum of Turin.

Drawing on a limestone chip of a standing female sphinx of rather 'Asiatic' appearance from the late New Kingdom. Cairo Museum.

the underside, wings that are raised from the body but folded down halfway along and an elegant head wearing the sort of crown made famous by a portrait bust of Akhenaten's queen, Nefertiti. Suspended on a ribbon or chain around the neck is a prominent rosette that links these female sphinxes to the Canaanite goddess Ashtoreth. Conquest and diplomacy brought foreign subsidiary wives, with their own religious traditions, to the courts of rulers like Amenophis III and Akhenaten. At about the same time, as we have seen, the Great Sphinx was being identified with a god, who was very possibly a Canaanite import, called Hwron, Hwrna or Hwl. Some of the stelae found by Professor Selim refer to the Great Sphinx as Hwrna Horemakhet, or speak of 'Adoration to Horemakhet, in his name of Hwrna'. Seti I, father of Ramesses II, extended the temple of Amenophis II at the Sphinx, recording that 'he made it as a monument to his father Hwl-Horemakhet'.

Royal interest in the Great Sphinx is attested into late New Kingdom times with the names of Ramesses IIII, IV and V mentioned on site. A further time of political confusion ensued in Egypt in about 1070 BCE, the Third Intermediate Period, lasting until about 700 BCE. The temple of Isis, from which came the Inventory Stela that misled nineteenth-century Egyptologists about the age of the Sphinx, was extended in this period (having been founded in New Kingdom times). More work was done there in the Saite Period, at around 600 BCE, when a self-conscious revival of the glories of the remote past led to the creation of such pious frauds as the Inventory Stela, which had Khufu restoring a pre-existent Sphinx along with many more anachronistic details, as we have seen. Some of the restoration work at the Sphinx belongs to this period, attributed to Khufu, but in reality carried out by some Saite king. By the end of Egypt's dynastic history, in 343 BCE when first the Persians and soon after the Greeks took control of the

Ramesses II offering a small
sphinx statue to the sun
god. In the garden of the
Cairo Museum.

Opposite: Greek sphinxes
on a sarcophagus in the
Archaeological Museum of
Istanbul.

Sphinx monstrosities
from the latter days of
ancient Egypt.

country, the whole Giza complex of pyramids, Sphinx, temples and tombs had
become, in Professor Selim's words, a debased amalgam of the cults of all sorts of
gods, home-grown and foreign, with a discredited priesthood in attendance. For
the Greeks and then the Romans, the place was as much a tourist attraction as
any sort of Mecca. The Sphinx came to bear the inevitable graffiti that went with
tourism: several Greek inscriptions have been found carved on its cladding blocks.

The ugliest of the casing work (before some of the misguided efforts of
modern times, that are now mercifully being rectified) was perhaps carried out in
Roman times: the outer repair blocks of the front paws for example. A stela not
from the site itself but from a nearby village records that the Sphinx was cleared
of sand in honour of the emperor Nero. Inscriptions found near the Sphinx show
that Hadrian's favourite Antinous reinforced the retaining walls that helped to
keep the sand out. The pavement of the Sphinx enclosure was restored during the
times of Marcus Aurelius and Septimus Severus.

By this time, the classical world had a sphinx icon of its own, the female,
winged and baleful monster of the Oedipus story, which began to be depicted in
Greece in the fifth century BCE. The riddle with which this sphinx challenged
travellers on the road to Thebes, until vanquished by Oedipus, still retained real
details from the ancient Egyptian religious beliefs about sphinxes, indeed about
the Great Sphinx of Giza itself. What goes on four limbs in the morning, on two

at noon and on three in the evening is the Egyptian sun-god in his manifestations as the crawling infant of the dawn, the upright strider of the noonday, the tottering old man of eventide in need of a stick to support him: Kheperi, Re, Atum. The sphinx of Thebes in Greece was also a guardian of sorts, vetting travellers on the road to that city; and, interestingly, even the theme of posing riddles might go back to ancient Egyptian times, for there are coffin texts of the intermediate period after the fall of the Old Kingdom that speak of two demon 'guardians of the bend' in the underworld who demanded correct answers to their questions before the souls of the dead could get past them. An old tradition of the Greeks said that the Theban sphinx had come from Ethiopia, by which name they called Africa where, indeed, in Egypt the sphinx was born. Professor Selim speculated that Phidias, the great Athenian sculptor who was active in the second half of the fifth century BCE, may have partly derived his design of a sphinx figure for the base of his statue of Zeus from Egyptian sphinx depictions on the lower sides of the pharaohs' thrones. Some of the later Egyptian sphinx images, particularly the winged females in which a foreign influence has been detected, certainly look like precursors of the Greek model. The emerging artistic tradition of the Greek world in its archaic phase was heavily influenced by Egyptian art: the pose of the Kouroi figures of the seventh and sixth centuries is obviously derived from Egyptian statuary, to give but one example. Solon's visit to Egypt, when he heard the tales that became the basis of the Atlantis story,

An early Greek sphinx with
a beautiful Archaic Smile.

took place early in the sixth century, when the Greeks were trading with Egypt
on a large scale. So the Greek world was in a position to absorb ideas like the
sphinx at an early date in its own development, while the native Egyptian culture
was still sufficiently keen on its own heritage to be able to pass it on. Perhaps
some elements of the Greek sphinx were at the same time derived from their own
Cretan and Mycenaean heritage and from the general Middle Eastern tradition
of sphinxes where the creatures were commonly winged and female after the
adoption of the idea from Egypt in about 1500 BCE. The Mesopotamian and
Levantine sphinx tradition, incidentally, also lies behind the cherubim of the
Jews. Evidently, it was the guardian role of the sphinxes that chiefly
recommended their image to the non-Egyptian world, and it is easy to see how a
guardian force that was primarily benevolent towards the righteous could come
in time to be seen rather as malevolent towards the unrighteous. Into very late
Egyptian times, people were being buried with little sphinx and lion guardians to
look after them in the next life, while the Greeks were picturing their sphinx as a
dire monster of terrifying threat.

When the Greeks conquered Egypt under Alexander the Great in 332 BCE, the
way was paved for the reintroduction of the sphinx idea into Egypt in the changed

form of the Theban throttler that the native Egyptians surely could hardly recognize as even remotely a product of their own civilization. Some of the early Greek sphinxes of the seventh and sixth centuries BCE (before the regular depiction of the hag-sphinx of Oedipus) had been very beautiful, with the Archaic Smile on their faces and elegantly curved wings, but the sphinxes of Hellenistic Egypt, in which the female Greek head was put atop a veritable menagerie of animal elements, could be a very different kettle of fish. There are real monsters here: full-face human heads on lions' bodies with solar discs and rams' horns on their rumps, tails ending in cobras, birds' wings and, quite grotesquely, crocodiles' heads at the creatures' breasts. Clearly, in a decadent time, the tatters of half-a-dozen or more different cults are incorporated into these all-purpose sphinxes. In other examples, the old falcon head persists – even on breasted female forms. But in some of these latter-day products, the Egyptian content is practically nil.

The Egyptian sphinx did not die along with the end of pagan Egypt. The Romans had taken sphinxes off to Rome as loot and copied them there. Some of these sphinxes remained on view through the Dark Ages of Christian Europe, inspiring further copies – patently of ultimately Egyptian inspiration, however distorted – even before the Renaissance got under way. With the Renaissance and the revival of interest in all antiquity including ancient Egypt, the sphinx image was re-established in the western artistic vision, from which it has never since wholly gone away.

At the Giza site of the Great Sphinx, the end of pagan antiquity saw the end of interest in keeping up the monument. There would be no more re-pavings, no more sand clearances. The tourist trade declined and the Christianized Egyptians, the Copts, were keen to neglect the monuments of their pagan ancestors. No doubt the sand was soon back to fill the Sphinx enclosure and bury most of the lion body, leaving only the head to weather the desert sandstorms. Most of the paint on face and body would have begun to fade and wear away. The somewhat poorer rock of the neck and the head-dress lappets would have started to succumb to the abrasion of the sand catapulted past it by the winds that sometimes roared over the surface of the dunes under the Sphinx's chin. The beard was perhaps soon broken off again, but the face was presumably intact when the Arabs conquered Egypt in their year 20 (642 of the Common Era). The final name by which the pagan world had known the Sphinx was Helios-Armachis, the Greek equivalent of Re-Horemakhet, but evidently the Christian locals of Giza still remembered the Hwl name at the time of the Arab conquest, causing their new rulers to dub the monument Abul Hol, Father of Terror, which in the circumstances might not have altogether displeased any spirit of Khafre that still retained an attachment to his pyramid complex at Giza, of which the Great Sphinx remains to this day the most wonderful component.

EPILOGUE

The pyramids of Giza and the Great Sphinx were built as long as four-and-a-half thousand years ago. There is inevitably much that we shall never be able to know about them, both on the grand scale of their ideological meaning for their builders and on the small scale of the precise order of events that went into their making. I hope this book has shown that, for all that, there is still much that can be learned about these ancient monuments by the application of careful research based on scholarly knowledge of Egyptology and archaeology, with the aid where appropriate of the findings of other sciences. Conversely there is precious little of worth to be learned from unscholarly speculations that neither know nor respect the extensive and detailed body of Egyptological knowledge so conscientiously put together by the professional students of the subject.

There are two areas in connection with the recent Sphinx controversies that offer lessons for the future of scholarly disciplines such as archaeology that have a large component of popular human interest to them. It is the interest we all have in the human past that encourages everyone, lay people as much as professionals, to feel somehow qualified to hold strong opinions where, quite possibly, real knowledge is slight; worst still, sometimes to undervalue the real knowledge that the professionals do wield, in favour of fanciful ideas or notions simplistically derived from other fields of study (geology and astronomy in this case).

There are few fields of science and scholarship in which non-experts would presume to know better than the experts to the degree that so many do where archaeology is concerned. The grandeur and colour of ancient Egypt has seen to it that Egyptology in particular should suffer in this way.

The sheerly fanciful speculators, with their pyramid builders from Atlantis, their 'encoded' astronomical messages from remote antiquity to the very times we live in, their secret chambers under the Sphinx, their 'ancient wisdom' by the bucketful, are to be sure an irritant to the Egyptologists, who see books and television programmes peddling what they know to be baseless and distorted versions of the past to people who are in no position to judge what they hear. It is worse than irritant, I believe: I think Egyptologists and archaeologists are truly sorry to see people being misled with nonsense when there is so much real knowledge to hand. All nonsense is unhelpful and I do not consider that any nonsense about the past can ever be regarded as harmless fun: the human race really does need to know what happened in history and prehistory in order to

Opposite: Work continues at the Sphinx, with cladding blocks of all periods on view: from possibly Old Kingdom originals through New Kingdom and later repairs to ugly Roman and more recent additions, currently being replaced with more sensitive work.

understand our place in the world and to avoid unnecessary illusions about ourselves. Besides, we surely want to know the real story, as far as we can. Some of the recent speculation about the Sphinx and pyramids is quite pernicious: we have been invited to picture the Atlantean supermen not just showing the poor old Egyptians how to build the pyramids but also conducting sexual relations with women lucky enough to be selected (on purely eugenic grounds, you understand), and then co-opting their superior children into a 'Secret Brotherhood' of the 'Ancient Wisdom'! Hitler would have been proud of them. This sort of thing exposes the ragbag of threadbare popular prejudice and ignorance that so often lies behind the whole genre. The entire 'proof' of the existence of this 'Secret Brotherhood' resides, incidentally, in the total absence of any evidence of its existence throughout Egyptian history.

The other lesson in the Sphinx debate concerns the too-frequent presumption of natural scientists who wander into fields of study perhaps more subtle than their own with no misgivings about the value of their own work and no evident faith in that of the professionals of the unfamiliar territory they enter. Where archaeology is concerned, the Sphinx debate is not the first time that natural scientists have presumed to lay down the law in controversial areas where their expertise can, at best, only make a contribution to the deliberations of the professional archaeologists.

The fraudulent site of Glozel in France is another case in point. 'Discovered' in the 1920s, the Glozel material purports to represent the transition from the Old Stone Age hunters to the writing and pottery-making age of the first farmers, as understood at the time. Its hotchpotch of bones with reindeer carvings, badly polished axes, worse made pots, inscribed tablets with garbled ancient letters and juvenile sex symbolism, constitutes a ludicrous realization of the archaeological theories of the 1920s, with some items that imitate the products of fifteen thousand years ago, some of eight thousand and some more of four or five. A scientific commission at the time of Glozel's discovery, and the local police's forensic laboratory, concluded that the whole thing was a fraud. But in the 1970s, dates for some of the pottery from Glozel were achieved by the thermoluminescence (TL) method, which gave on average an age of about two thousand years or so before present for the dated material. Now this date made no sense for the carvings that looked Old Stone Age, nor for the axes and pots that looked New Stone Age, nor for the inscribed tablets that looked Bronze Age or Iron Age. But none of this stopped the physicists who made the TL determinations from confidently declaiming that the items they tested were genuinely old, over two thousand years old at least – even in the case of the inscribed tablets, with their imitations of ancient Phoenician letters and so forth, that could have no context at all in the France of Roman times. The physicists stood by their graphs and measurements and their (perhaps narrow) faith in their technique in the face of all the evidence of fraud at Glozel; and they frequently seemed quite uninterested in the archaeologists' very real objections to Glozel, including its irrelevance to the known process of human development around the world, its unique incongruity with all the well-documented finds of real

archaeology, its lack of anything at all that would belong to Gallo-Roman or
Celtic France, to say nothing of its fraudulent background. Plainly, there was
something wrong with the TL dates, wrong in an aberrational way that the
physicists were not of an outlook to expect (to do with the bogus fabrication of
the Glozel pots). It reminds me powerfully of the geological case made for the
Sphinx's great antiquity: and just as Dr Schoch has speculated about Jericho as a
parallel for his Sphinx of nine thousand years ago, so the physicists of the Glozel
case speculated about Gauls and Greeks and travelling magicians and the like to
account for their findings, in the same spirit of amateur archaeologizing. Faced
with the Glozel puzzle, the eminent archaeologist Glyn Daniel remembered the
words of Sherlock Holmes in *A Study in Scarlet*: 'When a fact appears opposed
to a long train of deduction, it invariably proves to be capable of bearing some
other interpretation.' Geologists other than Dr Schoch have supplied some other
interpretation of the erosional features he held to demonstrate an age for the
Sphinx greater than the Egyptologists could entertain on the basis of their long
train of deduction. It really does behove the natural scientists to cross into the
territory of the archaeologists with a bit more respect for their learning than they
have sometimes shown, but I don't suppose the Sphinx will be the last time.

The Sphinx continues to smile his inscrutable smile above the controversy of
latter-day human beings, even if the smile's inscrutability owes more to old
vandalism and long erosion than to the artistic and religious intentions of his
makers, not to mention the antics of the tourists' camels all around him. (As a
matter of fact, he has been there twice as long as the camels, which were never a
feature of the ancient Egyptian scene.)

Erosion of the Sphinx body continues, as efforts to conserve him continue
likewise, and even the best-intentioned attempts at conservation have their
shortcomings. After some of the casing stones fell off the Sphinx in the early 1980s,
it was decided to replace much of the late repair work, done in Roman times or
some even later by Baraize, with incongruous larger stones. But some of this new
work turned out badly after a short time, with erosion and buckling out of the new
blocks, probably as a result of moisture coming out of the Sphinx body beneath.
Further new cladding was therefore planned in the late '80s, with a better quality of
stone and the provision of monitoring devices to keep a check on wind direction and
force, atmospheric humidity, condensation. It was soon evident that a strong sand-
bearing north-west wind is the chief cause of wind erosion on the Sphinx, to go with
the daily spalling as a result of condensation acting on the salts of the limestone.

The Sphinx has frequently presented a part-scaffolded appearance to its
visitors in the 1990s. Whether it will ever keep its age-old guard under a new,
retractable roof, we shall have to see. It seems unlikely that it will ever be
reburied in the sand or covered over with a glass pyramid, though both
suggestions have been made. Dr Lehner thinks that fears for the monument's
future can be exaggerated: a piece of the shoulder bedrock fell off a decade ago,
but the Sphinx will not crumble to dust in the next twenty years. Dr Zahi
Hawass would like to see Baraize's cement head-dress extensions removed: let us
hope that proves practicable.

And the Egyptological study of the Sphinx goes on too: not only directly at the monument, but also through a thousand byways of scholarship that might yet throw more light on the meaning and making of this still astonishing creation of the ancient Egyptian pioneers of civilization. In the end, the real meaning of the Sphinx for us is to show what human capacity and imagination could do in that dawn of civilization, and can do always. If people could do all that so long ago and we can find so much out about it, we should be encouraged. And we should use the example of the sort of careful and rational investigation of the past that the Egyptologists have achieved with the Sphinx as an inspiration for all our thinking about our world, and as a warning against mere speculation.

FURTHER READING

Introduction
Gardiner, Sir Alan. *Egypt of the Pharaohs*, Oxford University Press, 1961
Grant, Michael. *Myths of the Greeks and Romans*, London, Weidenfeld and
  Nicolson, 1962

Chapter 1
Baines, John, and Malek, Jaromir. *Atlas of Ancient Egypt*, Oxford, Phaidon,
  1980
Hassan, Selim. *The Sphinx, Its History in the Light of Recent Excavations*,
  Cairo, Government Press, 1949
Lehner, Mark, and Hawass, Zahi. 'The Sphinx – Who Built it and Why?',
  Archaeology 47:5 (Sept.–Oct. 1994), 30–47
Murnane, William J. *The Penguin Guide to Ancient Egypt*, London, Penguin
  Books, 1983
Shaw, Ian, and Nicholson, Paul. *British Museum Dictionary of Ancient Egypt*,
  London, British Museum Press, 1995

Chapter 2
Fagan, Brian M. *The Rape of the Nile*, London, Macdonald and Jane's, 1975
Greener, Leslie. *The Discovery of Egypt*, London, Cassell, 1966
James, T.G.H. *The Archaeology of Ancient Egypt*, London, The Bodley Head,
  1972
Jordan, Paul. *Egypt, The Black Land*, Oxford, Phaidon, 1976
Wilson, John A. *Signs and Wonders upon Pharaoh*, Chicago University Press,
  1964

Chapter 3
Gardiner, Sir Alan. *Egypt of the Pharaohs*, Oxford University Press, 1961
Haas, H. et al. 'Radiocarbon Chronology and the Historical Calendar in Egypt',
  Chronologies in the Near East, British Archaeology Report S379, Part II,
  1987, 586–606
Hassan, F.A., and Robinson, S.W. 'High Precision Radiocarbon Chronology of
  Ancient Egypt', *Antiquity* 61:231, March 1987, 119–35

Chapter 4

Renfrew, Colin. *Before Civilization*, London, Jonathan Cape, 1973

Sherratt, Andrew (ed.). *The Cambridge Encyclopaedia of Archaeology*, Cambridge University Press, 1980

The Times Atlas of Past Worlds, London, Times Books, 1988

Chapters 5 and 6

Aldred, Cyril. *Egypt to the End of the Old Kingdom*, London, Thames and Hudson, 1965

—— *The Egyptians*, London, Thames and Hudson, 1984

David, A. Rosalie. *The Egyptian Kingdoms*, Oxford, Elsevier-Phaidon, 1975

Edwards, I.E.S. *The Pyramids of Egypt*, London, Ebury Press and Michael Joseph, 1972

Hayes, William C. *Most Ancient Egypt*, Chicago University Press, 1964

Jordan, Paul. *Egypt, The Black Land*, Oxford, Phaidon, 1976

Rice, Michael. *Egypt's Making*, London, Routledge, 1990

Spencer, A.J. *Early Egypt – The Rise of Civilization in the Nile Valley*, London, British Museum Press, 1993

Chapter 7

Hassan, Selim. *The Sphinx, Its History in the Light of Recent Excavations*, Cairo, Government Press, 1949

—— *Excavations at Giza*, Cairo, Government Press, 1946

Lehner, Mark. 'Reconstructing the Sphinx', *Cambridge Archaeological Journal* Vol. 2, No. 1 (April 1992), 3–26

—— *The Complete Pyramids*, London & New York, Thames and Hudson, 1997

Lehner, Mark, and Hawass, Zahi. 'The Sphinx – Who Built it and Why?', *Archaeology* 47:5 (Sept.–Oct. 1994), 30–47

Howard Vyse, R.W. *Operations Carried on at the Pyramids of Gizeh*, London, J. Fraser, 1840–42

Chapter 9

Back issues of *KMT, A Modern Journal of Ancient Egypt* carry articles by Robert Schoch, Mark Lehner and James Harrell with associated correspondence. See in particular issues of Summer '92, Summer '94, Fall '94 and Fall '96. The Fall '96 issue has a useful article on 'The So-called Orion Mystery' by Robert Chadwick. *KMT* is published at 1531 Golden Gate Avenue, San Francisco, USA.

Malek, Jaromir, 'Orion and the Giza Pyramids', *Discussions in Egyptology* 30, 1994, 101–14

Tompkins, Peter. *Secrets of the Great Pyramid*, London, Penguin Books, 1973

Walker, Christopher (ed.). *Astronomy Before the Telescope*, London, British Museum Press, 1996

Chapter 10

See *KMT* articles and Lehner and Hawass as above

Gauri, K.L. et al. 'Geological Weathering and its Implications on the Age of the Sphinx', *Geoarchaeology*, Vol. 10, No. 2 (April 1995), 119–33

Chapter 11

Aldred, Cyril. *The Egyptians*, London, Thames and Hudson, 1984

Frankfort, H. *Ancient Egyptian Religion*, New York, Harper and Row, 1948

James, T.G.H. *An Introduction to Ancient Egypt*, London, British Museum Publications Ltd, 1979

Watterson, Barbara. *Gods of Ancient Egypt*, Stroud, Sutton Publishing, 1996

Wilson, John A. *The Culture of Ancient Egypt*, Chicago University Press, 1951

de Wit, C. *Le rôle et le sens du lion dans l'Egypte ancienne*, Leiden University, 1951

Chapter 12

Aldred, Cyril. *Egyptian Art*, London, Thames and Hudson, 1980

Baines, John, and Malek, Jaromir. *Atlas of Ancient Egypt*, Oxford, Phaidon, 1980

Hassan, Selim. *The Sphinx, Its History in the Light of Recent Excavations*, Cairo, Government Press, 1949

Epilogue

Jordan, Paul. 'Glozel', in *Chronicle* (Sutcliffe, R. ed.), London, British Broadcasting Corporation, 1978

INDEX

Italicized page numbers indicate illustrations.